John Webster provides a major scholarly analysis, the first in any language, of the final sections of the *Church Dogmatics*. He focusses on the theme of human agency in Barth's late ethics and doctrine of baptism, placing the discussion in the context of an interpretation of the *Dogmatics* as an intrinsically *ethical* dogmatics. The first two chapters survey the themes of agency, covenant, and human reality in the *Dogmatics* as a whole; later chapters give a thorough analysis of *Church Dogmatics* IV/4 and the posthumously published text *The Christian Life*. A final chapter examines the significance of Barth's work for contemporary accounts of moral selfhood. The book is important not only for a detailed analysis of a neglected part of Barth's *œuvre*, but also because it calls into question much of what has hitherto been written about Barth's ethical dogmatics.

BARTH'S ETHICS OF RECONCILIATION

BARTH'S ETHICS OF RECONCILIATION

JOHN WEBSTER

Professor of Systematic Theology,
Wycliffe College,
University of Toronto

CAMBRIDGE
UNIVERSITY PRESS

Published by the Press Syndicate of the University of Cambridge
The Pitt Building, Trumpington Street, Cambridge CB2 1RP
40 West 20th Street, New York, NY 10011-4211, USA
10 Stamford Road, Oakleigh, Melbourne 3166, Australia

© Cambridge University Press 1995

First published 1995

Printed in Great Britain at the University Press, Cambridge

A catalogue record for this book is available from the British Library

Library of Congress cataloguing in publication data

Webster, John
Barth's ethics of reconciliation / John Webster.
p.   cm.
Includes bibliographical references and index.
ISBN 0 521 47499 X (hardback)
1. Barth, Karl, 1886–1968. Kirchliche Dogmatik. 2 Christian
ethics – History – 20th century. 1. Title
BT75.B286W43   1995
230′044–dc20   94–34862
CIP

ISBN 0 521 47499 X hardback

WV

Contents

A note on references

Barth's *Church Dogmatics* (abbreviated where necessary to *CD*) is referred to by volume and part (for example, IV/I, p. I). *The Christian Life* is abbreviated to *ChrL*.

Introduction

In this book, I want to sketch a way of reading Barth's *Church Dogmatics* which takes at face value its claim to be an *ethical* dogmatics. Dogmatics, Barth proposes, 'has the problem of ethics in view from the very first'.[1] He has, however, rarely been taken at his word on the matter. The ethical sections of the *Church Dogmatics* have attracted far less attention than the more obviously dogmatic material; and even those who do give time to studying them frequently go away from the texts dissatisfied. It is as if the logic of Barth's thought, and especially the intensity of his adherence to certain understandings of the ontologically constitutive character of God's action in and as Jesus Christ, make serious consideration of human action superfluous, even, perhaps, a trespass on the sovereignty of grace.

Yet the fact remains that Barth devotes a great deal of space to ethics in the course of the *Church Dogmatics*. Moreover, the arguments which he there develops are no mere incidental excursuses in a properly dogmatic treatise; they are intrinsic to the design of the whole. It is arguable that one of the most serious obstacles to the reception of Barth's *magnum opus* is an inadequate grasp of the fact that the *Church Dogmatics* is a work of moral theology as well as a systematics. More closely, Barth's *Dogmatics* is, amongst other things, a moral ontology – an extensive account of the situation in which human agents act. Barth's ethics has, therefore, a very particular character, both materially and

[1] III/4, p. 3.

I

formally. It is primarily devoted to the task of describing the 'space' which agents occupy, and gives only low priority to the description of their character and to the analysis of quandary situations in which they find themselves. Barth's ethics tends to assume that moral problems are resolvable by correct theological description of moral space. And such description involves much more than describing the moral consciousnesses of agents. A Christianly successful moral ontology must be a depiction of the world of human action as it is enclosed and governed by the creative, redemptive, and sanctifying work of God in Christ, present in the power of the Holy Spirit. Consequently, such an ontology is not centred on the human agent, and especially not on moral reflectivity. Yet Barth pushes *this* kind of focus on moral selfhood out of the way in order to introduce in its place what is to him a more theologically – and humanly – satisfying account of the moral life as genuine action in analogy to prior divine action. Failure to take this point seriously often lies behind critiques of Barth's theology – as driven by near-obsession with noetic issues, for example, or as abstract from, or even hostile to, the world of human history and action. I want to show in some detail how such readings are all too often abortive from the beginning, since they routinely disregard tracts of Barth's argument which he considered an inherent part of his dogmatic work.

In essence, what follows suggests that Barth's *Dogmatics* is best approached by bearing in mind three characteristics of his argument, all of which are inter-dependent, and no single one of which can stand on its own without twisting the design of the whole. The three characteristics are these: (1) The *Church Dogmatics* as a whole is one lengthy exposition of the statement which in a very particular way is 'at once the basis and the content of all the rest', the 'hardest and most comprehensive statement', that 'God is'.[2] One of the ways in which the *Dogmatics* can be construed is as a massively ramified reassertion of the aseity of God: as an intense

---

[2] II/1, pp. 257–9.

pursuit of the truth that neither in the realm of being nor in the realm of knowledge is God contingent or derivative, but rather axiomatically real, true, and free. God is 'the One who is free from all origination, conditioning or determination from without, by that which is not Himself'.[3]

(2) Because – and only because – it is an exposition of the statement 'God is', the *Church Dogmatics* is also all along the line an anthropology. For the form of God's aseity, the chosen path of the divine being, is specified in the history of Jesus Christ; God's freedom is freedom for fellowship. As God *a se*, 'God can allow this other which is so utterly distinct from Himself to live and move and have its being within Himself. He can grant and leave it its own special being distinct from His own, and yet even in this way, and therefore in this its creaturely freedom, sustain, uphold and govern it by His own divine being, thus being its beginning, centre and end'.[4] And so part of Barth's exploration of the logic of 'God is' is an exploration of how a Christian doctrine of God cannot be simply a doctrine of God. 'We should still not have learned to say "God" correctly (i.e., as understood in the Christian Church on the basis of Holy Scripture) if we thought it enough simply to say "God". However well-grounded or critical our utterance, if it has a logical exclusiveness, if it is only "God", it will not suffice . . . We must not be so exact, so clever, so literal, that our doctrine of God remains only a doctrine of God.'[5] God moves towards humanity by establishing covenant fellowship between himself and his creatures; God is true God 'only in this movement'.[6] Dogmatics thereby acquires a double theme. As Barth put it at the beginning of a lecture in the late 50s:

'Theology,' in the literal sense, means the science and doctrine of God. A very precise definition of the Christian endeavour in this respect would really require the more complex term 'The-anthropology'. For an abstract doctrine of God has no place

---

[3] Ibid., p. 307.
[4] Ibid., p. 314.
[5] II/2, p. 5.
[6] Ibid., p. 7.

in the Christian realm, only a 'doctrine of God and of man', a doctrine of the commerce and communion between God and man.[7]

(3) Because the theme of the *Church Dogmatics* is *this* God in covenant with humanity, the *Dogmatics* is intrinsically an ethical dogmatics, and includes description of the human covenant partner as agent. For 'dogmatics asks concerning the covenant between the true God and true man established in Him from all eternity and fulfilled in Him in time. But true man is characterised by action, by good action, as the true God is also characterised by action, by good action. As dogmatics inquires concerning the action of God and its goodness, it must necessarily make thorough inquiry concerning active man and the goodness of his action. It has the problem of ethics in view from the very first, and it cannot legitimately lose sight of it.'[8]

In so far as it is a 'moral ontology', therefore, Barth's dogmatics can be construed as an extended inquiry into the moral field – into the space within which moral agents act, and into the shape of their action, a shape given above all by the fact that their acts take place in the history of encounter between God as prime agent and themselves as those called to act in correspondence to the grace of God. What Barth has to say about any topic in theology cannot adequately be grasped unless we bear in mind this larger scope of the argument of the *Church Dogmatics* as 'the-anthropology' and therefore as theological ethics. If 'in Jesus Christ the fact is once for all established that God does not exist without man',[9] then the task of Christian dogmatics includes ethics as a description of the human agent in relation to God.

So fundamental are these characteristics of Barth's theology that both his dogmatics and his ethics are seriously misunderstood if they are not kept in mind. Mistakes in interpreting Barth's thought often stem from deficiencies in

---

[7] K. Barth, 'Evangelical theology in the nineteenth century', in *The Humanity of God* (Collins, 1961), p. 11.

[8] III/4, p. 3.

[9] K. Barth, 'The humanity of God', in *The Humanity of God*, p. 50.

attending either to the sequence or to the interrelation of the characteristics we have identified. If we are alert to them, on the other hand, then much hasty critique of Barth's treatment of such topics as trinity, revelation, election, or Holy Spirit can be corrected by close attention to the kinds of arguments which Barth develops in his ethics. Two of many examples are ready to hand.

(1) In *The Making of Modern German Christology* and elsewhere, Alister McGrath restates a critical interpretation of Barth primarily associated with Gustav Wingren, namely that Barth construes God's relation to humanity in revelational or epistemological terms.[10] In restating the argument, McGrath claims that Barth's theology, despite its protestations to the contrary, is a mirror image of 'the Ritschl-Herrmann-Harnack tradition', in that

Barth . . . totally inverts the cognitive structure of the God–man relation, as expressed by the liberal school, insisting that man must be regarded as an *object* to whom the divine subject addresses his Word. By emphasising man's passivity and God's activity in the process of revelation, Barth believes it is possible to exclude *anthropological* considerations altogether from theology. Just as he believed the theologians of the nineteenth century to have been forced to reduce theology to anthropology by their insistence that man was subject and God object, so Barth believes that theology may maintain an intellectual autonomy if it is God who is treated as subject, and man as object, in the process of revelation . . . Barth thus effectively reduced the 'dialogue' between God and man to a 'monologue'.[11]

Moreover, Barth lays heavy emphasis 'upon the making known, or revealing, to man of something which has already happened from all eternity'.[12] Accordingly, McGrath argues,

---

[10] A. E. McGrath, *The Making of Modern German Christology. From the Enlightenment to Pannenberg* (Oxford, 1986), pp. 104–16; 'Karl Barth als Aufklärer? Der Zusammenhang seiner Lehre vom Werke Christi mit der Erwählungslehre', *Kerygma und Dogma* 30 (1984), 273–83; 'Karl Barth and the articulus iustificationis. The significance of his critique of Ernst Wolf within the context of his theological method', *Theologische Zeitschrift* 39 (1983), 349–61. See further G. Wingren, *Theology in Conflict. Nygren, Barth, Bultmann* (Edinburgh, 1958), pp. 23–44.
[11] *The Making of Modern German Christology*, pp. 105f.
[12] Ibid., p. 109.

the *Dogmatics* becomes preoccupied with a single epistemological question: How do human beings *know* 'what has
happened eternally'?[13] By locating all significant being and
action in God's eternity, it appears, Barth has unwittingly
made human consciousness into the centre of theological
interest:

> Although Barth inverts the nineteenth century subject–object
> relation in respect to God and man, his central interest remains
> the anthropologically conditioned question concerning man's
> knowledge of his situation ... The 'eternalization' (*Äternisierung*)
> of revelation, necessary for Barth on the basis of his presupposition
> of the divine freedom and the exclusion of anthropological con-
> siderations from theology, inevitably means that the emphasis is
> actually shifted from that revelation itself to man's recognition
> and appropriation of that revelation – and hence from God's
> activity to man's insights and knowledge (or, more accurately, to
> man's epistemic capacities and incapacities).[14]

Such alarmingly unrestricted and under-illustrated claims
about Barth would require a very detailed examination of
the *Dogmatics* both for their defence and their rebuttal. In
the present context, what is most striking is that the critique
proceeds entirely without reference to Barth's consistent
emphasis, steadily expounded throughout the *Dogmatics* but
especially in its ethical sections, on the *moral* character of
the relation of God to humanity. On McGrath's reading,
Barth does not present God and humanity as agents in a
differentiated fellowship as parties to the covenant of grace:
rather, God is sole agent, and humanity the utterly passive
recipient of divine disclosure. But – as I shall try to suggest –
no view of Barth is adequate which construes his understanding of revelation as simply 'epistemological', in the
sense of a deposit of knowledge of essentially a- or pre-
temporal states of affairs or divine acts. And to reduce
Barth's anthropology – indeed, his whole theology – to a
single question: how do human beings know God? is a
drastic oversimplification, achieved only by setting aside

[13] Ibid., p. 110.
[14] Ibid., pp. 110–12.

some very substantial tracts of Barth's writing in the *Dog-matics* and elsewhere. At the very least, I hope to show that we do well to take seriously Barth's claim that divine grace is not simply information, but action-eliciting divine activity:

When we see here [in Christ] the will of God being done, when, that is, we see His grace in action, the law is manifested to us. From what God here does for us, we learn what God wants with us and of us. His grace applies to us, affects us. Even in His grace, indeed just there, He shows that, while dealing for and with us, it is for and with us as His creatures ... His action does not revolve within Himself, but is aimed at *our* action, at getting our action into conformity with His.[15]

(2) More briefly, a second – and much better informed – example is Sheila Greeve Daveney's comparison of Barth and Hartshorne in *Divine Power*.[16] Unlike McGrath, Daveney's handling of Barth's doctrine of God is alert to the fact that, in Barth, God's freedom 'points to the capacity and possibility of relationship which is grounded in God's own self-relatedness',[17] and hence she is aware that in the *Dogmatics* 'God's determining knowledge and will do not cancel worldly self-determination but rather establish it.'[18] Her account goes awry, however, when she concludes despite this that Barth 'never conceives God's relationship with the world as truly social in nature', since, according to Barth, 'God is always cause, creatures effect; God is always active while creatures are ever and only reactive.'[19]

Once again, a reading of the ethical material in the *Church Dogmatics* makes this critique rather problematic. Partly this is because Barth's central categories for talking about the relation of divine and human agency – 'covenant' and 'corre-spondence' – are most fully explored in those sections which

---

[15] K. Barth, 'Gospel and law', in *God, Grace and Gospel* (Edinburgh, 1959), pp. 8f.

[16] S. G. Daveney, *Divine Power. A Study of Karl Barth and Charles Hartshorne* (Philadelphia, 1986). Daveney's findings are repeated in A. Case-Winters, *God's Power. Traditional Understandings and Contemporary Challenges* (Louisville, 1990), pp. 97–126.

[17] Ibid., p. 16.

[18] Ibid., p. 44.

[19] Ibid., pp. 230f.

Daveney does not examine. Partly it is because Barth's ethics offers the kinds of specifications of notions such as 'cause', 'effect', and 'action' which show that the critique is off target, because it misconstrues Barth's usage. For careful study of the ethical materials in the *Church Dogmatics* shows that concepts such as 'divine sovereignty' or 'omnipotence' are misunderstood and misapplied if their logic is thought to exclude the responsible life of the creatures of God. Moreover, one of the major reasons for Barth's inclusion of the ethical material in the *Church Dogmatics* is his conviction that the narration of God's mighty deeds cannot proceed without the narration of the corresponding deeds of God's fellow-workers, for grace evokes correspondences.

Critiques such as those of McGrath and Daveney miss the mark to the extent that they fail to take cognisance of the three structuring features of Barth's argument which we outlined above. McGrath simply ignores both the second feature – the principle of 'the-anthropology' – and the third feature – the *ethical* character of the *Church Dogmatics*. As a result, he seriously misunderstands the first feature – the sovereignty of God – by interpreting the statement 'God is' as logically exclusive. Daveney's analysis is more open to recognition of the second feature, but she continues to look for the wrong thing in the area of the third feature. Looking to Barth to provide an account of human agency as self-initiated or contra-causal to God rather than merely 'reactive', she is inevitably disappointed and has to interpret Barth's refusal as a return to an oppressive notion of divine power. Hence she can see no coherence between what he wants to affirm about divine action on the one hand, and what he says of human action on the other. Both critics, therefore, leave Barth feeling that any affirmation about human action and its significance which he might make runs counter to the logic of his fundamental – 'Christomonist' – axioms.

By way of contrast, I want to offer a reading of Barth which seeks to show that what he has to say about the freedom of divine action is fully coherent with, and inseparable from, what he says of the active life of humanity in correspondence to God. As a test case for such a reading, I take the unfinished ethics of reconciliation with which the fourth locus of the *Church Dogmatics* would have closed.

The material is found in two volumes: the so-called 'baptism fragment' of *Church Dogmatics* IV/4, and the posthumous material translated as *The Christian Life*.[20] These two volumes contain the last parts of the *Church Dogmatics* which Barth taught to his students in Basle. The baptism fragment contains paragraph 75, on 'baptism as the foundation of the Christian life', which stems from lectures in the summer semester of 1960. *The Christian Life* contains the material which immediately precedes and follows the treatment of baptism: paragraph 74, a general introduction to the ethics of reconciliation (lectures from the winter semester, 1959–60), and paragraphs 76–8, an unfinished exposition of the opening invocation and first two petitions of the Lord's Prayer (lectures from the summer semester, 1961). A planned section on the eucharist was never written. Paragraph 74 is a heavily revised version of the lecture texts, produced by Barth in the summer of 1960, in which the notion of 'invocation of God' replaces 'faithfulness' as the leading rubric for the Christian life.[21] Paragraphs 76–8 follow the lecture texts more closely.

Barth had intended to follow his usual custom of revising the lecture texts for publication as a further section of the *Church Dogmatics*. A number of considerations led him to abandon this intention in the case of all the material except paragraph 75. First, he was no longer teaching the material published as the *Dogmatics*. Though he taught in the winter

---

[20] *Die kirchliche Dogmatik, IV. Die Lehre von der Versöhnung, 4* (Zürich, 1967), translated as *CD* IV/4; *Das christliche Leben. Die kirchliche Dogmatik IV,4. Fragmente aus dem Nachlass. Vorlesungen 1959–61,* eds. E. Jüngel, and H.-A. Drewes (Zürich, 1976), translated as *The Christian Life. Church Dogmatics* IV/4. *Lecture Fragments* (Edinburgh, 1981).

[21] For an earlier stage of the manuscript, see *ChrL*, pp. 275–90, and the comments of the editors, p. xi.

semester 1961–2 (due to the failure to appoint his successor),
he lectured on that occasion on the material eventually
published as *Evangelical Theology*;[22] thereafter, he gave only
occasional seminars and colloquia, and with the cessation
of regular lecturing, Barth noted, 'there ended . . . an essential part of the impulse which lay behind my work thus
far'.[23] Second, Barth's 'faithful assistant' Charlotte von
Kirschbaum, who had become indispensable to Barth in the
production of the *Church Dogmatics*, fell permanently ill.[24]
Third, Barth himself suffered prolonged bouts of illness
during 1962–5, which left him exhausted and often
depressed, and rendered serious writing largely impossible.
For these reasons, all that Barth was able to prepare for
publication before his death in 1968 was paragraph 75,
leaving the rest to find their way into print as one of the
early volumes of the Swiss *Gesamtausgabe*.

The ethics of reconciliation, then, consists of a single
finished section, and a substantial body of material which
Barth did not oversee for publication. Certainly the unfinished material should not be overvalued; of the material
which he had prepared for the final part of the doctrine of
reconciliation, Barth chose to publish only the *Tauffragment*
and those texts which he himself oversaw for publication
must remain primary in interpreting his work. Nevertheless,
as Barth's last assistant points out, Barth did not destroy
the other materials, but preserved them;[25] they remain,
therefore, a very significant, if secondary, source for an
account of his thought.

Why choose this particular material to exemplify a reading
of Barth? Two main reasons can be adduced. First, these
closing sections of Barth's *magnum opus* have yet to receive
a full-scale commentary. Though the baptism fragment generated a very considerable literature in the late 1960s and

---

[22] London, 1963.
[23] IV/4, p. viii.
[24] Ibid.
[25] E. Busch, 'Introduction', in H.-M. Rumscheidt, ed., *Karl Barth in Re-View.
Posthumous Works Reviewed and Assessed* (Pittsburgh, 1981), pp. xixf.

early 1970s, most reaction focussed on its radical suggestions
in the area of sacramental theology and practice, and very
few paid attention to its place within the larger structure
of the *Church Dogmatics* and the doctrine of reconciliation,
where it is clearly a treatment of Christian *ethics*. In his
preface to the baptism fragment, Barth stressed that 'the
positive teaching which I have tried to give in this fragment
... is for me infinitely more important than this objection
to the baptismal practice which is still predominant. Except
on this positive basis the objection would make little sense,
just as my criticism of the sacramentalist theory of baptism
is intelligible only on the same positive basis'.[26] And he
went on:

I foresee that this book, which by human judgment will be
my last major publication, will leave me in the theological and
ecclesiastical isolation which has been my lot for almost fifty years.
I am thus about to make a poor exit with it. So be it![27]

His hunch proved largely correct, with respect not only to
the baptism fragment, but also to the other material on the
Christian life, which has gone largely unnoticed and has
had negligible impact on interpretations of Barth's thought.
A full-scale assessment of the texts is thus long overdue.[28]

---

[26] IV/4, p. xi.

[27] Ibid., p. xii.

[28] Three recent works devote some space to the ethics of reconciliation, though
none offers a full-length interpretation. J. Macken, *The Autonomy Theme in the
'Church Dogmatics': Karl Barth and His Critics* (Cambridge, 1990) contains a
critique of Barth's handling of human agency in the baptism fragment as part
of a larger account of the critique of Barth stemming from Rendtorff's work.
P. D. Matheny's study *Dogmatics and Ethics. The Theological Realism and Ethics of
Karl Barth's 'Church Dogmatics'* (Frankfurt/M, 1990) offers some very astute
characterisations of the ontological dimensions of Barth's moral theology, though
from a broader perspective. N. Biggar's recent and excellent study *The Hastening
that Waits. Karl Barth's Ethics* (Oxford, 1993) devotes some space to the ethics
of reconciliation (pp. 62–81), though it treats the baptism fragment only in
passing and, like Matheny, takes a more synoptic view of the issues than the
present study.
  On IV/4, perhaps the best starting point is E. Jüngel, 'Karl Barths Lehre von
der Taufe' and 'Thesen zu Karl Barths Lehre von der Taufe', in his *Barth-Studien*
(Gütersloh, 1982), pp. 246–94: Jüngel is particularly alert to the larger context of
IV/4. A selection of some of the better studies (most of which nevertheless focus
on the controversial questions of baptismal candidacy) would include R. Schlüter,

Second, these texts from Barth's unfinished ethics of reconciliation are an extraordinarily instructive source for the
reading of Barth which I am seeking to commend. More,
perhaps, than any other part of the *Church Dogmatics*, they
demonstrate how questions concerning human action were
by no means peripheral to Barth's dogmatic thought, but
very close to its heart. Moreover, they contain Barth's most
fully developed ideas on questions in which human agency
is at the forefront – questions of the voluntary nature of
our allegiance to, and confession of, Christ, questions of the

Karl Barths Tauflehre (Paderborn, 1973), especially pp. 56–107; the essays in
F. Viering, *Zu Karl Barths Lehre von der Taufe* (Gütersloh, 1971); and, among
others, the following: K. Aland, *Taufe und Kindertaufe* (Gütersloh, 1971); A. C.
Cochrane, review of IV/4, *Journal of Ecumenical Studies* 5 (1968) 745–57; and
'Markus Barth – an unBarthian Barthian. The place of the doctrine of baptism
in the *CD*', in D. Y. Hadidian, ed., *Intergerini Parietis Septum* (Pittsburgh, 1981),
pp. 39–50; A. Demura, 'Zwingli in the writings of Karl Barth – with special
emphasis on the doctrine of the sacraments', in E. A. McKee, and B. G.
Armstrong, eds., *Probing the Reformed Tradition* (Louisville, 1989), pp. 197–219;
H. Hartwell, review of IV/4, *Scottish Journal of Theology* 22 (1969), 10–29; H.
Hübert, *Der Streit um die Kindertaufe* (Frankfurt/M, 1972); H. Mottu, 'Les sacre-
ments selon Karl Barth et Eberhard Jüngel', *Foi et Vie* 88 (1989), 33–55; A.
Quadt, 'Die Taufe als Antwort des Glaubens' *Theologische Revue* 6 (1968), 468–
74; T. Rendtorff, 'Der ethische Sinn der Dogmatik', in *Die Realisierung der Freiheit*
(Gütersloh, 1975), pp. 119–34; E. Schlink, *Die Lehre von der Taufe* (Kassel, 1969);
H. Stirnimann, 'Karl Barths Tauffragment', *Freiburger Zeitschrift für Philosophie
und Theologie* 15 (1968), 3–28; T. F. Torrance, 'The one baptism common to
Christ and his church', in *Theology in Reconciliation* (London, 1975), pp. 82–105;
R. Weth, 'Taufe in den Tod Jesu Christi als Anfang eines Neuen Lebens', in
H. Deuser et al., eds., *Gottes Zukunft – Zukunft der Welt. Festschrift für Jürgen
Moltmann zum 60. Geburtstag* (Munich, 1986), pp. 147–58. G. Wainwright,
'Développements baptismaux depuis 1967', *Etudes Théologiques et Religieuses* 49
(1974), 67–93, gives a useful survey of the wider territory.

On *ChrL*, once again Jüngel gives a very good introduction in 'Invocation of
God as the ethical ground of Christian action', in *Theological Essays* (Edinburgh,
1989), pp. 154–72. Further studies of the posthumous material include
K. Blaser, 'L'Ethique en tant qu' ''Invocation de Dieu''. A propos des derniers
cours de Karl Barth', in *Karl Barth 1886–1968. Combats – Idées – Reprises* (Bern,
1987), pp. 171–81; J.-L. Blondel, 'Prayer and struggle: Karl Barth's *The Christian
Life*', *St. Luke's Journal of Theology* 23 (1980), 105–15; C. C. Dickinson, 'Church
Dogmatics IV/4', in H.-M. Rumscheidt, ed., *Karl Barth in Re-View* (Pittsburgh,
1981), pp. 43–54; T. Vogel, ' ''Unterweisung in der Kunst des richtigen Fragens
nach Gottes Willen und des offenen Hörens auf sein Gebot'': Ansatz der Ethik
und des ethischen Argumentation bei Karl Barth', in H. Köckert and
W. Krötke, eds., *Theologie als Christologie* (Berlin, 1988), 121–35; J. B. Webster,
'The Christian in revolt: some reflections on *The Christian Life*', in N. Biggar,
ed., *Reckoning with Barth* (Oxford, 1988), pp. 119–44.

nature of human moral maturity, questions of rebellion and resistance. A close reading of these texts will give the attentive reader a quite different version of Barth from that promoted by some interpreters, a reading in which the description of humanity's deeds as God's covenant partner is neither a concession to, nor a compromise of, Barth's point, but the outworking of some of his most deeply held theological convictions.

For these reasons, then, Barth's ethics of reconciliation offer a good entrée into a neglected feature of his work. However, they cannot be isolated from the whole argument of the *Church Dogmatics*, since the *Dogmatics* is, for all its detours, reconsiderations, and occasional retractions, a massively consistent argument, each part of which builds upon and helps interpret the other parts. Accordingly, the first two chapters of this book set the context of Barth's late ethical writings by tracing the theme of human agency as it emerges in the earlier parts of the argument of the *Dogmatics*, where Barth considers revelation, trinity, election, creation, and Christology, among other topics. These two chapters show extensively what is then shown intensively by reference to the final sections of the *Church Dogmatics* – namely, that Barth can make good his claim to have kept a firm eye on human persons as agents right from the beginning of his dogmatic argument.[29]

This book is, however, more than an exposition and interpretation of Barth. It also tries to identify some of the resources which his work offers for constructing a Christian theological account of human agency. Forty years ago, Donald MacKinnon remarked that 'it is simply not the

---

[29] Macken's proposal that what is found in the ethics of reconciliation is a late shift in Barth's development which emerges 'out of decades of struggle in which the affirmation of human and creaturely reality gradually won ground without contradicting the absolute claim of the divine subject' (*The Autonomy Theme*, p. 85) is not quite correct. Matheny (*Dogmatics and Ethics*, p. 5) is more on target when he suggests that '[v]ery early on in his career, Barth was convinced that a proper construal of the scriptural understanding of divine–human relationality could be used as a parable or model to provide a criterion and a point of reference that would set limits and furnish guidelines for human ethical agency'.

case that our theological understanding of human action is adequate to the perplexities of the present',[30] and his remark still holds true today. One – perhaps *the* most – persistent problem for Christian moral theology in modernity is that of developing an account of human persons as agents, active historical subjects rather than simply patients or recipients of the actions of others or Another. How can we talk of human action in such a way that we affirm both the reality of divine grace and the reality of action as a human moral project? Is it possible to affirm that human persons are subjects and agents in their own histories, and also to affirm that their subjectivity and agency are ultimately what they are by the gift of God? What range of languages about divine grace and human action do we need to attend to and develop in order to retain a sense of divine prevenience and yet of the substance of the human realm? And in what ways can our language beguile us into implicitly or explicitly undermining either the reality of our acts or the reality of their ultimate source in God? Elsewhere, MacKinnon phrased the issue thus:

A man's freedom is inalienable and imprescriptible; and we have to ask what becomes of his action if he takes the law of that action from outside himself to the extent not only of acknowledging that he receives *ab extra* its principle, but that he must regard its very accomplishment as something which he has received. True, he may point, as Paul does, to the range of his endurance; but is it his own? Is it tolerable for a serious morality to speak of 'our sufficiency as being of God'?[31]

MacKinnon's way of putting the question echoes a set of convictions about human subjectivity and liberty whose widespread acceptance and virtually axiomatic authority for Western understandings of morality are amongst the chief cultural fruits of the modern era from the seventeenth century onwards. These convictions have, in short, made any language about divine grace extremely difficult to sustain.

[30] D. M. MacKinnon, 'Christian and Marxist dialectic', in MacKinnon ed., *Christian Faith and Communist Faith* (London, 1953), p. 240.
[31] D. M. MacKinnon, *A Study in Ethical Theory* (London, 1957), p. 270.

Language about grace and language about human morality seem to pull in quite contrary directions, for to appeal to divine grace is to appeal for the action of an agent other than ourselves, and so to confess the inadequacy, even the uselessness, of our own moral endeavours. Consider, for example, a few remarks from Kant's *Religion Within the Limits of Reason Alone*. He writes thus of the idea of grace:

> The concept of a supernatural accession to our moral, though deficient, capacity and even to our not wholly purified and certainly weak disposition to perform our entire duty, is a transcendent concept, it is a bare idea, of whose reality no experience can assure us. Even when accepted as an idea in nothing but a practical context it is very hazardous, and hard to reconcile with reason, since that which is to be accredited to us as morally good conduct must take place not through foreign influence but solely through the best possible use of our own powers.[32]

Kant goes on to say that the idea of grace 'is wholly transcendent', so that it is 'salutary to hold it, as a sacred thing, at a respectful distance, lest, under the illusion of performing miracles ourselves or observing miracles within us, we render ourselves unfit for all use of reason or allow ourselves to fall into the indolence of awaiting from above, in passive leisure, what we should seek within'.[33] Kant's point is that grace is a morally subversive concept; reliance upon an external agency easily corrodes morality by transferring to another those tasks which it is our duty to perform. 'Grace dreamed of in slothful trust'[34] removes us from the real world of responsible action into a world of happy dependence upon 'foreign influence' where it matters little what we do.[35]

Does Barth offer us any help here? Most would answer in the negative, finding in him a restatement of the problem

---

[32] I. Kant, *Religion within the Limits of Reason Alone* (New York, 1960), p. 179.

[33] Ibid., p. 180.

[34] Ibid., p. 182.

[35] That Kant nevertheless retains a (minimal and not fully coherent) notion of divine grace, generated chiefly under pressure from his notion of radical evil, is shown by G. E. Michalson, 'Moral regeneration and divine aid in Kant', *Religious Studies* 25 (1989), 259–70.

rather than an attempt at its solution. It appears as if the logic both of Barth's doctrine of God and of his anthropology not only prevent him from making any substantial affirmations about human action, but also segregate the internally coherent world of his theology from the public realities of human history and action:

The later work of Barth, notably that of the *Church Dogmatics*, possesses a pathos ... strength and power were bought at the price of progressive isolation. This is a tendency chartable not only biographically through Barth's successive rejections of those with whom he came to disagree, but also within the inner logic of a theological system that struggles to regain reality through a strident theological rhetoric of the 'real'.[36]

Or again, this time in connection with Ernst Bloch:

The triumphalist pursuit of hegemony in either Bloch's 'Kingdom' or Barth's 'God' risks an intellectual absurdity most apparent where the systematic and ontological self-consistency of both is most complete. Thus the concluding passages of Bloch's *The Principle of Hope* and the third volume of Barth's *Church Dogmatics* risk *reductio ad absurdum* as on re-encountering contingency after their ontological adventures both writers face the charge that they represent merely the seamless rhetoric of transformation rather than an actual analysis of the possibility of translation of theory into social reality and practice. Their intellectual excursions into the grandiose inner logic of narratives extending, as it were into the future (Bloch) and the past (Barth), risk reduction to banal identity. Both have, in reality, reactivated quasi-idealist strategies that license massive literary self-advertisement but change little in any direct sense.[37]

In response to this most serious challenge to Barth, I want to suggest that his manner of theology remains a compelling option. However, its resourcefulness can only be seen if we are prepared to bear with Barth as he calls into question some of the most cherished and respected principles of modern Christian theology. One such principle is a commit-

[36] R. H. Roberts, 'Barth and the eschatology of Weimar', in *A Theology on Its Way? Essays on Karl Barth* (Edinburgh, 1991), p. 196.

[37] R. H. Roberts, *Hope and Its Hieroglyph. A Critical Decipherment of Ernst Bloch's "Principle of Hope"* (Atlanta, 1990), p. 222.

ment to historical contingency as ontologically superior to, or inclusive of, the world of the Christian confession. Whilst Barth's rejection of the principle undoubtedly seems 'quasi-idealist', we will make little headway until we acknowledge that he has a radically anti-modern moral ontology – that his map of the territory in which human action occurs is fundamentally different from those of his predecessors in the recent or more distant traditions of Western theology and moral philosophy. His work will remain opaque or obstinately unavailable unless we are prepared to follow him in looking at the contingencies of history as embraced within a more comprehensive context furnished by the confession of Jesus Christ as Lord.[38]

A second such principle which Barth challenges, closely connected with the first, is that the most responsible mode for Christian theology in modernity is 'apologetic' – or, at least, a co-ordination or correlation or integration of its concerns with its social, cultural, and intellectual milieu. But Barth does not 'answer' the kinds of critique developed by Kant and others; instead, he undermines their authority by undertaking to describe with unparalleled intellectual breadth and depth the very things which the critiques disallow. When I began this project, I half-hoped that Barth would say what some critics would have him say – that human beings are self-initiating agents whose dignity lies in their capacity for voluntary, responsible action. It is just possible to read his ethics of reconciliation in that way, viewing the final part of the *Church Dogmatics* as in some measure backing away from the apparently exclusivist theology of sovereignty thought to dominate his earlier work. But such a reading is, I now believe, a serious mis-reading, failing to take into account how thoroughly Barth's project,

---

[38] Matheny notes (*Dogmatics and Ethics*, p. 45) that 'Barth's conviction concerning the relation of dogmatics to ethics coincides and congrues with his rejection of all modern attempts to form a synthesis between theological and philosophical perspectives that place phenomenal reality in a position of primacy on the epistemological level ... To accomplish this task, he re-asserts the place of both revelation and eschatological reality in the scheme of human reality in such a way as to reconstruct their significance for theological thought.'

even in its early phases, calls modernity into question. From first to last – from the Wiesbaden lecture of 1922 on 'The Problem of Ethics Today'[39] to the discussion of resistance in *The Christian Life* – Barth is profoundly perturbed by one of modernity's primary images of the human person: that of the self as a centre of judgment, creating value by its acts of allegiance or choice, organising the moral world around its consciousness of itself as the ethical *fundamentum*. With great vigour, Barth resists – in the ethical sphere as much as elsewhere – the 'naively strong conviction that [humans'] self-awareness as human beings is superior to the totality of those things which differ from it, which are in some way outside it'.[40] It is, I hope to show, most helpful to read the ethics of reconciliation as an exercise in such resistance. He refuses to concede that modernity sets definitive limits to what may be said and thought, not because he fears that modernity has said too much and left Christian theology with nothing further to say, but because it has said too little, disregarding the reality to which Christian faith and action bear witness and which is alone properly to be called 'real'. In making such affirmations, and in making them in the way and on the basis that he does, Barth refuses to succumb to resignation about the possibility of theological discourse. He simply breaks the rules of modernity, according to which, as Kathryn Tanner puts it, 'freedom and power are had by the creature only in independence from God's creative agency for them'.[41]

All this makes Barth's texts demanding to read: like any 'classic' texts, they question and unsettle their readers. 'Classics command attention' by resisting 'our engrained laziness and self-satisfaction'.[42] I want to try to show that

[39] K. Barth, 'The problem of ethics today', in *The Word of God and the Word of Man* (London, 1928), pp. 136–82.

[40] K. Barth, *Protestant Theology in the Nineteenth Century. Its Background and History* (London, 1972), p. 74.

[41] K. Tanner, *God and Creation in Christian Theology. Tyranny or Empowerment?* (Oxford, 1988), p. 162.

[42] D. Tracy, *Plurality and Ambiguity. Hermeneutics, Religion, Hope* (San Francisco, 1987), p. 15.

what commands attention in Barth's ethics of reconciliation is a twofold claim: that the followers of Jesus Christ are invited and entitled to act, and that the invitation and entitlement to action are truly grasped only by those who live in his fellowship and under his good and gracious rule.

CHAPTER ONE

Revelation and God

The final sections of Barth's *Dogmatics* offer a theological description of the grounds and nature of the Christian life and of the Christian agent engaged in that life. Making sense of his description involves us in retracing a number of decisions which Barth has worked through in the earlier volumes of his massive argument. Amongst these decisions are formal or methodological proposals about the nature of theological ethics, but these are important for Barth only in so far as they reflect substantive decisions about major topics in Christian doctrine: revelation, trinity, Christ, Spirit, creation, humanity, covenant, salvation. We cannot begin to understand Barth's theological ethics until we see that he construes both the human agent and the sphere within which human agency occurs by reference to an entire vision of reality of which the centre is the manifestation of God's creative and regenerative purposes in the history of Jesus Christ. Our first task, then, before turning directly to the ethics of reconciliation, is to sketch some of the primary moves of the preceding argument of the *Dogmatics* as they bear upon both the task of Christian ethics and the subject-matter to which it addresses itself: free human acts in correspondence to God's free and liberating act.

But expounding Barth is no easy task. The *Dogmatics* is a work of extraordinary beauty and moral seriousness as well as scholarly depth, and the temptation to reduce its conceptual and rhetorical complexities to the 'one-dimensionality of what passes for scholarly expression' is always crouching at the interpreter's door.[1] Barth himself sounded more than one warning against casual interpretations and critiques of his work. Moreover, for all its twists and turns, the *Dogmatics* displays a high degree of internal consistency, such that each part of the argument simultaneously draws from and expands the other parts; and so to expound one theme is almost inevitably to expound the whole. But underlying these difficulties is the fact that, because the extensive (on some readings, overextensive) *use* of primary Christian language and concepts is an essential part of how Barth undertakes to recover the vocation of Christian theology, summaries of his writing rarely get off the ground.[2] Even though the attempt at exposition has to be made if we are to get some purchase on Barth's thinking, we would be unwise to consider it as anything other than a set of fairly unsatisfactory markers to help make sense of an argument that best speaks for itself.

REVELATION AND THEOLOGY

'Ethics', he writes at the beginning of his exposition of the ethics of reconciliation in paragraph 74, 'is an attempt to answer theoretically the question of what may be called good human action. Theological ethics such as is attempted here finds both this question and its answer in God's Word. It thus finds it where theological dogmatics as the critical science of true church proclamation finds all its answers and questions. Theological ethics can be understood only as an integral element of dogmatics.'[3] Our initial orientation concerns the way in which Barth understands the nature of theology (and hence theological ethics) and its responsibility to revelation.

---

[1] E. Jüngel, *Karl Barth. A Theological Legacy* (Philadelphia, 1986), p. 12.
[2] As Hans Frei puts it (*Types of Christian Theology* (New Haven, 1992), p. 157), '[A]s one tries to restate it afterwards the material dies on one's hands. It can be done, but there is nothing so wooden as to read one's own or others' restatements of Barth's terms, his technical themes and their development.'
[3] *ChrL*, p. 3.

'Theological existence is exclusively and without compromise *theological* existence – nothing more and nothing less.'[4] That tautologous definition from a peerless contemporary interpreter catches precisely Barth's understanding of the theological task. Dogmatics (of which ethics is a part) is, on this account, irreducible, in the sense that it is a discipline with its own grounds, grounds to which alone its language and its procedures are responsible, grounds which are not secured by any considerations drawn from a more comprehensive context within which they might be located, grounds which are only successfully disclosed in the actual pursuit of theological thinking rather than in any antecedent rationale or theoretical description. The immense intellectual and spiritual force of Barth's work – as well as most of the severe problems which characteristically attend its reception – stem from the astonished, insistent (to the jaundiced reader, obsessive) single-mindedness with which he pursues his task as one which is answerable to no other reality than that which has brought it into being, namely the Word of God. 'I believe that it is expected of the Church and its theology – a world within the world no less than chemistry or the theatre – that it should keep precisely to the rhythms of its own relevant concerns, and thus consider well what are the *real* needs of the day by which its own programme should be directed.'[5]

Barth's orientation of his *Dogmatics* in 'The Doctrine of the Word of God', especially in volume I/I, is best read as an extended attempt to do just that: to recover for theology 'the rhythm of its own ... concerns'. Dogmatics, he proposes, has to go 'its own way sincerely and with no pretence'.[6] More concretely, dogmatics has to be characterised by both a 'confessional attitude' and a 'church attitude',[7] since it is an undertaking 'within the framework of the

---

[4] E. Jüngel, 'Theologische Existenz – Erinnerung an Karl Barth', *Evangelische Kommentare* 19 (1986), 259
[5] I/I, p. xvi.
[6] Ibid., p. 31.
[7] I/2, pp. 822, 840.

Church' in which the hearing and teaching church reminds itself that 'there exists prior to and above and after every *ego dico* and *ecclesia dixit* a *haec dixit dominus*'.[8] And, above all, Barth repeatedly distances himself from apologetic investigation of the *possibility* of Christian dogmatics by reference to some more general realm of human piety or some theory of knowledge or ontology. He refuses, that is, to advance anything in the way of an extra-theological argument in favour of theology. Especially in Anglo-Saxon response to Barth, this refusal of apologetics is frequently (and rather lamely) construed as a tiresome inability to see the epistemological and moral resources for theology and ethics in a notion of natural order. But such a response scarcely catches what Barth is about: his point is much more far-reaching than simply a denial of generally available knowledge of God upon which revelation in Christ builds. In the end Barth is constructing a full-scale alternative to a notion which has been firmly established 'since the days of the Enlightenment' in what he calls 'Modernistic dogmatics', namely the notion that 'the Church and faith are to be understood as links in a greater nexus of being'.[9] The whole of Barth's dogmatic *œuvre* can be seen as a huge attempt to refute that Enlightenment notion, not so much by arguing against it as by reversing its terms and describing how things look if the 'greater nexus of being' is relocated *within* the framework to which church and faith testify.

Barth is concerned to contradict the principle that, in giving an account of 'the way of knowledge pursued in dogmatics', we can take up a superior position 'which is somewhere apart from this way or above the work of dogmatics', in 'an ontology or anthropology as the basic science of the human possibilities among which consideration is somewhere given to that of faith and church.'[10] Barth believed this principle to be embedded in liberal Protestant dogmatics, in theological existentialism, and in what he took

[8] Ibid., p. 801.
[9] I/I, p. 36.
[10] Ibid., p. 32.

to be classic Roman Catholic teaching concerning the *analogia entis*. But it is important to realise that Barth's point is more than epistemological. His objection to pre-theological inquiry into the possibility of dogmatic knowledge is that to adopt the stance from which such an inquiry is conducted is in effect to take up a position which subverts the absoluteness of God in his self-manifestation in Jesus Christ. By definition, that self-manifestation, precisely because it is the self-manifestation of *God*, cannot be handled as if it were a contingent feature of a more comprehensive reality; it simply *is*, and any attempt to adopt a position apart from, or over against, it in order to discuss its possibility overturns the very reality which it seeks to secure. 'The possibility of revelation is actually to be read off from its reality in Jesus Christ.'[11] Here Barth is putting into effect what he learnt from his study of Anselm at the beginning of the 1930s:[12] if God in self-revelation is sheerly necessary being, then 'the place from which the way of dogmatic knowledge is to be seen and understood can be neither a prior anthropological possibility nor a subsequent ecclesiastical reality, but only the present moment of the speaking and hearing of Jesus Christ Himself, the divine creation of light in our hearts'.[13]

It is from this perspective that we are to interpret Barth's interweaving of the doctrines of revelation and divine triunity. Revelation is not primarily an *epistemological* doctrine for Barth. It only furnishes an answer to the question 'How do we know God?', from within its answer to the question 'Who is God?' In revelation, God identifies himself; and so the concern of the doctrine of revelation is not first and foremost to develop a theory of knowledge, but to offer an account of the divine being. 'If we really want to understand revelation in terms of its subject, that is, God, then the first thing we have to realise is that this subject, God, the Revealer, is identical with His act in revelation and also

[11] I/2, p. 31.
[12] This study culminated in the 1931 interpretation of the *Proslogion*, translated as *Anselm: Fides Quaerens Intellectum* (London, 1960).
[13] I/2, p. 31.

identical with its effect. It is from this fact . . . that we
learn we must begin the doctrine of revelation with the
doctrine of the triune God.'[14] It is certainly an important
question whether this approach to the doctrine of the trinity
tends (at least in the first volume of the *Dogmatics*) to
conceive of God quasi-monistically as the single divine subject of a completed act of self-manifestation.[15] That question
aside, however, the whole thrust of Barth's doctrine of revelation is against the loading of that doctrine with cognitive
or experiential questions prior to consideration of the being
of God: language about revelation puts us firmly in the
province of the Christian doctrine of God and the acts of
God.

In sum, in 'The Doctrine of the Word of God' Barth is
advancing, in Hans Frei's phrase, 'an internal prolegomena
to dogmatics . . . in which he unfolds the concept of revelation descriptively rather than constructing an argument for
its conceptual possibility.'[16] Frei goes on to note how

Barth was looking for ways to show that the correlation of distinctive Christian concepts with concepts derived from general human
experience inevitably leads in the direction of the reduction of
Christian concepts. Mediating theology is an unstable compromise
between a Christocentric theology properly at risk because stripped
of all external foundational support, and a theology that has put
itself at the mercy of consistent conceptual 'demythologization',
on the other. Mediating or apologetical theology has a superior
standpoint from which to mediate between these two extremes on
even and harmonious terms . . . but of course Barth thought that
it was a place which did not, or should not, really exist.[17]

This is an acute observation. By the time he began (for the
second time) to write the prolegomena to a *Dogmatics*, Barth
was able to turn his back on the paradigm of theology

---

[14] I/1, p. 297.
[15] See here, for example, R. Williams, 'Barth on the triune God', in S. W. Sykes,
ed., *Karl Barth. Studies of his Theological Method* (Oxford, 1979), pp. 147–93; and
'Trinity and revelation', *Modern Theology* 2:3 (1986), pp. 197–212.
[16] H. Frei, 'Barth and Schleiermacher: divergence and convergence', in *Theology
and Narrative. Selected Essays* (Oxford, 1993), p. 180.
[17] Ibid., p. 183.

which had governed Protestantism since at least the end of
the eighteenth century, and to offer an extensive exposition
of the nature of the discipline which consistently declined
to locate faith, church, and their intellectual expressions
within a larger class of realities ('knowledge', 'religion',
'history'), realities of which the particulars of Christian
conviction are examples and into which they may be by
and large resolved as contingent expressions of generic states
of affairs. In this sense at least, the Barth of the early
Dogmatics is no foundationalist: he is entirely reluctant to
sever the identity between 'the absolute' or 'that which is
of ultimate significance' and the content of the Christian
faith, above all its trinitarian and Christological
content.[18]

Underlying all this is Barth's theological *realism*. His rejection of non-theological prolegomena to dogmatics, his 'maxi-
mization of the difference between *Wissenschaftslehre* and
theology',[19] is much more than an attempt to secure cognitive
privileges for the theologian by separating theology from the
'non-theological' disciplines. It is grounded in an assertion
of the *ontological* supremacy of God in his self-manifestation:
'being' may only be ascribed to realities other than the
reality of the self-revealing God in a wholly derivative sense.
And so whilst Barth is not a foundationalist (at least in the
sense noted above), nor is he a pluralist or relativist or
idealist. His refusal to situate the Christian faith and theology within a larger class of realities does not mean that
he sees faith and its theological articulation as (to use
contemporary idiom) one of a number of incommensurable
'worlds of meaning' constituted 'intratextually' and held
together by linguistic procedures and 'intrasystematic' conventions. Though Barth is increasingly pressed into service

---

[18] The point can also be illustrated with considerable success by reference to
Barth's later use of Christological narrative, especially in his doctrine of reconciliation. See here two readings of Barth, both of which are indebted to Frei's
work: D. Ford, *Barth and God's Story* (Frankfurt, 1981) and B. Marshall, *Christology
in Conflict. The Identity of a Saviour in Rahner and Barth* (Oxford, 1987).

[19] H. Frei, 'Barth and Schleiermacher', p. 196.

for theological proposals along these lines,[20] such interpretations in the end break down because they pay scant attention to Barth's realist understanding of the world of faith.
Christian faith and theology are 'realist' in the sense that
they testify to an absolute act of divine self-positing, in
whose self-establishing veracity they participate by grace.
Barth would have little patience with interest in immanent
worlds of meaning, and perhaps would have associated it
with the wearisome business of ecclesial subjectivism which
often filled him with dismay. Such speculation apart, Barth's
emphasis that faith and theology cannot be deduced from
other realities by transcendental argument is *toto caelo* different from agnosticism concerning their objective grounds,
and from any suggestion that the dynamics of faith's production are basically internal. If Barth refuses to submit
theology to the pressures of the 'Cartesian anxiety', the
nervous search for justifications, it is because theology
already has an absolute justification in its given ground:
like faith, it needs no other foundation than that which is
given in the divine self-manifestation from which it comes.
It is for *this* reason (rather than on the basis of cognitive
relativism) that Barth presses that 'theology does not have
to begin by finding or inventing the standard by which it
measures. It sees and recognises that this is given with the
Church. It is given in its own peculiar way, as Jesus Christ
is given, as God in His revelation gives Himself to faith.
But it is given. It is complete in itself. It stands by its

---

[20] Notably by G. Lindbeck, both in a hint at the end of *The Nature of Doctrine.
Religion and Theology in a Postliberal Age* (Philadelphia, 1984), p. 135, and in his
essay, 'Barth and textuality', *Theology Today* 43 (1986), 361–76; H. Frei writes
appreciatively of Lindbeck towards the end of his essay, 'The "literal reading"
of biblical narrative in the Christian tradition: does it stretch or will it break?',
in *Theology and Narrative*, pp. 117–52. For some critical appraisal of Lindbeck
on this point, see R. Thiemann, 'Response to George Lindbeck', *Theology Today*
43 (1986), 377–82, and G. Hunsinger, 'Beyond literalism and expressivism: Karl
Barth's hermeneutical realism', *Modern Theology* 3:3 (1987), 209–23, especially p.
222, n. 20; *How To Read Karl Barth. The Shape of His Theology* (Oxford, 1991),
pp. 165–73; and 'Truth as self-involving. Barth and Lindbeck on the cognitive
and performative aspects of truth in theological discourse', *Journal of the American
Academy of Religion* 61 (1993), 41–56.

claim without discussion.'[21] Or, as he puts it later in a
statement of the 'analytic judgment' which is, in effect, both
the epistemological and the ontological axiom of the whole
Dogmatics: 'God reveals Himself as the Lord.'[22]

Barth's realism is of a very distinct kind, because of the
reality to which it is oriented, the self-revealing God. His
insistence on the underivability of Christian faith and theology is rooted in a conviction that the reality by which
they are encountered and to which they are a response –
the reality which in this early part of the *Dogmatics* he
designates 'the Word of God', and which he will later
describe with ever-increasing focus as the narratable identity
of Jesus Christ – *is reality*. That is to say, it is real in a
way and with a force which entirely eclipse all other claimed
realities, realities which it absolutely transcends and encloses
within itself, but by which it is in no sense comprehended.
'It is He, He who is the reality!'[23] To be encountered by
that reality in its self-positing and radically *new* character
is to be faced with a challenge to transgress and reorganise
habitual perceptions of the norms for human experience
and expression.[24] The ruthless consistency with which Barth
pursues the logic of this ontological claim has often evoked
the charge of monism. As we look at what Barth has to
say about the Christian as agent, we shall see that in many
respects that charge trades on a misunderstanding. Barth
is not claiming that God in Christ is 'the reality' in an
exclusive sense, in a way which amounts to an ontological
disenfranchisement of all other 'realities'. The reality of

---

[21] 1/1, p. 12.

[22] Ibid., p. 306. In similar vein, Hunsinger asks: 'Can it be irrelevant . . . that
Lindbeck finds it possible to define the necessary and sufficient conditions for
the truth of a theological assertion, without once referring to the role of divine
agency?', 'Truth as self-involving', p. 49. See further R. Thiemann, 'The significance of Karl Barth for contemporary theology', *The Thomist* 50 (1986), 530.

[23] 1/2, p. 368.

[24] G. Hunsinger ('A response to William Werpehowski', *Theology Today* 43 (1986),
359) comments: 'The world announced in the biblical narratives, as Barth read
them, is a world beyond ordinary comprehension and experience, because it is
a world in which the very conditions of experience are to be transfigured and
made new.'

Jesus Christ as the self-positing of God includes within itself all other realities, and it is in him and from him that they have their inalienable substance. Barth's apparent ontological exclusivism is in fact an inclusivism: *solus Christus* embraces and does not suspend or absorb the world of creatures and their actions.[25]

Barth's *Dogmatics*, then, is to be read as in its entirety a single extended realist claim that God in his self-manifestation has both epistemological and ontological priority, and that it is to that self-establishing reality that faith and theology *refer*. The notion of 'reference' is one which has sustained severe damage in recent philosophical writing, most of all in those versions which propose that 'reality' is made up of a set of objects independent of minds, languages, concepts, and theories, and whose true description would involve correspondence between sign and thing signified.[26] Barth, too, is cautious about the reach of human acts of referring, but the reason he advances for his caution is not simply the historical or contingent character of cognitive acts. Though he is always sharply aware of the negative dynamics of projection, his caution has more to do with the fact that both the reality to which we refer (God) and the process by which we come to refer to that reality of God lie wholly outside the range of our human possibilities. Certainly we may talk of 'a reference to the event of the real knowledge of the Word of God'; but 'the power of this reference does not lie in itself; it lies in that to which it refers . . . In no respect, then, does the force of our reference lie in our hands.'[27] Nevertheless, Barth is not content to rest at that point; he wishes to press on to affirmations of the reliable character of Christian language in its referential function, even if that to which it refers is incomprehensible.

[25] On this theme, see I. U. Dalferth, 'Karl Barth's eschatological realism', in S. W. Sykes, ed., *Karl Barth. Centenary Essays* (Cambridge, 1989), pp. 14–45; and 'Theologischer Realismus und realistische Theologie bei Karl Barth', *Evangelische Theologie* 46 (1986), 402–22.

[26] For one of the very best summary statements of this critique, see H. Putnam, *Reason, Truth and History* (Cambridge, 1981).

[27] I/1, p. 197.

The point is one which he makes at some length in his discussion of 'the limits of the knowledge of God' in II/1.[28] There he freely acknowledges that human knowledge of God is an enterprise which shares fully in the formal character-istics of all human cognition (what he calls 'views' and 'concepts'), and that such 'viewing and conceiving are not at all capable of grasping God'.[29] God is 'hidden', then, in the sense that 'God does not belong to the objects which we can always subjugate to the process of our viewing, conceiving and expressing and therefore our spiritual over-sight and control'; or again, 'God is not a being whom we can spiritually appropriate.'[30] Hence all language ('even the language of ecclesiastical dogma and the Bible') stands 'under the crisis of the hiddenness of God'.[31] Barth's argu-ment, however, is not that of an anti-realist for whom we can never transcend the 'internal' or conventional character of all mental and linguistic representation. Whilst such trans-cendence is in no way a human possibility, an impulse to true human thought and speech about the incomprehensible God is effected by God himself in his revelation: 'He Himself has given us permission and command to see and speak.'[32] And, hence, in 'a bestowal which utterly transcends all our capacity', it happens that 'our viewing of the unviewable God and conceiving of the inconceivable God are made by God's own capacity a genuine viewing and conceiving, the whole truth of which is the truth of God, and that in such a way that by the capacity of its object it is a true viewing and conceiving'.[33]

---

[28] II/1, pp. 179–254. For some reflections on the larger context of this paragraph from the *Dogmatics*, see C. Gunton, 'No other foundation. One Englishman's reading of *Church Dogmatics*, chapter V', in N. Biggar, ed., *Reckoning with Barth* (Oxford, 1988), pp. 61–79.

[29] II/1, p. 182.

[30] Ibid., pp. 187, 188.

[31] Ibid., p. 195. In this respect, G. Hunsinger is correct to suggest that Barth's understanding of the way in which the biblical text refers is not 'literalist', in that Barth denies any 'perfect coincidence' between the text and its mysterious, ineffable referent. See 'Beyond literalism and expressivism', pp. 209, 220.

[32] Ibid., p. 190.

[33] Ibid., p. 198.

This kind of 'participation in the veracity of the revelation of God'[34] is supremely to be attributed to Scripture, which is for dogmatics and ethics 'the basic text upon which all the rest and everything of our own can only wait and comment'.[35] But why so? Because Barth is refusing 'the basic error' of thinking that 'the realities of which the Bible speaks are found in doctrinal, metaphysical, moral, experimental or historical domains above, behind, beneath or in front of the text'?[36] Hardly. Because the text 'absorbs the world, rather than the world the text'?[37] Perhaps. Or – more subtly – because the 'linguistic, textual world is . . . not only the *necessary* basis for our orientation within the real world, according to the Christian claims about this narrative, and this narrative alone; it is also *sufficient* for the purpose'?[38] Such statements reach towards what Barth is doing, and certainly find some echoes in some statements of his own, notably from the period of his intense recovery of Scripture whilst in the pastorate at Safenwil.[39] But they miss the target to the extent to which they fail to see that, for Barth, it is not Scripture as *text*, and certainly not Scripture in its *use* by a determinate religious community,[40] which is of overarching significance, but Scripture as normative *testimony* to the absolute act of God's self-manifestation in free grace. Barth's understanding of Scripture as the 'basic text' is inseparable from his emphasis on the divine action by which it becomes God's Word: 'The Bible is God's Word to the extent that God causes it to be His Word', so

---

[34] Ibid., p. 213.

[35] I/I, p. xii.

[36] G. Lindbeck, 'Barth and textuality', p. 365.

[37] G. Lindbeck, *The Nature of Doctrine*, p. 118.

[38] H. Frei, 'The "literal reading" of biblical narrative', p. 143.

[39] See, for instance, two classic early addresses: 'The strange new world within the Bible' and 'Biblical questions, insights, and vistas', in *The Word of God and the Word of Man* (London, 1928), pp. 28–96.

[40] Barth's refusal to identify the truth-content of Scripture (and of other forms of Christian language) with its use has been pointed out by G. White, 'Karl Barth's theological realism', *Neue Zeitschrift für Systematische Theologie und Religionsphilosophie* 26 (1984), 60.

that what is central is 'God's action in the Bible'.[41] Expressed as a thesis: 'Revelation engenders Scripture which attests it.'[42] Once again, the argument rests on realist convictions about the character of God's self-revealing, of which Scripture is a function. The 'biblical character' of dogmatics and Christian ethics is, thus, not a matter of conformity to the 'cultural-linguistic' world of Christian faith, textually encoded; it is rather a matter of adopting the attitude of the biblical witness as one 'exclusively controlled by the realities which it is his duty to indicate and confirm'.[43]

In sum: Barth's disavowal of apologetic prolegomena to dogmatics, and his replacement of it by what is partly a treatise *De scriptura sacra*[44] and partly a treatise *De deo trino*, is rooted in his sense of the sheer noetic and ontological preponderance of the reality of God in his self-gift to humanity. This is why it is true to say that 'the *Church Dogmatics* is one long ontological treatise, one great vision of unified reality'.[45] But because that lovingly described reality is 'Jesus Christ in the divine-human unity of his being and work', then 'we are dealing both with God and with man'.[46] This inherent twofoldness of the reality with which Christian theology is concerned becomes increasingly fascinating to Barth as the *Dogmatics* unfolds, and will culminate in his discussion of the Christian agent in the ethics of reconciliation. But it is present from the very start in his

---

[41] I/1, pp. 109, 110. It is at this point that Lindbeck's interpretation of Barth in 'Barth and textuality' has been heavily criticised. See, for example, R. Thiemann, 'Response to George Lindbeck', p. 378; G. Hunsinger, 'Beyond literalism and expressivism', p. 222, n. 20, and 'Truth as self-involving', passim. Both Thiemann and Hunsinger are disposed to take *CD* I/1 and I/2 seriously, unlike Lindbeck, who dismisses Barth's early volumes as the importation of bad epistemology (see ibid., p. 368). For a perceptive statement of the need for an account of divine agency in the theology of Scripture and its functioning, see J. Sykes, 'Narrative accounts of biblical authority: the need for a doctrine of revelation', *Modern Theology* 5:4 (1989), 327–42.

[42] I/1, p. 115.

[43] I/2, p. 817.

[44] Cf. the discussion in I/1, p. 43.

[45] R. Jenson, 'Karl Barth', in D. Ford, ed., *The Modern Theologians*, vol. I (Oxford, 1989), p. 28.

[46] *ChrL*, p. 3.

account of the human recipient of revelation, to which we now turn.

In an essay on Barth's hermeneutics, Werner Jeanrond observes how 'Barth begins his *Church Dogmatics* with the hermeneutical-theological question: What is the Word of God and who am I in relationship to God's Word?'[47] It could equally well be said that Barth's initial question is an ethical-theological question, since the relation to itself which the Word of God establishes for its human recipient is not simply noetic, a matter of interpretation, but ethical, a matter of action. Put another way: *from the very beginning, Barth's theme is God and humanity as agents in relation.* Even at the furthest reaches of his protest against anthropocentric reduction of God to a function of human piety, consciousness or moral projects, Barth is attempting to safeguard not only the axiomatic divinity of God, but also the authenticity of the creature. Barth's later 'the-anthropology' (of which the ethics of reconciliation is the last substantial expression) already has its roots in his doctrine of revelation.

From the outset, then, Barth is concerned to point out that the Word of God sets before us 'the so-to-speak anthropological problem'.[48] How is that problem raised? It is worth pausing over Barth's answer to that question, not only because it remains consistent throughout the *Dogmatics*, but also because it gives us important clues to the way in which he sets about thinking about the human agent.

All along the line, Barth resists two notions. First, he refuses any suggestion that revelation can be considered in isolation from its directedness to human recipients: 'we cannot speak or think of it at all without remembering at once the man who hears and knows it'.[49] Abstracted from

[47] W. Jeanrond, 'Karl Barth's hermeneutics', in N. Biggar, ed., *Reckoning with Barth*, p. 84.
[48] I/1, p. 191.
[49] Ibid.

the fellowship which it seeks to establish with the hearers
of the Word, God's self-manifestation would not be what it
is: *manifestation*. But, second, Barth also refuses any idea that
this directedness of revelation presupposes the existence of
some realm which is relatively autonomous in respect of
God's manifestation of himself, a realm alongside, or even
prior to, the occurrence of the Word of God, which forms
a condition for the possibility of that Word. This is why
Barth gives such rough handling to suggestions that the
human creature is *capax infiniti*: 'God's Word is no longer
grace, and grace itself is no longer grace, if we ascribe to
man a predisposition towards this Word, a possibility of
knowledge regarding it that is intrinsically and independently native to him.'[50] Or again, 'the possibility of knowledge corresponding to the real Word of God . . . represents
an incomparable *novum* compared to all his ability and
capability'.[51] Crucially, however, this denial does not lead
Barth to exclude consideration of the human recipient of
revelation, but rather to ground the necessity of such a
consideration in the occurrence of revelation itself. It is the
procession of God's being in the history of its enactment
which raises the question of human being and history and
action. This means (1) that it is *exclusively* on the basis of
God's procession that humanity becomes a theological
theme, and (2) that on the basis of God's procession
humanity *really does* come into consideration. Barth will later
root this in substantive Christological dogma: in the doctrine
of the hypostatic union, and in his extensive reflections on
resurrection and the Holy Spirit. The logical and theological
structure of this development is already in place, however,
very early in the *Dogmatics*, providing one of the essentials
for his later ethical concentration.

    An early example of this pattern of argument occurs in
the section of I/I on 'The Word of God and Experience'.[52]
'By the experience of God's Word which is possible for

[50] Ibid., p. 194.
[51] Ibid.
[52] Ibid., pp. 198–227.

men on the presupposition of its reality, we understand the determination of their existence as men by God's Word.'[53] In explaining what he means here, Barth is at pains to point out that God's determination of human existence is not a factor which has to be set alongside human self-determination in some kind of coexistence or synthesis of two equal or comparable powers. But, on the other hand, divine determination does not issue in 'a state of potential or total receptivity or passivity',[54] precisely because such passivity 'involves a misconception of the nature of the encounter between God and man. If God is seriously involved in the experience of the Word of God, then man is just as seriously involved too.'[55] Thus 'the man who really knows God's Word . . . can understand himself only as one who exists in his act, in his self-determination',[56] in which 'very self-determination' we are 'subject to determination by God'.[57] In effect, what this means is that 'the self-determination of man as such takes place at a specific point in a specific context. It has found its beginning and its basis in another higher determination. In the act of acknowledgement, the life of man, without ceasing to be the self-determining life of this man, has now its centre, its whence, the meaning of its attitude, and the criterion whether this attitude really has the corresponding meaning – it has all this outside itself, in the thing or person acknowledged.'[58] Here we have *in nuce* all the major elements of Barth's characteristic way of entering into questions of human subjectivity and agency: a refusal of an independent realm of human being apart from God's Word (this will later be fully expressed in the account of the Word's assumption of humanity); an affirmation of the essentially reciprocal nature of the encounter between God and humanity brought about

[53] Ibid., p. 199.
[54] Ibid., p. 200.
[55] Ibid.
[56] Ibid.
[57] Ibid., p. 201.
[58] Ibid., pp. 207f.

by the Word (this will be developed most of all in the
handling of covenant); an emphasis that being human means
active existence in the context of God's history with
humanity (a point taken up in each of the ethical sections
of II/2, III/4 and IV/4).

Intrinsic to all these discussions, however, is a theology
of the Holy Spirit, already described in Barth's first full-dress
treatment of the topic in the *Dogmatics* as 'the subjective
side in the event of revelation',[59] God liberating *homo peccator*
to become *capax verbi divini*.[60] And, when Barth moves on to
look in detail at 'The Freedom of Man for God' as part of
his account of 'The Outpouring of the Holy Spirit',[61] the
discussion once again falls into the pattern just identified.
'In what freedom of man's is it real that God's revelation
reaches him?'[62] In answering the question, Barth from the
outset denies that a bridge into the realm of human subjectivity pre-exists the event of God's self-manifestation: there
are, simply, no 'natural' conditions for the reception of
revelation, and examining the possibility of such reception
does not entail moving into 'quite a different sphere of
inquiry' from that of the objective content which is
received.[63] Clearly Barth is combating neo-Protestant use of
'Spirit' as a bridge-term through which a synthesis of objective and subjective can be effected, and insisting instead
that 'the subjective reality of revelation as such can never
be made an independent theme. It is enclosed in its objective
reality'.[64] In the realm of the Spirit, we remain, therefore,
in the realm of the Christological *ephapax* and its application
by Jesus Christ himself in his high-priestly office.[65] Yet, even
here, the concern is not to abolish the subjective so much
as to establish it on proper grounds, thereby displaying the
true ordering of God and humanity, objective and subjective.

[59] Ibid., p. 449.
[60] Cf. ibid., p. 456.
[61] I/2, pp. 203–42.
[62] Ibid., p. 204.
[63] Ibid., p. 207.
[64] Ibid., p. 240.
[65] On this theme, see the discussion of 'The Readiness of Man', II/1, pp. 128–78.

'Not God alone, but God and man together constitute the content of the Word of God attested in Scripture.'[66] This almost incidental statement takes us near the heart of what Barth is about in his various accounts of the Spirit: the relation between God and humanity is fundamental, in that God is what he is in this relation. Certainly, the relation is 'not reversible', in the sense that '[i]t is not a relation in which man can be ... the partner and workmate of God'.[67] But, alongside the reality of '*God* with us', we have to affirm the further reality of 'God with *us*',[68] a reality which is, strictly speaking, not subordinate to the objective element 'because any subordination in principle would indirectly call into question the *homoousia* of the Holy Spirit'.[69] At least in the light of these passages, one of the major contemporary charges against Barth's trinitarian theology – its alleged adherence to 'the Latin, psychological model, which tends to isolate God from the drama which he initiates with man as his partner'[70] – can be seen to be rather wide of the mark.

There is a very important consequence: 'God with *us*' is an *ethical* reality, for in the outpouring of the Spirit in which God's revelation meets a specific person, 'the Word of God becomes unavoidably his master'.[71] As life in the Spirit, human life is determined for, and obligated to, obedient action, 'utterly and absolutely commanded'.[72] This command

---

[66] I/2, p. 207.
[67] Ibid., p. 207; cf. ibid., p. 235. Later, Barth will revise the antipathy to the notion of partnership, largely under pressure from the notion of covenant. On this, see W. Krötke, 'Gott und Mensch als "Partner". Zur Bedeutung einer zentralen Kategorie in Karl Barths Kirchlicher Dogmatik', in E. Jüngel, ed., *Zur Theologie Karl Barths, Zeitschrift für Theologie und Kirche* Beiheft 6 (1986), pp. 158–75.
[68] I/2, p. 207.
[69] Ibid., p. 208.
[70] P. J. Rosato, *The Spirit as Lord. The Pneumatology of Karl Barth* (Edinburgh, 1981), p. 137. The criticism has been made at some length by J. Moltmann in *The Trinity and the Kingdom of God* (London, 1981), pp. 139–44, and (much more carefully) by W. Pannenberg in *Grundfragen systematischer Theologie. Gesammelte Aufsätze II* (Göttingen, 1980), pp. 80–128.
[71] I/2, p. 265.
[72] Ibid., p. 272.

means both 'an ultimate and profound irresponsibility',[73] in
the sense of release from 'the spiritual cramp which always
results when men think and act as if the *causa dei* were
really their own anxiety and concern',[74] and also 'a definite
formation and direction' in conformity to Christ,[75] for 'the
aim of His action is that out of man's life there should
come a repetition, an analogy, a parallel to His own being –
that he should be conformable to Christ'.[76] The terms there
('repetition', 'analogy', 'parallel') hint towards a conviction
which will emerge with much greater force and clarity once
Barth has the notion of 'correspondence' (*Entsprechung*) more
firmly in place: the conviction that *because* (and *only* because)
God's enactment of his own life is what it is, then humanity
in its active life is an intrinsic theme of Christian dogmatics.
To affirm that this is so, as Barth does in the *Dogmatics*'
first lengthy section on ethics, under the title 'The Life of
the Children of God',[77] is not to detract from the perfection
of Christ's work, but to specify both that in which that
work consists and how it reaches its soteriological goal in
the establishment of the Christian life. 'It is the grace of
revelation that God exercises and maintains His freedom to
free man.'[78]

As Barth returns to methodological issues at the end of
1/2, he draws out of his discussion of revelation a principle
which he had struggled to articulate in the opening section
of his ethics lectures in 1928 in Münster and then in Bonn
in 1930:[79] '[T]he theme of dogmatics is always the Word
of God and nothing else. But the theme of the Word of
God is human existence, human life and volition and
action.'[80] Indeed, 'dogmatics loses nothing more nor less

[73] Ibid., p. 274.
[74] Ibid., p. 276.
[75] Ibid.
[76] Ibid., p. 277.
[77] Ibid., pp. 362–454. Barth took the title from a remark of Harnack's in the
course of a private conversation in 1925: see ibid., pp. 367f.
[78] Ibid., p. 365.
[79] See *Ethics* (Edinburgh, 1981), pp. 3–19.
[80] 1/2, p. 793.

than its object, and therefore all meaning, if it is not continually concerned as well with the existence of man and the
realities of his situation', with 'the problem of the Christian
life of man, i.e., the life of man as determined by the Word
of God: the problem what we ourselves must do'.[81] Critics
of this theme in Barth (especially in its much fuller presentation in the section in II/2 'Ethics as a Task of the Doctrine
of God'),[82] usually inveigh against the denial which underlies
what he has to say about the intrinsically ethical character
of dogmatics – the denial of any general ethical sphere or
set of problems, which are the object of common attention
and to which theological ethics in its turn also addresses
itself.[83] The core (and, from Barth's perspective, the
weakness) of the objection is the assumption – to which the
Dogmatics as a whole is an extended challenge – that we
know in advance of revelational-Christological considerations
the meaning of primary ethical concepts ('command',
'decision', 'history', 'self', 'action'), and that the Christian
meaning of those concepts is only a modulation of what is
more generally available. Whether we find Barth's ethics as
a whole satisfactory will depend to some degree upon willingness to follow him at this point. Nevertheless, we would be
unwise to assume that the logic of his position is such that
he can only talk seriously about the world of human action
by sidestepping his founding principles. Far from it: like the
Christian proclamation upon which it reflects, Christian
dogmatics 'undeniably has to do with the relationship *founded
and completed in the Word of God* between the true God and
true man, i.e., man in his totality and therefore as an active
agent'.[84]

Our next task is to explore some aspects of the doctrine
of God which is bound up with this proposal.

---

[81] Ibid., p. 792.
[82] II/2, pp. 509–51.
[83] For a recent example of this line of critique, see T. Rendtorff, *Ethics*, vol. 1 (Philadelphia, 1986), pp. 14–19.
[84] I/2, p. 788.

GOD, ELECTION AND ETHICS

The doctrine of the Word of God in the first four chapters of the *Dogmatics* is a proposal that 'God is known through God and through God alone':[85] the divine self-manifestation is a highly specific and absolutely unconditioned act of self-positing which by its occurrence creates knowing human subjects to correspond to itself. As we have seen, Barth declines to locate Christian knowledge of God in some more comprehensive setting, since, as knowledge of the absolute, it carries its own conditions with it and stands in need of no ancillary or antecedent states of affairs. Language about revelation, we might say, *particularises*, making Christian knowledge of God follow a specific path, marked out by the specific procession of God's being in self-bestowal. Barth's doctrine of God is an attempt to define with ever-increasing density the singular being of God who makes himself known *thus*.

'In the doctrine of God we are to learn what we are saying when we say "God" ',[86] Barth writes at the beginning of his account. The exposition which follows is in effect an elaborate set of descriptions of the Christian meaning of the term 'God'. Such descriptions are not merely descriptions of Christian *use*, for such use is no more sanctified than any other human attempt to speak of God. Like all attempts to know and speak of God, Christian knowledge and speech lie exposed to the constant temptation to make God into simply one of a series of objects for our cognisance, a basically apprehensible, manageable reality. Barth is undertaking, rather, an account of the *given* Christian meaning of the term, the conditions of which are generated from without, wholly determined by 'the particular and utterly unique objectivity of God'.[87]

Put more concretely: Barth is seeking to map out a meaning for the term 'God' which is controlled by unswerving

[85] II/I, p. 44.
[86] II/I, p. 3.
[87] Ibid., p. 14.

fidelity to the first commandment, which consistently recalls itself from the idolatrous drift towards the general away from the specificity of God's self-utterance.[88] In this regard, it is instructive to note Barth's consideration of the unity of God in his account of the divine perfections. Weaving together the notions of uniqueness (*singularitas*) and simplicity (*simplicitas*), Barth presents the unity of God in terms of God's sheer self-positing *Istigkeit*, God's irreducible *this-ness*. In an excursus on monotheism, for example, he rejects any idea that God's uniqueness can be grasped by entertaining an idea of God as the last and highest example of what we might call 'comparative uniqueness', so that God becomes one to whom 'uniqueness accrues or is ascribed as a kind of embellishment drawn from the stores of creaturely glory'.[89] 'He is not a unique being in the way in which there are many such. He is *this* unique being. As this unique being He is *the* unique being.'[90] God's uniqueness is God's particularity; God stands in need of no context of comparison for his uniqueness to become manifest. It is simply a matter of 'God Himself in the actuality, the superior might, the constancy, the obviousness, or even more simply, the factuality, in which He is present as God and deals as God with the creature, with man.'[91] The point here is not simply a vigorous pressing home of the principle that *Deus non est in genere*: because God is a unique subsistent, 'God' and 'membership of a class' are both logically and theologically contradictory. Barth is also wanting to affirm that the singularity of God, his sheer factuality, includes God's presence to, and dealings with, his creature. The character of God's simplicity cannot, therefore, be caught through some

---

[88] Behind what Barth has to say in the *Dogmatics* here lies an important essay from 1933 (the same year as *Theological Existence Today*), 'The first commandment as an axiom of theology', translated in H.-M. Rumscheidt, ed., *The Way of Theology in Karl Barth. Essays and Comments* (Allison Park, 1986). See further H.-M. Rumscheidt's analysis of the essay in 'The first commandment as axiom for theology', in J. Thompson, ed., *Theology Beyond Christendom* (Allison Park, 1986), pp. 143–64.

[89] II/1, p. 452.

[90] Ibid., p. 455.

[91] Ibid., p. 457.

abstract 'idea of the absolutely simple',[92] but only from the
closest adherence to 'the Word and work of God'.[93]

God's utter uniqueness is revealed in the gracious movement of his being towards his creature; God's inexhaustible
liberty is the act in which as Father, Son, and Spirit he
constitutes himself by electing to be our creator, reconciler,
and redeemer – such are the fundamental themes of Barth's
doctrine of God. But, as we shall see, they contain a further
implication of considerable ethical import. If in the Christian
doctrine of God we are concerned with the Christian meaning of the term 'God' as it is given in the enactment of
God's own life in self-revelation, then that meaning will be
partly shaped by a reference to the world of the creature
who is the object of God's grace. As Barth puts it later on,
at the beginning of the second volume of the doctrine of
God:

We should still not have learned to say 'God' correctly (i.e., as
understood in the Christian Church on the basis of Holy Scripture)
if we thought it were enough simply to say 'God'. However
well-grounded or critical our utterance, if it has a logical exclusiveness, if it is only 'God', it will not suffice. For if it is true that
in Jesus Christ there dwells the fullness of the Godhead bodily
(Col 2.9), then in all the perfection with which it is differentiated
from everything that is not God, and thus exists for itself, the
Subject God still cannot, as it were, be envisaged, established and
described only in and for itself. We must not be so exact, so
clever, so literal, that our doctrine of God remains only a doctrine
of God.[94]

And so 'to be truly Christian, the doctrine of God must
carry forward and complete the definition and exposition of
the Subject God. It must do this in such a way that quite
apart from what must be said about the knowledge and the
reality of God as such, it makes the Subject known as One
which in virtue of its innermost being, willing and nature

---

[92] Ibid.
[93] Ibid., p. 454.
[94] II/2, p. 5.

does not stand outside all relationships, but stands in a definite relationship *ad extra* to another.'[95] God so construed is a *moral* reality.

How does Barth arrive at this position? The first move (after a lengthy reinforcement of some of the earlier epistemological considerations in paragraphs 25-7)[96] is an interpretation of the statement 'God is'.[97] The core of the discussion is Barth's particularisation of the being of God: as the *ens concretissimum*, God is to be defined by reference to his own chosen path of self-definition: 'God is who He is in His works.'[98] And this means that 'God is who He is in the act of His revelation.'[99] Thus Barth enunciates the rule which will find expression throughout his doctrine of God: 'What God is as God, the divine individuality and characteristics, the *essentia* or "essence" of God, is something which we shall encounter either at the place where God deals with us as Lord and Saviour, or not at all.'[100]

God, then, is '*actus purissimus et singularis*'.[101] This singular act is the act in which the triune God seeks fellowship with the creature. What Barth calls God's 'name' (that is, God's 'unsubstitutable' identity as the one who is *thus*, in *this* life-act) is an utterly gratuitous movement towards created reality.

As it is revealed to us as the definition of that which confronts us in His revelation, this name definitely has this primary and decisive thing to say to us in all its constituents – that God is He who, without having to do so, seeks and creates fellowship between Himself and us. He does not have to do it, because in Himself without us, and therefore without this, He has that which He seeks and creates between Himself and us. It implies so to speak an overflow of His essence that He turns to us.[102]

[95] Ibid., pp. 5f.
[96] II/1, pp. 3–254.
[97] Ibid., p. 257.
[98] Ibid., p. 260.
[99] Ibid., p. 262.
[100] Ibid., p. 261.
[101] Cf. ibid., p. 264.
[102] Ibid., p. 273.

And so to the very depths of his eternal being, God 'is the one who loves': ' "God is" means "God loves".'[103]

This love is unconstrained; having no necessity beyond itself, it is 'a seeking and creation of fellowship without any reference to an existing aptitude or worthiness on the part of the loved',[104] and is therefore the actuality of God's freedom. God's freedom, the aseity of God's loving works, is not to be envisaged as a kind of depth *behind* those works: seeing it in such terms disrupts the identity of the *essentia dei* and the *opera dei ad extra*, and nearly always leads to a negative definition of divine freedom as independence, absence of constraint, freedom from, rather than freedom for, love. By contrast, Barth defines God's freedom by reference to a basic rule: to ask 'What is God?' is to ask 'Who is God?'[105] Far from seeking to determine the nature of divine aseity by looking for 'a characteristic mark of divinity which this God will have in common with other gods',[106] it is a matter of identifying 'the freedom which is proper to and characteristic of Him'.[107] That freedom is the freedom in which God *loves* the creature. In a statement rich in ethical ramifications, Barth writes that 'God can allow this other which is so utterly distinct from Himself to live and move and have its being within Himself. He can grant and leave it its own special being distinct from His own, and yet even in this way, and therefore in this its creaturely freedom, sustain, uphold and govern it by His own divine being, thus being its beginning, centre and end.'[108] God's freedom is thus actual as the loving gift and preservation of the creature's life.

Barth's account of the divine perfections (a term he prefers over the more formal notion of 'divine attributes') does much to fill out this primary notion of God's freedom in

---

[103] Ibid., pp. 275, 283.
[104] Ibid., p. 278.
[105] Cf. ibid., pp. 299f.
[106] Ibid., p. 299.
[107] Ibid., p. 304.
[108] Ibid., p. 314.

the act of love. The account is prefaced in paragraph 29 by what is apparently a set of remarks on how to organise a complex body of material, but which turns out to contain some important substantive proposals. Barth chooses to treat the perfections of God under two heads: the perfections of the divine loving (paragraph 30) and the perfections of the divine freedom (paragraph 31). The distinction is, however, merely heuristic: in their diversity, love and freedom are not different themes, but the same theme differently considered. Barth's insistence on the point is telling, for he is at pains to avoid a contradiction of the principle that God's freedom *is* his love. There can be no question of

a separation between a God in Himself and a God for us, in which the essential being of God will probably be decisively sought in His sovereign freedom and the perfections proper to it, eternity, omnipotence and so on, while the love of God and its perfections, holiness, justice, mercy and so on, are treated nominalistically or semi-nominalistically as a question of mere economy, as non-essential, as perhaps purely noetic determinations, so that the final and decisive word in our doctrine of God is the affirmation of God as the impersonal absolute.[109]

This same decision is expressed in the way Barth expounds the divine perfections through a series of paired concepts: grace and holiness, mercy and righteousness, patience and wisdom (in paragraph 30); unity and omnipresence, constancy and omnipotence, eternity and glory (in paragraph 31). The first concept of each pair characterises the perfection under the aspect of the divine loving, the second under the aspect of freedom (though, once again, there is no essential change of theme as we move from one to the other). Thus, of the first pair, for example, Barth writes, 'When we speak of grace, we think of the freedom in which God turns His inclination, good will and favour towards another. When we speak of holiness, we think of this same freedom which God proves by the fact that in His turning towards the other He remains true to Himself and makes

---

[109] Ibid., p. 345.

His own will prevail.'[110] The aim of this elaborate patterning is to secure from the beginning a point of critical importance about Christian belief in God, namely that God's lordship or absoluteness is to its very depths specified by a turning to humanity.

Thus the formal structure of the account of the perfections of God expresses the same point made more substantively by the doctrines of election and covenant: God *is* God for us. As in his handling of those doctrines, Barth here eschews a polarisation of God *pro se* and God *pro nobis*, and the frequent corollary that the reality of the *pro nobis* can only be procured by making the reality of God a function of some more primary anthropological state of affairs.[111] The identity of God's aseity and his loving being for us is well-rehearsed in interpretation of Barth. What is less often remarked is the ethical import of what he undertakes. If the perfection of God's freedom is the perfection of his capacity to love, then God is essentially one whose act is directed towards the reciprocal active life of humanity. In this regard, what Barth writes of the patience of God is instructive:

We define God's patience as His will, deep-rooted in His essence and constituting His divine being and action, to allow another – for the sake of His own grace and mercy and in the affirmation of His holiness and justice – space and time for the development of its own existence, thus conceding to this existence a reality side by side with His own, and fulfilling His will towards this other in such a way that He does not suspend and destroy it as

---

[110] Ibid., p. 360.

[111] It is this issue which lies at the heart of Barth's dispute with Bultmann, most of all in the 1950s, and which surfaced in the debate between Herbert Braun and Helmut Gollwitzer in the early 1960s. See H. Braun's two essays, 'The meaning of New Testament Christology', *Journal for Theology and Church* 5 (1968), 89–127, and 'The problem of a New Testament theology', *Journal for Theology and Church* 1 (1965), 169–83, along with his study *Jesus of Nazareth* (Philadelphia, 1979). Gollwitzer's critique, translated as *The Existence of God as Confessed by Faith* (London, 1965), evoked Braun's response 'Gottes Existenz und meine Geschichtlichkeit im NT', in E. Dinkler, ed., *Zeit und Geschichte* (Tübingen, 1964), pp. 399–421. The inadequacies of both protagonists in view of Barth's doctrine of God are brilliantly sketched in E. Jüngel, *The Doctrine of the Trinity* (Edinburgh, 1975).

this other but accompanies and sustains it and allows it to develop in freedom.[112]

Precisely because God is such, it is unnecessary to establish the reality of the world of human acts by making the term 'God' into a sort of dispensable cipher for some purely immanent obligation or engagement. 'About God one can only speak in reference to the carrying out of certain actions, the actions of obedience and humility'[113] – lurking within Braun's statement is precisely the abstract notion of divine transcendence to which Barth's doctrine of God offers an explicit Christological correction.

So understood, the account of the perfections of God prepares the ground for the presentation of election in *Dogmatics* chapter 7. The general outline of Barth's radical reshaping of the Reformed tradition at this point is well known. Election is pushed back into the doctrine of God; instead of treating of the determination of created reality by a God who is essentially defined in isolation from creation, the doctrine of election concerns God's decision to be God *for* creation: 'God makes a self-election in favour of this other.'[114] More specifically, election is expounded in the closest proximity to the doctrine of the two natures of Christ: the heart of the doctrine of election is 'Jesus Christ, electing and elected', for '[i]n Him God stands before man and man stands before God, as is the eternal will of God, and the eternal ordination of man in accordance with this will'.[115] As such, election concerns the covenant of grace, God's indefatigable competence to institute, direct, and fulfil all his good purposes for us.

The root of this entire recasting of the concept of election is the specification of the doctrine of God which has already found expression in the treatments of the being and attributes of God in II/1. Here, however, the specification is undertaken with even more explicitly Christological content

---

[112] II/1, pp. 409f.
[113] H. Braun, *Jesus of Nazareth*, p. 128.
[114] II/2, p. 10.
[115] Ibid., p. 94.

than the earlier phases of the argument. 'When Holy Scripture speaks of God it concentrates our attention and thoughts upon one single point and what is to be known at that point.' And that point is, in the last analysis, identical with 'the name of Jesus Christ', so that election is nothing other than God's history with humanity 'under this name'.[116] This is what lies behind Barth's protest against classical Reformed accounts of election in terms of the divine decrees, in which there is an isolation of the formal characteristic of election: choice, irresistible sovereign choice.[117] For Barth, on the other hand, it is all-important that election be construed, not through some notion of 'infinite power in an infinite sphere' (which is 'the characteristic of the government of ungodly and anti-godly courts'),[118] but as the *dominium* which is proper to God as 'He has concretely determined and limited Himself after the manner of a true king (and not of a tyrant).'[119] And if election is the good rule of the true king, then its exposition is a matter of an unambiguous declaration of 'the sum of the Gospel',[120] a 'proclamation of joy'.[121] Election means 'God for us';[122] it means that 'God wills neither to be without the world nor against it';[123] in election, God 'does not say No but Yes'.[124] And so we do not here face an inscrutable divine decision, but rather the unbroken continuity between God's enactment of his own life in Jesus Christ and his disposing of his creatures to life and blessedness.

---

[116] Ibid., pp. 52f.

[117] In this study *Christ and the Decree. Christology and Predestination in Reformed Theology from Calvin to Perkins* (Grand Rapids, 1986), Richard Muller correctly points out that, unlike many contemporary critics of the classical Reformed tradition, Barth does not see predestination as the basic tenet of Reformed scholasticism (see Muller, pp. 130f, and II/2, pp. 72f). Muller underemphasises, however, Barth's serious critical reserve concerning 'the tenet of the decree of God in general' (II/2, p. 78).

[118] Ibid., p. 50

[119] Ibid.

[120] Ibid., p. 24.

[121] Ibid., p. 13.

[122] Ibid., p. 26.

[123] Ibid.

[124] Ibid., p. 28.

Once again, it would be easy to miss the ethical significance of Barth's recasting of divine election. On Barth's
reading, election is a teleological act on the part of God,
having as its end the life-act of the creature whom God
elects into covenant with himself: as Colin Gunton puts it,
'Election is to a particular kind of life.'[125] This directedness
towards, and claim upon, the human creature and the creature's act, in which God elects a path for himself and elects
us as partners, is very close to the centre of what Barth
wants to say about God and God's covenant. For 'grace
does not will only to be received and known. As it is truly
received and known, as it works itself out as the favour
which it is, it wills also to rule . . . There is no grace without
the lordship and claim of grace. There is no dogmatics
which is not also and necessarily ethics.'[126] Election is not
a decree imposed and, as it were, complete in its imposition,
requiring no corresponding attitude and activity on the part
of the one determined; it is, instead, the movement of the
being of God, carrying with it, and establishing, the human
agent. Certainly election confronts us with 'the omnipotent
and unsearchable Therefore of God' – with a definitive
conclusion about who we are. But that very conclusion
'drives us forward', in that it 'summons to obedience'.[127]
This is not to qualify the sovereignty of election in such
a way that God's conclusion concerning the creature is
transformed into a mere incitement to further acts of self-
determination on the creature's part, for 'dispositions concerning our conduct have already been made.'[128] Yet election
is election to action; Barth is as uneasy with the moral
passivity which results from the abstract fatalism which
afflicts the notion of divine decrees as he is with the opposing
idea of absolute human indeterminacy. Starting from God's

---

[125] C. Gunton, 'The triune God and the freedom of the creature', in S. W. Sykes,
ed., *Karl Barth. Centenary Essays*, p. 51. See further P. D. Matheny, *Dogmatics
and Ethics*, pp. 166–70, on the ethical dimensions of Barth's doctrine of election.
[126] II/2, p. 12.
[127] Ibid., p. 31.
[128] Ibid., p. 32.

intratrinitarian life and the overflow of that life 'in the form
of the history, encounter and decision between Himself and
man',[129] Barth can move on to speak of how 'the fulfilment
of the election involves the affirmation of the existence of
elected man . . . There is . . . a simple but comprehensive
autonomy of the creature which is constituted originally by
the act of eternal divine election and which has in this act
its ultimate reality.'[130] 'Theonomy' is accordingly a matter
of God's gift of Himself in 'willing and recognising the
distinct reality of the creature, granting and conceding to
it an individual and autonomous place side by side with
Himself'.[131] And – in a move which will be fundamental to
the whole presentation of the ethics of reconciliation at the
end of *Dogmatics* volume iv – Barth identifies *prayer* as the
most characteristic act of the creature:

God's eternal will is the act of prayer (in which confidence in
self gives way before confidence in God). This act is the birth of
a genuine human self-awareness, in which knowledge and action
can and must be attempted; in which there drops away all fear
of what is above or beside or below man, of what might assault
or threaten him; in which man becomes heir to a legitimate and
necessary and therefore an effective and triumphant claim; in
which man may rule in that he is willing to serve.[132]

All that we have said so far should serve to show why it
is entirely fitting that the doctrine of God should culminate
in the lengthy treatment of ethics in chapter 8, under the
rubric 'The Command of God'.[133] Because it is a doctrine
of *this* God, its theme is the covenant, without which God
simply 'does not exist'.[134] And the covenant is not only an
indicative reality: it is a summons. 'For who can possibly
see what is meant by the knowledge of God, His divine
being, His divine perfections, the election of His grace,

---

[129] Ibid., p. 175.
[130] Ibid., p. 177.
[131] Ibid., p. 178.
[132] Ibid., p. 180.
[133] The ethical section forms slightly under one-fifth of the whole of the doctrine
of God in i/i and ii/2.
[134] ii/2, p. 509.

without an awareness at every point of the demand which is put to man by the fact that this God is his God, the God of man?'[135]

Grace is imperatival. And – as always in Barth – the imperatival character of grace, its character as command, is emphasised in order to confirm the place of the human agent in response to grace. This quite crucial point is not always grasped, usually because Barth's notion of command is easy to misconstrue in too abstract a way by isolating it from the context in which alone its proper meaning can be discerned. Barth's understanding of command is precise and distinctive, and does not lend itself to being translated into some general deontological principle such as 'moral imperatives are orders addressed to moral agents by God, the moral law-giver'.[136] Everything depends on the specific connotations of terms such as 'order', 'moral agent', 'law', and (most of all) 'God'. It is certainly incontestable that there are passages (and they are not infrequent) where Barth appears to work with an almost purely heteronomous notion of obligation as 'something alien ... the command of another',[137] which could attract such an interpretation. But, even here, Barth is at pains to point out that 'true and genuine obligation, law and duty voiced by another than ourselves'[138] emerges from a specific history in which obligation is redefined: the *saving* events of the death and resurrection of Jesus Christ. The intelligibility of Barth's discussion of 'The Command of God' as a whole turns upon his refusal to identify his account with some generic ' "theonomous ethics" ',[139] and upon his counter-assertion that terms such as 'command', 'law' or 'claim' are Christianly construed by reference to the nameable history of Jesus Christ. Everything hangs upon the fact that God's

[135] Ibid., p. 512.
[136] G. de Graff, 'God and morality', in I. T. Ramsey, ed., *Christian Ethics and Contemporary Philosophy* (London, 1966), p. 32.
[137] II/2, p. 651.
[138] Ibid.
[139] Ibid., p. 365.

command is specified in that history, that God 'demands
our obedience in and with the fact that He is gracious to
us in Jesus Christ':[140]

> We must seek the command of God only where it has itself torn
> off the veil of all human opinions and theories about the will of
> God and manifested itself unequivocally. We must seek it only
> where He has revealed Himself as grace and therefore in His
> truth. We must seek it only in what happened in Bethlehem, at
> Capernaum and Tiberias, in Gethsemane and on Golgotha, and
> in the garden of Joseph of Arimathea. In this event God uttered
> His command.[141]

> The history of Jesus Christ – *this* subject, *this* sequence –
> forms a series of events in which the claim and command
> of God can appropriately be specified, and so distanced
> from ideas of simple *power*, 'absolute predominance'.[142]

Barth is not usually taken seriously here.[143] Not only is
this because of the proximity of his language of command

---

[140] Ibid., p. 559.

[141] Ibid. From this perspective, W. Werpehowski is correct to insist that, for
Barth, 'The notion of command finds its meaning within the framework of
what he calls the "Whence?" and the "Whither?" of theological ethics, i.e.,
the sovereign grace of the electing God in Jesus Christ and the radical need
of his rebellious creature': 'Command and history in the ethics of Karl Barth',
Journal of Religious Ethics 9 (1981), 301. Werpehowski is also largely correct (as
the passage cited from Barth shows) to say that Barth's use of 'command'
terminology is 'determined by a reflection which is bound in principle to the
narrative depiction of the history of God's dealings with humanity in Jesus
Christ' (p. 302) – though I suspect that Werpehowski's appeal to the notion
of narrative depiction may have more restricted application than he supposes,
especially in the earlier volumes of the *Dogmatics* (on this last point, see also
W. Werpehowski, 'Narrative and ethics in Barth', *Theology Today* 43 (1986),
334–53). More generally, Barth's use of the language of command relates to
Cavell's comment on 'modal imperatives' ('ought', 'must', etc): ' "Ought" and
"must" . . . are modes of presenting the very reasons you would offer to support
them, and without which they would lack meaning altogether . . . What makes
their use rational is their relevance to the person confronted, and the legitimacy
your position gives you to confront him or her in the mode you take responsibility for': S. Cavell, *The Claim of Reason. Wittgenstein, Skepticism, Morality, and
Tragedy* (Oxford, 1979), p. 323.

[142] II/2, p. 553.

[143] David Nicolls, for example, makes the extraordinary claim that Barth's construal of the notion of divine command out of God's grace in Christ 'is very
similar to Schmitt's justification of the *Führerprinzip* on the grounds of the
familial relationship between the leader and his people': *Deity and Domination*.

to that of heteronomous domination; it is also because the very Christological doctrine by which he seeks to purify the notion of command is itself articulated in ways which apparently threaten to undermine the reality of the human subject and agent which it seeks to establish. This happens, for instance, when Barth appeals (explicitly or implicitly) to 'being in Christ' or to the 'vicarious' nature of Jesus Christ's humanity, or to Christ's substitutionary work 'in our place'. Thus the person in Christ

exists because Jesus Christ exists. He exists as a predicate of this Subject, i.e., that which has been decided and is real for man in this Subject is true for him.[144]

It is to be noted that primarily and properly it is Jesus Christ who has rendered this obedience, for primarily and properly He is the elect of God, sanctified man. It is He, and not Adam, who is in the state of original innocence. It is He, and not we, who is in the state of eternal innocence, righteousness and holiness ordained for us.[145]

His person, the person of the Son of God and therefore of God Himself, is by God's gracious and righteous will *the* human person, our common Head and Representative. In Him God has seen each human person from all eternity. As He judges Him, and He is judged by God, judgment is executed on every human person. He is the Word that was in the beginning with God. He is, therefore, the Word that is true of every man. He is our sanctification for God and eternal life as it is unshakably and irrevocably accomplished.[146]

If all this is true, and if good human action is only an 'endorsement'[147] of these states of affairs, does not the moral agent vanish, resolved into the prior divine decision? Perhaps one could argue that the very texture of morality requires that we say something like the following:

Images of God and the State in the Nineteenth and Twentieth Centuries (London, 1989), p. 116.
[144] Ibid., p. 539.
[145] Ibid., p. 740.
[146] Ibid., p. 778.
[147] Ibid., p. 540.

'Whatever happens, it is *by my agency* that everything must happen.' Even if he let himself be carried off like an old sack of coal, he would have chosen his own damnation; he was free, free in every way, free to behave like a fool or a machine, free to accept, free to refuse, free to equivocate . . . He could do what he liked, no one had the right to advise him, there would be for him no Good or Evil unless he brought them into being. All around him things were gathered in a circle, expectant, impassive, and indicative of nothing. He was alone, enveloped in this monstrous silence, free and alone, without assistance and without excuse, condemned to decide without support from any quarter, condemned for ever to be free.[148]

– so Mathieu in Sartre's *The Age of Reason.* How would Barth respond?

In a way the whole of the *Dogmatics* is an implicit response. Some aspects of this already have been identified: the ontological inclusivity of the human reality of Jesus Christ which grounds (rather than displaces) all other human realities; the directedness of the ways and works of God towards the life-act of the human creature. In the present context, a further element emerges: a radical interrogation of some of the most firmly established conventions of post-Enlightenment moral thought in the West. More than anything else, Barth strives to displace the deliberative consciousness from its sovereign place as the moral fundamental (what Sartre calls 'free and alone'). One way of interpreting Barth would be to read his work as an exploration of what Paul Ricoeur calls 'nonethical ethics' – as propounding a view of human agency which does not see the moral life in terms of a competition between a superior will which commands, accuses and condemns and an inferior will which, if it is not to submit to the abasement of obedience, must struggle to match and supplant the will by which it is opposed.[149] One extension of this schema is the idea that

---

[148] J.-P. Sartre, *The Age of Reason* (Harmondsworth, 1961), pp. 242f. See also Sartre's essay 'Cartesian freedom', in *Literary and Philosophical Essays* (London, 1968), pp. 169–84.

[149] 'To think nonethically, we must start at a point where the autonomy of our will is rooted in dependence and an obedience which are not infected by

moral authenticity can only be attributed to a quasi-absolute consciousness, to an indeterminate self, without constraints, characterised above all by an infinitely regressive interiority: in effect, moral Cartesianism.[150] For Barth, however, the moral life is not a matter of a competitive drama, some clash of wills between an infinite source of obligation and a finite moral self which has to win its subjectivity by aspiring to infinity. The notion of God's election of humanity to covenant, with its corollary notion of human life as *essentially* participation in a history with God, suggests a very different understanding of moral selfhood.

In an important phrase, Barth speaks of humanity as encountered by God's claim which, as *permission*, is 'the granting of a very definite freedom'.[151] With this, Barth severs the bond between moral authenticity and indeterminacy. To exist as a moral being is to exist in a given shape, to act *within certain limits*. Those limits are not a set of arbitrarily imposed *barriers*, closing off what are, in fact, genuine human possibilities. Rather, they are the *form* within which and as which the human moral agent may exist, and outside which it is not meaningful to speak of good human conduct at all. Being a human moral agent means existing in this way, not as a hindrance to liberty, but as the shape in which human life is itself. The opposite to the idea of the contingency of moral selfhood – that of the absolute, undetermined moral self – Barth regards as morally destructive, because it abstracts the agent from the covenant relation to God which alone integrates human life into a wholesome project. Outside the form of that relation, the

---

accusation, prohibition, and condemnation': 'Religion, atheism, and faith', in *The Conflict of Interpretations* (Evanston, 1974), p. 449.

[150] This tradition is now, of course, sustaining serious criticism: see, for example, E. Tugendhat, *Self-Consciousness and Self-Determination* (Cambridge, Mass., 1986), and the (strongly-drawn) critiques of F. Kerr, *Theology after Wittgenstein* (Oxford, 1986) or R. Rorty, *Contingency, Irony and Solidarity* (Cambridge, 1989), especially pp. 23–43. For a nuanced account of interiority incorporating some of these perspectives, see R. Williams, 'The suspicion of suspicion: Wittgenstein and Bonhoeffer', in R. H. Bell, ed., *The Grammar of the Heart. New Essays in Moral Philosophy and Theology* (San Francisco, 1988), pp. 36–53.

[151] II/2, p. 585.

human person becomes 'judge of good and evil':[152] the final
given of the moral life is not a history in which the agent
is called to participate and to which he or she gives
allegiance, but rather the realm of interiority. Occupying
this 'office as the judge of good and evil' is for the agent a
'retreat into himself',[153] an attempted transcendence of fini-
tude into unrestricted moral consciousness.

It is this process of absolutising the activity of moral
reflectivity into an inner life untouched by relation to God
which is the heart of Barth's unease about moral deliberation. Barth is not (as is sometimes thought) denying any
place to moral consciousness – to what he calls 'awareness',
that which distinguishes moral conduct from simple natural
events.[154] But he is denying that moral awareness offers us
a place to stand outside our history with God, prior to
engaging in that history and the command which it issues
to us. That command, he writes, 'drives us from the last
of these neutral refuges – an ethics which tries not to be
an ethos'.[155] This is not to make moral action into a mere
reflex; but it is to deny that moral authenticity has its
ultimate ground in transcendent moral consciousness, in 'the
self-willed desire of man to know good and evil'.[156]

---

[152] Ibid., p. 596.
[153] Ibid.
[154] Ibid., p. 658. See also the emphasis on the need for moral self-examination,
ibid., p. 636. Barth's account of deliberation is criticised by R. E. Willis in
'Some difficulties in Barth's development of special ethics', *Religious Studies* 6
(1970), 147–55. See also the balanced appraisal of N. Biggar, 'Hearing God's
command and thinking about what's right: with and beyond Barth', in N.
Biggar, ed., *Reckoning with Barth*, pp. 101–18.
[155] Ibid., p. 660.
[156] Ibid., p. 645. What Barth has to say here takes up a line of thinking already
present in the famous 1922 address to a pastors conference at Wiesbaden, 'The
problem of ethics today', in *The Word of God and the Word of Man*, pp. 136–82.
The address is in large part a dismantling of the notion of an absolute moral
subject, of the view that '[t]he moral personality is the author both of the
conduct with which the ethical question is concerned and the question itself'
(p. 153). Barth dismantles that notion by insisting that ethical consciousness
does not transcend, but is rather radically relativised by 'the ethical question',
which, properly speaking, is addressed to us by God and *limits* the moral self
by exposing it to 'perfect timelessness' (p. 139).

Barth's much-criticised reticence about the role of moral deliberation does not have its roots, therefore, in some idea of immediate moral certainty which bypasses the need for agents to engage in reflection. Rather, the reticence is the result of the deep differences between Barth and some dominant modern images of the moral self. Such is Barth's rhetoric that he could be construed as condemning *all* moral reflection as a kind of grasping after absolute knowledge of good and evil, or as an attempt theoretically to evade obedience by objectifying and inspecting the conditions of possibility for God's command. When combined with his reluctance to go beyond general principles into particular examples, the rhetoric can almost seem to subvert any genuine sense of moral perplexity. A quite different way of reading Barth, however, would suggest that he has already made the shift for which David Kelsey has called, in a programmatic essay on Christian anthropology: a shift 'from the person as patient or subject of consciousness to the person as agent'.[157] On Barth's terms, moral responsibility is not defined by reference to an inner deliberative sanctum, but by the closely allied notions of 'response' and 'correspondence'. 'We live in responsibility, which means that our being and willing, what we do and what we do not do, is a continuous answer to the Word of God spoken to us as a command.'[158] The metaphor of 'answer' catches exactly what Barth wants to say about human morality: it is finite, brought into being by an external summons, and yet as such a real, reciprocal act. In effect, the model of summons and answer rules out both abstract divine monergism and pure human autonomy. More concretely, the human response is a matter of a proper correspondence or conformity between our life-act and the divine action from which it derives. 'The grace of God wills

---

[157] D. H. Kelsey, 'Human being', in P. Hodgson and R. King, eds., *Christian Theology. An Introduction to Its Traditions and Tasks* (Philadelphia, 1982), p. 163. Kelsey quite correctly points out that for Barth the relation of humanity to God 'does not consist of a mode of consciousness and cannot be discovered by an analysis of the structure of consciousness' (ibid.).

[158] II/2, p. 641.

and creates the covenant between God and man. It therefore determines man to existence in this covenant. It determines him to be the partner of God. It therefore determines his action to correspondence, conformity, uniformity with God's action.'[159] Once again, the language of 'correspondence' (so central to Barth's understanding of the relation of God to the human creature) effects a delimitation, a 'placing' of human conduct which identifies how both in origin and form it is derivative but none the less substantial.[160] As a 'following', the human action which corresponds to God's action is an acknowledgment of the divine act which embraces and sustains it, and of its own consequently contingent nature. For, above all, '[w]hat we have to do is to accept and maintain what he regards as true of our life against our own opposition and to let our action be illumined and ruled by this acceptance. This is the required conformity of our action with that of the gracious God.'[161]

To sum up what has been of necessity a somewhat lengthy discussion: Barth's doctrine of God has argued that, because (and, for Barth, *only* because) of the Christian construction to be put upon the statement 'God is', Christian theology and ethics can affirm that 'the creature itself may be actual within its limits'.[162] What account of creation is entailed here?

---

[159] Ibid., p. 575.
[160] For a very illuminating set of reflections along these lines, see G. Outka, 'Following at a distance: ethics and the identity of Jesus', in G. Green, ed., *Scriptural Authority and Narrative Interpretation* (Philadelphia, 1986), pp. 144–60.
[161] Ibid., p. 581.
[162] III/3, p. 86.

CHAPTER TWO

Creation and reconciliation

CREATION

Part of the fate of Christian theology in the modern era has
been its virtual displacement as a comprehensive account
of the orders of nature and human history. Instead of furnishing an all-embracing interpretation of 'natural' reality
through its doctrines of creation, human being, and provi-
dential governance (as they are shaped by a theology of
redemption), Christian theology has found itself relativised
by modes of inquiry apparently more universal in reach,
less tradition-specific in their procedures. One effect of this
has been to place a very great burden of apologetic responsibility on those tracts of the corpus of Christian doctrine
which treat of the created order (the doctrines of creation,
providence, humanity): they have frequently come to bear
the brunt of offering a foundation for subsequent theological
discourse about the being and acts of God, demonstrating
from within a theory of nature or history or human consciousness the necessity and legitimacy of theological categories concerning the ultimate or the transcendent. The
difficult passage which it is the task of the doctrines of
creation and humanity to negotiate is, accordingly, one from
known natural realities to the reality of God, the success of
the move being dependent upon the perceived measure of
overlap between natural experience of the world and that
which is articulated in Christian doctrine.

Barth's doctrine of creation knows no such move: in its
entirety it is a disavowal of the legitimacy of the procedure,
since Christian language about creation and humanity

follows rather than precedes language about God. At the opening of *Dogmatics* iii, he writes that:

the assertion of creation is a statement of faith, i.e., a statement which can never be more than a hypothesis apart from its foundation in God's self-witness, not only on the side which maintains that *God* is the Creator of the world, and which therefore asserts the reality of *God*, but also on that which asserts that God is the Creator of the *world*, and which therefore asserts the distinctive reality of the *world*. It is only too easy to suggest that, while the reality of God as the Creator is uncertain, and therefore needs proof or revelation, the reality of the creature is all the more certain, so that the one is to be treated as a factor which is not given but has still to be sought, whereas the other may be presupposed *rocher de bronche . . . Nihil constat de contingentia mundi nisi ex revelatione . . .* If the world is not created by God, it is not. If we do not recognise that it has been created by God, we do not recognise that it is . . . [I]t is primarily the creature and not the Creator of whom we are not certain . . .[1]

Barth's doctrine of creation, then, construes the reality of the created order in a very specific way. Not only does it deny that Christian theological language about creation has to find a home in a larger theory of the contingency of the world or of humanity; it also proposes that the 'realness' of the created order is not as it were a 'natural' property. The creation is truly 'real' as a function of the encounter which God inaugurates with humanity; its reality is not antecedent to the event of that encounter. 'We must not think of trying to discover, construct, and define for ourselves the field of "reality" to which we can look from this event and from which we can then look back upon the event', Barth writes at the beginning of the ethics of creation, for

what does reality mean? We have to realise that the introduction of the concept at this point might carry a dangerous implication. Are we not dealing with reality in the event of the encounter of the God who commands with the man who acts as this is set before us in the Word of God? Can the reality of this event be different from that which it has in and by itself? Must it acquire

---

[1] iii/1, p. 6.

its reality by its relationship to another reality? If we understand by the God who commands and the man who acts the two partners revealed to us in the Word of God, is not the reality of their encounter the fullness, epitome and standard of all reality?[2]

From this primary conviction – that the covenantal encounter between God and the human creature is the 'fullness, epitome and standard of all reality' – much of Barth's doctrine of creation falls into place: its focus on the human creature, its stress on the priority of covenant over nature, its refusal to undertake a phenomenology of the human, its apparent ontological and ethical occasionalism. From this, too, can be seen why Barth's ethics of creation develops in the way it does, since it starts not from some 'ethical reality of life, the perception of which constitutes the task of an ethical theology',[3] but from the *event* of the covenant in which the meaning of terms like 'action' or 'life' first receives its Christian theological determinacy.

Volume III of the *Dogmatics* is, of course, an enormously complex and wide-ranging treatment of creation, anthropology, providence, and ethics. It is also the least accessible of the volumes of Barth's work, containing what are probably the two most difficult sections of the *Church Dogmatics*, the treatment of human temporality in paragraph 47 ('Man in His Time'),[4] and the ontological discussion of 'God and Nothingness' (paragraph 50).[5] It is in this volume, however, that Barth expounds some crucial decisions which affect the shape of the later ethics of reconciliation, of which the most significant is an insistence on the priority of participation in the humanity of Christ for a definition of human nature and action.

Two delimitations which Barth makes at the beginning of volume III are of critical importance for the whole. First, the doctrine of creation (and thus of the existence and activity of the human creature) is part of the *Credo*, and

[2] III/4, p. 27.
[3] T. Rendtorff, *Ethics*, vol. I (Philadelphia, 1986), p. 31.
[4] III/2, pp. 437–640.
[5] III/3, pp. 289–368.

thus a doctrine of faith. The primary datum, therefore, of a Christian account of created order is not the creature's existence, but God; ascription of existence to the creaturely realm follows from confession of God's self-existence. For 'if we dare to take the not unimportant step of ascribing its own reality to that which is distinct from God, i.e., heaven and earth and ourselves; if we are of the bold opinion that we ourselves, and with us the so-called world, are and are not *not*, we have to realise that this is always an undemonstrable hypothesis . . . unless we have accepted the divine self-witness and therefore confessed with the whole of Christendom that in the beginning God created heaven and earth and ourselves and therefore gave to the world distinct from Himself a demonstrable and indisputable reality.'[6] This reversal of the accustomed (Cartesian) direction from creatureliness to Creator leads to a second, epistemological point. Knowledge of God as Creator does not take its rise in human experience – a sense of contingency or an awareness of ultimacy within human history – but in confession of Jesus Christ whose humanity is the guarantee of the independent existence of the creation. 'The person of Jesus Christ is the proof that although the creature is not a second God beside the One, although it is not of the nature of God and therefore self-existent, it does exist after its own fashion by the will of God. It is the proof that the creature is not excluded and denied, but established and determined by Him.'[7] The humanity of Jesus (not our own) is thus the *fundamentum inconcussum veritatis*. From the very beginning, then, we are faced with the central and contentious claim of Barth's doctrine of creation: what is axiomatic is not created consciousness but the Word's assumption of creaturely existence at the incarnation. And we are thereby introduced to its most characteristic procedure for the construction of doctrine about the created realm: 'reckoning

[6] III/1, p. 5.
[7] Ibid., p. 25.

with Jesus Christ as with a known human quality and on this basis assuring ourselves of the reality of creation'.[8]

It is, further, in this light that we are to interpret Barth's account of the relation of creation and covenant which, together with his exposition of Genesis 1 and 2, forms the bulk of III/1. As is well known, Barth organises the material under two heads: 'Creation as the External Basis of the Covenant' and 'The Covenant as the Internal Basis of Creation'. Creation is the external basis of the covenant in the sense that creation is defined in terms of its end: God's works of creation 'have in view the institution, preservation and execution of the covenant of grace, for partnership in which He has predestined and called man',[9] so that 'Creation sets the stage for the story of grace.'[10] Though Barth might be read to be compromising the original goodness of creation, it is more accurate to say that, for him, the goodness of the creation is 'teleological' rather than simply 'original'. The creation is good in so far as it functions as 'equipment for grace':

Creation is one long preparation, and therefore the being and existence of the creature one long readiness, for what God will intend and do with it in the history of the covenant. Its nature is simply its equipment for grace. Its creatureliness is pure promise, expectation and prophecy of that which in His grace, in the execution of the will of His eternal love, and finally and supremely in the consummation of the giving of His Son, God plans for man and will not delay to accomplish for his benefit. In this way creation is the road to covenant.[11]

Later, in a discussion of 'Creation as Benefit', Barth reiterates the point (over against Marcion and Schopenhauer): 'That God's creation has the character of benefit derives everywhere . . . from the fact that its fundamental purpose

---

[8] Ibid., pp. 31f.
[9] Ibid., p. 43.
[10] Ibid., p. 44.
[11] Ibid., p. 231.

lies in the covenant between God and man.'[12] If Barth's
point eludes us or seems to undermine the dignity and value
of the created order, it is because we frequently use the
notion of 'creation' in order to interpret our natural human
history as contingent upon a transcendent reality, on which
basis we then go on to speak of God's redemptive purposes.
For Barth, on the other hand, 'creation' is not to be thought
of as the necessary *ground* of the other works of God, a
ground which is complete in itself and can be defined without reference to the history of redemption. Quite the contrary: creation is the necessary *implication* of God's primary
work of grace in Jesus Christ. For Barth, in other words,
creation is wholly ordered towards its redemptive fulfilment:
its meaning lies not in its original ordering *per se*, but in
that ordering as the external condition for covenantal grace.

This is why Barth goes on to speak of covenant as the
internal basis of creation:

The fact that the covenant is the goal of creation is not something
which is added later to the reality of the creature, as though the
history of creation might equally well have been succeeded by
any other history. It already characterises creation itself and as
such, and therefore the being and existence of the creature. The
covenant whose history had still to commence was the covenant
which, as the goal appointed for creation and the creature, made
creation necessary and possible, and determined and limited the
creature.[13]

'Creation itself and as such', we might say, is not for Barth
a general reality within which the saving works of God also
have their place as part of a more comprehensive, less
particular, history. Rather, 'creation' is wholly enclosed
within the redemptive covenant, in the history of which
creation becomes itself. For '[t]he aim of creation is history';
and

[w]hat is meant is the history of the covenant of grace instituted
by God between Himself and man; the sequence of the events in

[12] Ibid., p. 332.
[13] Ibid., p. 231.

which God concludes and executes this covenant with man, carrying it to its goal, and thus validating in the sphere of the creature that which from all eternity He has determined in Himself; the sequence of the events for the sake of which God has patience with the creature and with its creation gives it time – time which acquires content through these events and which is finally to be 'fulfilled' and made ripe for its end by their conclusion. This history is from the theological standpoint *the* history.[14]

In sum: Barth's discussion disallows the use of categories such as 'creation' or 'history' as a means of securing *remoto Christo* the existence of the human creature. Noetically, 'creation' and 'history' are not 'natural' categories, nor are they the fruit of human consciousness of contingency or temporal passage. Ontologically, the content of such terms is Christologically determined. And this means, accordingly, that neither category can offer an independent apologetic entrée into discourse about redemption:

There is absolutely no external basis that this covenant can have which was not posited by the God who here enters into covenant with man. There is no existence of the creature in which it can originally belong elsewhere than to this compact. It has no attributes, no conditions of existence, no substantial or accidental predicates of any kind, in virtue of which it can or may or must be alien to the Founder of this covenant.[15]

For:

If the covenant of grace is no illusion, if the love of God and the fact that we are loved in Jesus Christ is no dream, neither is the existence of God, nor our own existence, nor that of the world around us; neither is our consciousness that we are and that things outside us also are; neither is our consciousness of self or the world; neither is even our consciousness of God, however problematical this may be in itself. As a sure revelation of the covenant, the self-disclosure of the Creator is also the sure revelation of His reality as Creator and therefore of our reality as His creatures.[16]

[14] Ibid., p. 59.
[15] Ibid., p. 96.
[16] Ibid., p. 365.

Just how far-reaching the implications of this proposal are can be seen from the anthropology which follows as the next stage of Barth's argument.

HUMAN BEING

The earlier parts of *CD* III/2 devote much space to securing one conviction which is basic to Barth's anthropology and ethics: the conviction that because human persons cannot be defined *remoto gratia*, apart from the covenant of grace which is the creature's end, attempts to reach self-definition through self-reflection yield only delusion. 'The self-contradiction resulting from our contradiction of God is serious. It really prevents us from understanding ourselves. We are not clear nor transparent to ourselves, nor can we see ourselves from any higher standpoint. We are totally and not just partially incapable of occupying any independent vantage point from the height of which we might penetrate and judge ourselves.'[17] The point here is not simply that Barth, like Calvin, has a profound sense of the ruinous effects of sin on human self-knowledge. It is also that in laying out a procedure for constructing anthropological doctrine, Barth declines to set theological language about humanity in a wider context of human self-reflection. Rather than undertaking what Pannenberg calls 'a fundamental-theological anthropology' looking for 'implications that may be relevant to religion and theology' in the natural and human sciences,[18] Barth presses insistently upon one point which is the positive side of his refusal of correlation: 'The nature of the man Jesus alone is the key to the problem of

---

[17] III/2, p. 30.
[18] W. Pannenberg, *Anthropology in Theological Perspective* (Philadelphia, 1985), p. 21. Pannenberg proposes that theology's use of anthropological findings will be a matter of 'critical appropriation', since 'modern anthropology has been historically characterised by a certain tendency and will not allow theologians to claim it as a neutral basis for theological reflections making use of its results' (ibid.); yet it is unclear how this relates to his earlier and much stronger assertion that 'Christian theology in the modern age must provide itself with a foundation in general anthropological studies' (p. 15).

human nature. This man is man. As certainly as God's relation to sinful man is properly and primarily His relation to this man alone, and a relation to the rest of mankind only in Him and through Him, He alone is primarily and properly man.'[19] Thus:

The ontological determination of humanity is grounded in the fact that one man among all others is the man Jesus. So long as we select any other starting point for our study, we shall reach only the phenomena of the human. We are condemned to abstractions so long as our attention is riveted as it were on other men, or rather on man in general, as if we could learn about real man from a study of man in general, and in abstraction from the fact that one man among all others is the man Jesus. In this case we miss the one Archimedean point given us beyond humanity, and therefore the one possibility of discovering the ontological determination of man. Theological anthropology has no choice in this matter. It is not yet or no longer theological anthropology if it tries to pose and answer the question of the true being of man from any other angle.[20]

'Humanity' is used in a highly specific sense by Barth, a sense which is both non-phenomenological and highly objectivist. It does not refer to 'immediately accessible and knowable characteristics of the nature which man thinks he can regard as that of his fellows and therefore of man in general',[21] since the description of such characteristics gives us only 'knives without edges, or handles without pots, or predicates without subjects'.[22] Rather the content of the term 'humanity' is to be filled out by reference to a 'source outside'.[23] More closely, the Christian theological use of the term is to be construed through the history in which God encounters us: 'We pass beyond the limits of autonomous human self-understanding ... to a genuinely different level of thought, only when we realise that the conjunction "God and man" or "God with man" or "man with God" means

[19] 111/2, p. 43.
[20] Ibid., p. 132.
[21] Ibid., p. 75.
[22] Ibid., p. 76.
[23] Ibid., p. 122.

noetically and ontically that God *acts* towards man, and when we rigidly confine our view to the history which takes place between God and man.'[24]

This history is not a modulation of some pre-existent, generally perceptible *humanum*; it is a *definitive* history, that in which humanity comes to be. To give one example from the course of Barth's unfolding of the point: he posits that human being 'consists in listening to the Word of God',[25] such that the human person is 'the creaturely being which is addressed, called and summoned by God'.[26] Barth's assertion would be quite misunderstood if it were read as a phenomenological statement, a Christian theological symbolisation or interpretation of a state of affairs open to common inspection. On the contrary: Barth insists on the utter particularity of the claim. For 'the sum of the divine address' is 'the man Jesus';[27] and what the man Jesus says as God's address is, simply, 'Himself'.[28] To claim that human persons are essentially 'listeners' is thus to make a claim about *this* (and *only* this) summons, behind which there is no antecedent 'natural' reality. 'When the reality of human nature is in question, the word "real" is simply equivalent to "summoned".'[29] God's summons of humanity in Jesus is, in the last analysis, *creatio ex nihilo*, and not the shaping or modification of pre-existent human receptivity.

On many counts, Barth's persistence in the point seems a perverse kind of idealism, an isolation of theological language about human nature and history from the 'phenomena of the human' to which he grants no real definitive role in discovering what he calls 'real man'. And, in ethical terms, Barth's discussion seems to point towards an alienation of Christian action from its natural human conditions. The core of the issue is the relation of the general to the particular: is

[24] Ibid., p. 124.
[25] Ibid., p. 147.
[26] Ibid., p. 149.
[27] Ibid., p. 147.
[28] Ibid., p. 148.
[29] Ibid., p. 150.

Christian theology to begin its definition of the human agent from pre-theological reflection on human nature and history, subsequently applying or correlating (perhaps critically) the fruit of such reflections with Christian anthropological and ethical symbols? Or is it to define the human agent exclusively out of the event in which God commands and humanity is called to obedient action? For Barth, the alternatives are very sharply posed, and only the latter route is viable, since the whole thrust of his doctrine of created being is that outside the encounter between God and humanity it is not theologically meaningful to speak of humanity at all. This is why, at the beginning of his treatment of special ethics at the end of the doctrine of creation, he insists that 'special ethics cannot proceed except in the framework of this reference to the event of God's concrete command and man's concrete obedience or disobedience. Whatever it may have to say regarding the concrete form of the command and its bearing upon man's concrete action, it will always have to repeat and underline and sharpen this reference. It will always have to be on its guard against trying to give more than such a reference.'[30] Christian ethics thus involves what Barth calls ' "formed" reference':[31] reference to two subjects in encounter (God and the human agent) and to the event of their encounter, which constitutes the object of Christian ethical inquiry. The two subjects – God as Creator, Reconciler, Redeemer, the human partner as creature and as object of, and respondent to, reconciling and redemptive activity – are specific, perceptible, describable realities in Jesus Christ, whose history is not illustrative but definitive of the content of the terms 'God' and 'humanity'. The history of Jesus prescribes both the inner content of those terms and the outer limits beyond which their Christian usage evaporates. On this basis, the task of Christian ethics will be highly particular. It will be neither foundational nor comparative, but will restrict itself to offering a kind of

[30] III/4, pp. 15f.
[31] Ibid., pp. 18, 23: the phrase is picked up again in the recapitulation of paragraph 52.1 in *ChrL*, p. 6, where it appears as 'formed and contoured reference'.

commentary on the covenant-establishing acts of God: 'comprehensively understood, its task will be to accompany this history of God and man from creation to reconciliation and redemption, indicating the mystery of the encounter at each point on the path according to its own distinctive character'.[32] Above all, Christian ethics will be characterised by its conviction that it is in this history (to which 'formed reference' is made), and not by virtue of some more primary 'creatureliness', that human persons are *real*:

> Neither with the aid of creation nor without it ... do we need to seek a reality distinct from that of the ethical event. We need only consider and state how the latter represents and characterises itself. We need only pursue the history in which each ethical event has its place and forms its moment – the history in which God is Creator, Reconciler and Redeemer and man is that which corresponds to this divine action, His creature, the one who is accepted in grace and has a part in His promise. This history is the reality in which the ethical event takes place, to which we look from the event, and from which we must look back to the event to see it in its concreteness. We may confidently refer to this history because we have to do simply with the self-unfolding of this event.[33]

And, further, in this event 'it is always a question of God in His articulated and differentiated action, and of man in his correspondingly articulated and differentiated being in relation to this God'.[34] What picture of the human agent emerges from this?

HUMAN AGENCY

First, contrary to what sometimes is alleged, Barth's anthropology gives considerable weight to the human person as intrinsically an agent. The human person 'exists and lives as he deliberately posits himself in some way in relation to God, to his fellow-men, and to his environment. His actions

[32] Ibid., p. 26.
[33] Ibid., p. 28.
[34] Ibid., pp. 28f.

are this deliberate positing of himself. His life is neither a mere duration of his existence nor a mere vegetative nor animal course of events. It is the sequence, nexus or history of his self-positing and therefore of his acts.'[35] This assertion that the human person is *essentially* and not *accidentally* an agent will be of very great significance for the ethics of reconciliation and the ethical interpretation of Christian baptism.

Second, the human agent exists in limitation, that is, 'within the limits which correspond to its creaturely existence'.[36] Once again, the point is fundamental to understanding Barth's anthropology and ethics, and worth pausing over. At first blush, 'limitation' suggests 'confinement', whereas Barth means something closer to 'specificity' or 'particular shape'. The human creature is limited, to be sure, in the sense that it is not an indeterminate, quasi-infinite moral self; but its limitedness by God is not its being hemmed in by an alien will, but rather its formation into *this* good creature. And so, Barth argues, the relation between God and humanity is best understood 'as a limitation, i.e., as God's ordaining and man's accepting of a limit'. But 'we must divest ourselves of the idea that limitation implies something derogatory, or even a kind of curse or affliction. When the reference is to the limitation which comes from God, limitation is not a negation but the most positive affirmation. Limitation as decreed by God means circumscription, definition, and therefore determination.'[37]

The point is made a number of times in the discussion of providence in III/3, where God's lordship over and in creaturely occurrence is presented not as *restrictive*, but as what might be called an act of *purposive integration*, through which the definiteness of the creature is upheld. Hence,

---

[35] III/4, pp. 470f. On this theme in Barth, see the perceptive comparison of Luther and Barth by E. Jüngel in 'Gospel and law: the relationship of dogmatics to ethics', in *Karl Barth. A Theological Legacy* (Philadelphia, 1986), pp. 105–26, especially 121f.

[36] III/3, p. 61.

[37] III/4, p. 567.

under the rubric of the divine preserving (*conservatio*), Barth writes:

That the creature may continue to be by virtue of the divine preserving means that it may itself be actual within its limits: actual, and therefore not a mere appearance engendered by some heavenly or hellish power; itself actual, and therefore not an emanation from the being of God and certainly not from non-being. God preserves the creature in the reality which is distinct from His own. It is relative to and dependent upon His reality, but in its relativity and dependence autonomous towards it, existing because it owes its existence to Him, as a subject with which He can have dealings and which can have dealings with Him.[38]

Or, later, in the account of the divine ruling (*gubernatio*), God's rule is expounded as God's 'ordering' of the creature and its acts ('God rules creaturely occurrence by ordering it'[39]) in the sense that by permissive acts God enables the creature to move towards its particular given end, since 'the very meaning of creaturely activity, its effect, and the goal or end in which it culminates, are all the gift and dispensation of God. The activity can exist at all only on the basis of the divine preservation of the creature. It is constantly formed and directed by the permission given to it by God.'[40] Crucially, this ordering and forming of creaturely activity is the glorification, not the degradation, of the creature, on the basis of the principle which underlies not only Barth's account of providence, but in a certain sense his anthropology and ethics in their entirety: 'the individual thing receives its particular dignity and value on the basis of a formative economy which assigns to all things a place and time and function'.[41] Limitation, then, is not about deficiency, still less about some divine force inhibiting legitimate human flourishing; it is rather the creature's quite specific path to glory assigned and maintained by the ordering acts of God.

---

[38] III/3, p. 86
[39] Ibid., p. 164.
[40] Ibid., pp. 166f.
[41] Ibid., pp. 192f.

One of the most fully elaborated presentations of these
related themes of 'limitation' and 'formative economy' (as
well as one which has evoked very heavy critique) is Barth's
lengthy set of reflections on human temporality.[42] A central
notion in those very nuanced reflections is that of 'allotted
time' – temporal limitation as the given shape or form
(and therefore the boundary) in which human life finds its
determinateness. God is

the One in relation to whom our life has its limit and our time
is allotted ... the One who has created and wills to have us
within this limit and allotted span. The final longing for an
unlimited life in unallotted time necessarily falls away once we
realise that the limit and set span of our existence is the condition
which must be fulfilled in order that He, the eternal God, may
be our Counterpart and our Neighbor ... and that we may be His
counterparts and His neighbors. Limit in the creaturely dimension
means a clear-cut outline and contour. Man would not be this
man, here and now, the concrete subject of this history, if his life
did not have this outline and contour, if it did not have these limits
and boundaries. A being in unending time would be centrifugal.[43]

Behind this passage lies a belief that true human temporality
is not a natural *habitus*, something in which the creature is
'inviolably self-subsistent',[44] but an ever-fresh gift of grace
through God's making himself present to the creature. This,
in turn, is bound up with an exclusion of the human self
and the sequence of its acts as the measure of time. Time
is not measured by the succeeding moments of human
experience or self-projection into the world, nor by temporal
self-consciousness. To have a history is thus not to be able
to make our history present to ourselves, either in its entirety
or in its specific present, for the human person 'cannot
review or interpret himself even in the present moment, let

----

[42] III/2, paragraph 47 ('Man and His Time'), pp. 437–640, and III/4, paragraph
56.1 ('The Unique Opportunity'), pp. 565–94. For criticism of Barth's understanding of time, see R. H. Roberts, 'Barth's doctrine of time: its nature and
implications', in *A Theology on Its Way?*, pp. 1–58.
[43] III/2, p. 565.
[44] Ibid., p. 556.

alone in the future or in the totality of his past'.[45] Rather, the entire economy of human being, including temporality, is contingent upon the act of God in Christ assuming and thereby validating human time. Once again, then, Jesus' humanity is axiomatic for constructing doctrine about human being: 'the existence of the man Jesus in time is our guarantee that time as the form of human existence is ... willed and created by God, is given by God to man, and is therefore real'.[46] More sharply: 'Primarily it is not we who are now but God who is now.'[47]

The evident lack in Barth's account of human temporality of the element of 'the permanent continuity of substantial form'[48] has often raised the question of whether his account of moral identity is too atomistic, too reticent about the durable aspects of moral selfhood (character, growth, *acquired* wisdom).[49] Barth is clearly reticent about such notions because of his highly objective interpretation of the temporality of the human agent as the agent's acceptance of an assigned place in an external narrative or sequence. This sequence is the large-scale narrative of the acts of God which create a relation with the creature. The self's temporality derives primarily from its occupation of a place and role within this overarching historical order organised around the unfolding of God's covenant purpose. It is '[t]his history of God and man' which Barth considers to be 'the constant factor and therefore the connection or context of all ethical events',[50] – rather than some independently grounded under-

---

[45] III/4, p. 608.
[46] III/2, p. 520.
[47] Ibid., p. 529.
[48] The phrase is Georges Poulet's, from *Studies in Human Time* (Baltimore, 1956), p. 5.
[49] The clearest statement of this critique is S. Hauerwas, *Character and the Christian Life* (San Antonio, 1975). See also W. Werpehowski's critique of Hauerwas in 'Command and history in the ethics of Karl Barth', *Journal of Religious Ethics* 9 (1981), 298–320, and Hauerwas' response in 'On honour: by way of a comparison of Barth and Trollope', in N. Biggar, ed., *Reckoning with Barth* (Oxford, 1988), pp. 145–69; N. Biggar, *The Hastening that Waits*, pp. 27f.
[50] III/4, p. 26.

standing of human temporal extension or continuity. Clearly this relativises the importance of small-scale biographical narrative in our conception of human agency: the Christian life under the call of God is not presented as a sequence of evolving stages or a biographical progression, but more episodically, with the determinative place given to the claim of God which we encounter *now*:

The determination of the age in which every man exists can obviously be truly meaningful and important only as the divine determination of the *Now*, as the constantly changing *Henceforth*, from which he has to set out for new shores according to the command as though it were for the first and last time. The criterion of our action resulting from this determination cannot consist in the difference of this or that age from another. It consists rather in the secret and yet real coinherence of the differing stages, implicit in the fact that it is the same commanding God who always speaks concretely and differently at the various stages, in order that He will and may be heard by the same man concretely and therefore in the specific form of his one being.[51]

As we shall see in more detail in looking at the ethics of reconciliation, the effect of this presentation of temporal determinacy upon Barth's understanding of ethical agency is twofold: at one and the same time it accords considerable significance to human action and yet also relativises our acts, preventing them from assuming absolute status in the definition of personhood. Barth's treatment of the matter produced, moreover, some of his most acutely felt, humane writing. The accounts of 'The Unique Opportunity' and of 'Vocation' in the course of the discussion of 'Freedom in Limitation'[52] are imbued with a sense of the *density* of particular human history – its irretrievability and yet, by divine grace, its wholesomeness as an 'ineffable benefit'.[53] Moreover, Barth commends a proper – unanxious, unharassed –

[51] Ibid., p. 611.
[52] Ibid., pp. 565–647.
[53] Ibid., p. 578.

urgency which ought to characterise humanity under the command of God: 'The opportunity must be grasped'; 'We have no time to lose.'[54] On other occasions, Barth sometimes expressed an extraordinarily powerful sense of death as obliteration of all human possibilities: 'Some day a company of men will process out to a church-yard and lower a coffin and everyone will go home; but one will not come back, and that will be me. The seal of death will be that they will bury me as a thing that is superfluous and disturbing in the land of the living.'[55] Yet Barth's image of the human agent is not of a race *against* temporal contingency, in which we have somehow to shape ourselves by unconditioned creativity or establish the meaning of the moral situation by seizing hold of the present and making it our own. Much more is Barth's image that of the agent's entry into a given form, of cheerful, unpossessive acknowledgment of determinacy and limitedness, there to find space for freedom and flourishing and for the modest 'little steps' which correspond to God's command.[56]

PRAYER AND ACTION

Two final themes from Barth's doctrine of creation are important background to the ethics of reconciliation: prayer and the active life.

[54] Ibid., pp. 580, 587.
[55] K. Barth, *Dogmatics in Outline* (London, 1949), pp. 117f. A parallel passage in the *Dogmatics* runs: 'It is indeed unpleasant to think that some day I shall be a corpse whom others will leave and go home chatting after they have heaped wreaths and flowers and poured out kind words and music upon me. It is indeed unpleasant to think that my place will then be in a coffin or urn a few feet below the surface of the ground. It is indeed an unpleasant thought that for a time I will then be missed up above in the daylight, but that I will be finally extinguished from human memory when the last of those who knew me has gone the same way' (III/4, p. 589). There are striking similarities between what Barth says here and the deeply felt reflection on mortality in T. Nagel, *The View from Nowhere* (Oxford, 1986), pp. 223–31.
[56] III/4, p. 666. This notion of the 'modesty' of human acts will be greatly expanded in *ChrL*, under the rubric of 'The Precedence of the Word of God', pp. 168–204.

Prayer is treated in volume III of the *Dogmatics*[57] as 'the most intimate and effective form of Christian action',[58] more specifically as the paradigmatic instance of the significant and yet the properly modest compass of human activity. In this respect, the earlier treatment clearly foreshadows Barth's use of petition as the primary image for restored human ethical agency in the exposition of Christian baptism and of the Lord's Prayer, which provide the structure for the fragments of the ethics of reconciliation.

In linking prayer to ethos, Barth's interest is not in cultic or liturgical formation of moral dispositions, but in prayer as a human venture.[59] 'Prayer . . . is simply asking.'[60] Barth begins here because petition focusses his account of the relation between God's acts of divine grace and the corresponding human activity which grace evokes. Prayer as petition, in so far as it demonstrates this understanding of grace and its human answer, leads us to 'the innermost centre of the covenant between God and man'.[61] Because it is an asking which flows from the prior divine gift, prayer cannot be conceived of as a self-directed human venture, a kind of positioning of the self before God which draws forth divine response. On the contrary: the one who asks 'is doing that which corresponds and answers to the situation in which he finds himself placed by the Word of God' – petition is 'simply the taking and receiving of the divine gift and answer as it is already present and near to hand in Jesus Christ'.[62] Yet this is not to deny that petition is a real act –

---

[57] The theme is handled (along with faith and obedience) as part of the account of 'The Christian Under the Universal Lordship of God the Father' (III/3, pp. 265–88) and later in III/4, pp. 87–115 as part of the account of 'Freedom before God'. J. Kelsay is correct to note that 'Barth's discussion of prayer is tied to his general discussion of theological ethics': 'Prayer and ethics: reflections on Calvin and Barth', *Harvard Theological Review* 82 (1989), 174.

[58] III/3, p. 264.

[59] This distinguishes his work from recent accounts such as T. Sedgwick, *Sacramental Ethics. Paschal Identity and the Christian Life* (Philadelphia, 1987), or F. J. van Beeck, *God Encountered I: Understanding the Christian Faith* (San Francisco, 1989), pp. 234–49.

[60] III/3, p. 268.

[61] III/4, p. 93.

[62] Ibid., pp. 270, 274.

indeed, the very core of human agency. For

we have to do with the will of God not only over but with the
creature. We have to do with His covenant with man. We have
to do with His grace directed towards man as an autonomous
being distinct from himself. We have to do with His work, in
which man has an animate and not an inanimate subject. We
have to do with His Word, which man can hear and answer. In
short, we have to do with the freedom in which man himself can
live.[63]

Beneath this lies another level to the argument (one which
will become increasingly important in the doctrine of
reconciliation): a complex Christological statement, which
both strongly affirms the vicarious character of Jesus' human
action and yet does not suppress the reality of genuine
human analogies to that which is accomplished outside the
realm of our agency. On the one hand, the human act of
supplication takes its rise in a fact concerning Jesus: 'This
man prayed.'[64] Prayer is, then, 'not merely . . . a creaturely
movement',[65] because 'the first and proper suppliant is none
other than Jesus Christ Himself'.[66] But – and at this point
the vicarious humanity model is expanded – 'He is not
alone in doing this.'[67] That last statement is not primarily
an anthropological statement, nor is it a qualification of the
non-transferable character of Jesus Christ's office as high
priest in which he is 'the Representative and Substitute for
all others'.[68] Rather, it is a statement that, *because* Christ's
prayer is his action 'for others', we may also pray 'with him',
on the basis of his achievement and its self-representation in
the Spirit. Barth here is articulating in condensed form
what will become the overarching dogmatic structure of his
account of the relation of Christology and the Christian life
in the next volume of the *Dogmatics*: 'at the very heart of

---

[63] III/3, p. 274.
[64] Ibid., p. 276.
[65] Ibid., p. 288; cf. III/4, p. 108.
[66] III/3, p. 274.
[67] III/3, p. 276.
[68] Ibid.

creaturely occurrence' there lies 'an asking which has to be understood in the light of the divine gift and answer . . . an asking which is done in this order'.[69]

Barth's account of 'the active life' expounds a closely parallel understanding of the relation of prevenient grace to human activity. Two aspects of his handling of the topic deserve comment. First, Barth refuses to see 'work' (social labour) as the entirety of the active life which is commanded by God: '[W]e can hardly say that work in itself and as such is the active life which God requires.'[70] Barth has already prepared for this relativising of the place of work in his interpretation of the Sabbath commandment in the early part of III/4: the command means 'a clear delimiting and relativising of what man can and should will and do of himself'.[71] By making rest prior to work, the Sabbath command accords priority to divine grace and so once again sets limits to human self-positing by demanding of the agent a 'renunciation of himself, of all that he thinks and wills and effects and achieves'.[72] Barth's lengthy critique of the work ethic (for its failure to pursue only worthy ends, its inhuman contribution to 'the reign of empty and inordinate desires',[73] its lack of reflectivity, its capacity to enslave by tension and excessive seriousness) is a countermovement against forgetfulness that 'one's active affirmation of existence is only relative . . . [since] it is surrounded and upheld by the absolute active affirmation of existence whose Subject is God and not oneself'.[74]

Lest this shift of work from the centre to the periphery seem to undermine what Barth's larger argument seeks to uphold – that the Christian life is indeed a *vita activa* – it is important to underline the stress which Barth places on the proper 'correspondence' between God's activity and

---

[69] Ibid., p. 284.
[70] III/4, p. 471. On this theme in Barth, see P. West, 'Karl Barth's theology of work: a resource for the late 1980s', *Modern Churchman* 30 (1988), 13–19.
[71] Ibid., pp. 53f.
[72] Ibid., p. 59.
[73] Ibid., p. 538.
[74] Ibid., p. 558.

human acts. 'An active life in obedience must obviously consist in a correspondence to divine action.'[75] Here, as elsewhere, the term 'correspondence' bears a good deal of weight. It furnishes a way of affirming both the unique, incommunicable nature of God's action (of which there can never be any human continuation or supplementation or adornment), and the reality of the human 'venture of action'.[76] To embark on that venture is not to aspire to become co-regents with God, but rather to enter into and act out an order which, in its specificity and limitation, receives and testifies to the generative action of God in Christ. 'As man is summoned to this active participation, he will accept the strict and salutary distinction between God and man.'[77] That, in sum, is what it means to be creature and covenant partner of the God and Father of our Lord Jesus Christ.

RECONCILIATION

Barth's doctrine of reconciliation is one of a handful of post-Reformation theological works with clear title to classic status. He began work on it at age 65, and it consumed the largest share of his attention and energies until work on the *Dogmatics* all but ceased with his final lectures on the subject. Barth approached the subject of the doctrine of reconciliation with a particular joy and yet with a measure of apprehension, being 'very conscious of the special responsibility laid on the theologian at this centre of all Christian knowledge. To fail here is to fail everywhere.'[78] The authority of the resulting text derives most of all from the fact that Barth writes as one who is supremely *interested* in his subject: God in Christ, 'the axiom of all axioms':[79]

---

[75] Ibid., p. 474.
[76] Ibid., p. 473.
[77] Ibid., p. 483.
[78] IV/1, p. ix.
[79] IV/2, p. 794.

[T]he basic note in the life of the Christian as the man who loves God is that the One above, the Crucified and Risen, is – how shall we put it? – important to him; that everywhere and constantly and repeatedly, with a definiteness which cannot be excelled, in a way which cannot be said of the other things and factors which interest and claim and gladden and trouble him, or of other men or the whole world or even himself, He has significance.[80]

This sense of the supreme and urgent significance of the object of theological reflection pervades *Dogmatics* iv, as does the sense that Barth is constantly struggling to *concentrate*, to attain that specificity in his thought and speech which, as he put it in a letter, 'comes only out of the matter itself and with our faces set towards Jerusalem'.[81]

For all its expansiveness, the doctrine of reconciliation is elaborately ordered in a way which itself expresses funda-mental theological convictions.[82] In the Christological sec-tions, Barth eschews the divisions of the material traditional in Protestant dogmatics, and interweaves person and work, exaltation and humiliation, prophet, priest, and king. The purpose of this ordering is to penetrate behind the conven-tional dogmatic structures to reach the matter of which they are, properly speaking, merely analytic. That matter is the enacted sequence of the history of Jesus, for: 'To say "Jesus" is necessarily to say "history", His history, the history in which He is what He is and does what He does.'[83] Moreover, the doctrine of reconciliation is much more than a treatise on Christology. As a Christology, it is also a soteriology, a pneumatology, an ecclesiology, an anthropology, and an ethics. For Barth, these loci are inseparable because the history of Jesus is, once again, the history of the covenant.[84] Narrating that history is not only recounting its specificity *illic et tunc*; it is also speaking of its universal self-

---

[80] Ibid., pp. 793f.
[81] *Letters 1961–8* (Edinburgh, 1981), p. 61; cf. p. 64.
[82] Busch records how the structure of the doctrine of reconciliation has its surpris-ing origin in a dream: *Karl Barth*, p. 377.
[83] iv/3, p. 179.
[84] Busch, again, records (*Karl Barth*, p. 377) that Barth nearly chose 'covenant' for the title of volume IV, rather than 'reconciliation'.

manifestation in the power of the Spirit (pneumatology). Moreover, narrating that history is recounting not simply the history of the one man Jesus, but the history of all humanity in him (soteriology, ecclesiology, anthropology, and ethics). Thus, *precisely because* it is a Christological treatise, the doctrine of reconciliation has as part of its internal structure a reference to the re-establishment of the human world. On its own distinct grounds and in a very distinct sense, it is, in part at least, an 'existential' or 'moral' Christology.

'The atonement is history. To know it, we must know it as such. To think of it, we must think of it as such. To speak of it, we must tell it as history.'[85] Barth does not go about his doctrine of reconciliation primarily by offering extended conceptual analysis – though parts of it are severely conceptual – but by undertaking what is, in effect, a massive descriptive expansion of the person and works of the central subject in the history of reconciliation: Jesus. All other interests in the treatise (historical, dogmatic, ethical, and so forth) are strictly subservient to the primary *passion* – the word is not too strong – for the depiction of the event of Jesus as the enacted sequence in which the covenant is fulfilled and the reconciliation of God and humanity accomplished. The subject-matter of reconciliation, then, is 'not a state, but an event'[86], and 'a single and particular event which has a definite importance for all time and space, but which takes place once and for all in a definite *hic et nunc*'.[87]

This specificity is underscored by Barth's increasing concentration on the 'name' of Jesus, on what Hans Frei called the 'unsubstitutable' identity of Jesus as *this* one and none other, whose living and dying and rising again constitute an absolutely primitive sequence, of which all concepts are merely analytic.[88]

[85] IV/I, p. 157.
[86] Ibid., p. 6.
[87] Ibid., p. 8.
[88] H. Frei, *The Identity of Jesus Christ* (Philadelphia, 1975), p. 49 and passim.

We must realise that the Christian message does not at its heart express a concept or an idea, nor does it recount an anonymous history to be taken as truth and reality only in concepts and ideas ... [I]t recounts this history ... in such a way that it declares a name, binding the history strictly and indissolubly to this name and presenting it as the story of the bearer of this name. This means that all the concepts and ideas used in this report (God, man, world, eternity, time, even salvation, grace, transgression, atonement and any others) can derive their significance only from the bearer of this name and from His history, and not the reverse.[89]

As he spirals round his theme, Barth refuses to let this point pass; there is a constantly reiterated 'He Himself' in the text which signifies Barth's fierce adherence to the unqualified primacy of the story of Jesus. It is as if the name of Jesus constantly prevents the argument from tugging away from its moorings and drifting into generalities. That name is, therefore, not a basically detachable mode of signifying a reality which could be signified with different names, perhaps, or known under more abstract descriptions. The name 'is not merely a cipher, under which that which it really means and has to say leads its own life and has its own truth and actuality and would be worth proclaiming for its own sake, a cipher which can at any time be omitted without affecting that which is really meant and said, or which in other ages or climes or circumstances can be replaced by some other cipher'.[90] Rather, the name 'Jesus' adverts to the specific and irreducible set of events in which he has his identity as *this* person. That is why, as he puts it later, '[w]e can speak of the being, activity and speech of Jesus Christ only in relation to specific events, only in the form of a narration of a history and histories. If Christology as the depiction of this being, activity and speech is to be anything more than an obscure metaphysics, in all its parts and aspects it can only be the unfolding of a drama.'[91]

Barth's doctrine of reconciliation is, then, striking above all for its *narrative density*, its ceaseless vigilance against

---

[89] IV/1, p. 16.
[90] Ibid., p. 21; cf. IV/3.2, p. 797.
[91] IV/3.1, p. 136.

conceptual takeover, its refusal to go beyond the simple 'It
came to pass . . .'[92] Part of the discipline of such vigilance
is an unsettling of easy familiarity with the gospel story, for
'we must try to find some way of making the accustomed
unaccustomed again, the well-known unknown and the old
new: that is, the outline of the evangelical history with
which we are so familiar and the stimulating singularity of
which we may so easily overlook.'[93] In both its overall
structure and in its details, *Dogmatics* IV is an invitation to
'consider this history carefully once more.'[94] In terms of
overall structure, Christology and soteriology (along with
the corresponding material on ecclesiology, anthropology,
and ethics) are organised around the narrative sequence of
Jesus' life, death, and resurrection, patterned after the twofold movement of exile and homecoming from the story of
the prodigal and – in a dependent way – after the descent–
ascent motif from Philippians 2. And in its details, *Church
Dogmatics* IV constantly returns to the particulars of Jesus'
story. The exposition of the kingly office of Christ in paragraph 64.3, 'The Royal Man', for example, is an extended
account of 'the evangelical tradition concerning Jesus'.[95] Or,
again, a brief exposition of John 3.16 in the introductory
summary section of the doctrine of reconciliation in IV/1
stresses how 'ἠγάπησεν tells a definite story, gives news of
a unique event.'[96] And the examples could be multiplied
many times.

It is very important, however, that we do not interpret
Barth as applying to the story of Jesus some general theory
about the narrative structure of personal identity: Barth
simply has no interest in considering any such broad claims.
His point is simple and restricted: the core of a Christian
account of God's dealings with humanity is Jesus in his
historical progress from Bethlehem to Calvary. Barth's insist-

---

[92] IV/1, p. 223.
[93] Ibid., p. 224.
[94] Ibid.
[95] IV/2, p. 156.
[96] IV/1, p. 70.

ence on the irreducibility of that history does not express
general convictions about narrativity: it is a *theological* claim
about Jesus and his life, a theological claim which is at the
same time an ontological claim and an epistemological claim.

The *theological* claim is that Jesus' history is the actuality
of divine grace. Jesus' history is primary, not because it
shares in the irreducibility of all narratives, but because it
is the sovereign act of God himself. Ultimately, the reason
why the content of the history of Jesus is not available under
any other description than that afforded by the canonical
narratives is that *this history* is that of God himself. It is
irreducible because, as divine action, it cannot be circumscribed within some larger scheme. Barth's narrative Christology, then, does not allow him to sit loose on the ontological categories of classical incarnational Christology. Quite
the reverse: such conceptuality, properly understood, is an
attempt to articulate the fact that Jesus' historical progress
is no mere contingent event, but the absolute act of God's
self-positing, God's 'high humility'.[97] Because *God* is subject
and agent in this history, it cannot be resolved into something higher or more general: as God's act, Jesus' history
simply *is*. For 'if the atonement is an act of divine sovereignty, we are forbidden to try to deduce it from anything
else . . . we are commanded to accept and acknowledge it
in all its inconceivability as something that has happened,
taking it strictly as it is without thinking round it or over
it'.[98] The story of Jesus cannot be supplanted because it
presents itself as having the axiomatic status of the necessary
being of God himself.

From this fact that, 'when we say all these things about
the man Jesus we say them about God',[99] there follows an
ontological claim. Because it is the history in which the
covenant between God and humanity is fulfilled from both
sides, Jesus' history is the true essence of created being. As
our saving history, Jesus' history is 'fulfilment, the supreme,

[97] Ibid., p. 159.
[98] Ibid., pp. 80f.
[99] Ibid., p. 194.

sufficient, definitive and indestructible fulfilment of being'.[100]
Created human being *is* in so far as it participates in the
covenant with God which is established in the irreplaceable
history of Jesus Christ. As we have seen, Barth's entire
presentation of the doctrines of creation and humanity in
Church Dogmatics III has prepared us for just this point; but
its sheer enormity as a claim is not to be underestimated.
For so much hangs on so little: an entire ontology of created
being rests upon a mere fragment. That fragment can bear
the weight with which it is loaded only because we may –
without any compromise of its utter specificity – ascribe to
it that pure absoluteness which is proper to God alone.
'Jesus Christ, very God and very man, born and living and
acting and suffering and conquering in time, is as such the
one eternal Word of God at the beginning of all things.'[101]
In effect, then, the doctrine of reconciliation is a further
expansion of the earlier claim: He is the reality! As Barth
puts it in his discussion in IV/3.2 of 'The People of God in
World-Occurrence', 'in Jesus Christ we do really have the
new reality of world-history'.[102] As the act of God himself,
Jesus' life-act grounds, frames and limits all other histories
as their *ratio essendi*, but is itself in no way grounded, or
framed, or limited.

Finally, an *epistemological* claim is also at work here: as
axiomatic and sheerly necessary reality, this history itself
establishes the conditions under which it may be known as
what it is. 'The actuality of this new being and occurrence,
grounded in the divine act of majesty, creates the possibility
of a special perception to meet it, a perception which is
controlled and mastered by it, attaching itself to it, following
and accompanying it, imitating and repeating it.'[103] As *divine*
action, it cannot be a matter for what Barth calls 'demon-
stration':[104] for construction on grounds external to the sub-

---

[100] Ibid., p. 8; cf. ibid., p. 13, and IV/3.1, p. 43.
[101] IV/1, p. 49.
[102] IV/3.2, p. 712.
[103] IV/2, p. 120.
[104] Ibid.

ject-matter of the possibility of knowledge of that matter.
For knowledge of this history is knowledge of 'the divine
act of majesty in virtue of which it is actual and may be
known', an act which is such that 'the basis and the *de jure*
of its perception cannot lie or operate outside the fact itself'.[105] Once again, this is bound up with the narrative
density of Barth's treatise: knowledge of the history of Jesus
is not a speculatively constructed reassurance of *how* these
things can be so, or *why* 'it came to pass', but something
of an entirely different order. It is a matter 'of reading and
expounding a definitely given text'.[106] And 'text' here means
not only the canonical narrative of the gospel record, but
something more – what Barth calls 'the basic text', which
is 'the fact created by the divine act of majesty to the extent
that it has the character, not only of being and occurrence,
but also, as this fact, of revelation. In this character it
reveals and discloses itself. It gives itself to be known. It
creates the possibility of a seeing and hearing and understanding of it.'[107] And so '[w]e can only read and expound
that basic text . . . We can only act as those to whom it is
given. We cannot try to get "behind" it, either behind the
fact that it is given, or behind the way in which it is
legitimate and possible for us to act in correspondence to
this fact.'[108]

This explains why Barth's account of our *knowledge* of Jesus
Christ is so slight, indeed almost cavalier, in its handling of
the two major preoccupations of twentieth-century Christology: history and hermeneutics. As we shall see, Barth
replaces these formal preoccupations with *doctrinal* affirmations: about the resurrection as the luminosity of the
Christ-event, and about the Holy Spirit as the *doctor veritatis*.
Because, again, of what he takes to be the absolute and
therefore self-positing character of the object of Christology,
Barth locates the bridge between Jesus' history and our

[105] Ibid., p. 121.
[106] Ibid., p. 122.
[107] Ibid.
[108] Ibid., p. 123.

own not in some cognitive or interpretative or experiential processes, but in the self-manifestation of the risen Jesus in the power of the Spirit, as a reality which we can only acknowledge.

What is the shape taken by anthropology within such an account, in which the events of Jesus' career are accorded ontological and noetic primacy? And how will this anthropology prepare us for the presentation of the ethics of reconciliation with which the volume closes?

From the very beginning, Barth is at pains to establish two points: that the doctrine of reconciliation includes a statement about humanity, and that it does so only on the basis of God's election of us in grace. Reconciliation means: God with us, and therefore the restoration of the proper ordered mutuality between God and the creatures of his grace. 'Emmanuel' cannot be construed as a statement having God for its exclusive logical subject, for the God who is 'with us' is 'the God who does not work and act without His people':[109]

If the fact that God is with us is a report about the being and life and act of God, then from the very outset it stands in a relationship to our own being and life and acts. A report about ourselves is included in that report about God ... To put it in the simplest way, what unites God and us men is the fact that He does not will to be God without us, that He creates us rather to share with us and therefore with our being and life and act His own incomparable being and life and act, that He does not allow His history to be His and ours to be ours, but causes them to take place as a common history. That is the special message which the Christian message has to proclaim at its very heart.[110]

Precisely because the atonement is about the fulfilment of the covenant, then any such formula as 'God everything and man nothing' is 'complete nonsense'.[111] For the *telos* of the work of God in Christ is not simply God's self-glorification, but his self-glorification in the glorification of

[109] IV/I, p. 6.
[110] Ibid., p. 7.
[111] Ibid., p. 89.

humanity. Here 'God is indeed everything but only in order
that man may not be nothing, in order that he may be His
man, in order that as such he, too, may be everything in
his own place, on his own level and within his own limits
. . . This creating and grounding of a human subject which
is new in relation to God and therefore in itself is, in fact,
the event of the atonement made in Jesus Christ.'[112]

The second point which Barth is at pains to establish is
that the necessary inclusion of this anthropological dimension does not involve any retraction of the primacy of grace:
we do not, as it were, shift into a different sphere when we
take up these anthropological concerns. Humanity's exaltation by being drawn into the covenant is a statement
included within the Christian message of God's grace in Christ,
a message which is 'primarily a statement about God and
only then and for that reason a statement about us men'.[113]

To see how seriously Barth takes these concerns, we need
look no further than the opening pages of IV/2, where Barth
moves to the treatment of what he calls the second problem
of the doctrine of reconciliation, namely the exaltation of
humanity to fellowship with God. Barth clearly is aware
that he faces a risk in treating this theme: the risk of a
return to 'theological humanism, moralism, psychologism,
synergism, and ultimately anthropocentric monism'.[114] His
strategy for handling the risk is, in essence, an equal emphasis on the pure gratuity of the Word's assumption of human
nature and on the full reality of our participation in the
covenant by virtue of the Word's *assumptio carnis*. For, on
the one hand, '[w]e have to do with the eternal beginning
of all the ways and works of God when we have to do with
Jesus Christ – even in His true humanity. This is not a

---

[112] Ibid. From this point of view, the accounts of Jesus' 'unsubstitutable' identity
offered by Frei and Marshall need considerable expansion, since they tend to
treat the *inclusivity* of Jesus' humanity rather lightly. In the case of Frei, at
least, this may be bound up with his reticence in spelling out the wider
dogmatic concerns of the doctrine of the two natures, most of all in terms of
the anthropological dimensions of the Word's assumption of human nature.

[113] Ibid., p. 5.

[114] IV/2, p. 8.

"contingent fact of history".[115] But, on the other hand, '[t]he humanity of Jesus is not a secondary moment in the Christ-event. It is not something which happens later, and later again will pass and disappear ... Like His deity, it is integral to the whole event'.[116] The doctrine of the hypostatic union affords an affirmation that the absolute unconditionedness of the God of grace *and* our exaltation to full humanity are both integral to the same movement of Jesus' history. And, from the side of humanity and its life-in-act, this means that 'we are lifted up, that we are awakened to our own truest being as life and act, that we are set in motion by the fact that in that one man God has made Himself our peacemaker and the giver and gift of our salvation ... This ... does not mean the extinguishing of our humanity, but its establishment ... It is not for us a passive presence as spectators, but our true and highest activation.'[117]

What are the implications for how Barth understands Christian existence?

The most important implication – and one which immediately distances Barth from the mainstream of contemporary theological reflection – is that Christian existence is not the point at which the gospel of reconciliation first becomes 'real'. The 'reality' of the gospel is not something of which it comes to be possessed by virtue of our existence and acts; our existence and acts come to possess 'reality' in so far as they share in the axiomatic reality of God with us, set forth in the gospel. One of the most remarkable (and yet, strangely, less well-noticed) features of the doctrine of reconciliation is Barth's extensive recovery of the prophetic office of Christ, above all in *Church Dogmatics* IV/3. Barth uses the notion of the 'prophetic' character of Jesus' history to say that 'as reconciliation takes place, it also declares itself', that it is 'outgoing and self-communicative'.[118] The point is

---

[115] Ibid., p. 31.
[116] Ibid., p. 35.
[117] IV/1, pp. 14f.
[118] IV/3.1, p. 37.

partly the epistemological one to which we have already
referred; but it is also a larger affirmation of how reconciliation includes not only its objective accomplishment, but
also its subjective realisation as the truth of human existence.

As often in *Church Dogmatics* IV, Barth's hidden dialogue
partner is Bultmann. Already in the Foreword to IV/I,
Barth remarked that 'throughout I have found myself in an
intensive, although for the most part quiet, debate with
Rudolf Bultmann',[119] and Barth's critical distance from
Bultmann here, as earlier, revolves around the question of
how and on what grounds the reality of God impinges upon
our existence. The distance between the two dates back at
least as far as Bultmann's critical remarks on Barth's
Christliche Dogmatik for working with 'uncritically adopted
concepts of an older ontology'.[120] By 1930, Barth had come
to see the rift between the two as one concerning the entire
grounds of Christian faith and theology: writing of
Bultmann, Gogarten and Brunner, he says:

From my standpoint all of you, though your concern differs from
mine in different ways, represent a large-scale return to the flesh-
pots of Egypt. I mean that if I am not deceived, all of you – in
a new way different from that of the nineteenth century – are
trying to understand faith as a human possibility, or, if you will,
as grounded in a human possibility, and therefore you are once
again surrendering theology to philosophy.[121]

Where Bultmann read Barth as a return to post-Reformation
scholasticism, Barth came to read Bultmann as espousing
a relatively independent sphere of human existence and its
capabilities with which faith and theology must be co-
ordinated, thus compromising the absolute originality and
gratuity of the basis of faith. By the time Barth came to
deliver his famous response in the early 1950s, *Rudolph
Bultmann – An Attempt to Understand Him*, he presented his
quarrel with Bultmann in terms of a widely divergent understanding of the place of the *pro nobis* aspect of the Christ

[119] IV/I, p. ix.
[120] Karl Barth/Rudolf Bultmann, *Letters 1922–1966* (Edinburgh, 1982), p. 39.
[121] Ibid., p. 49.

event. For Bultmann (in the tradition of Schleiermacher, Melanchthon, and the young Luther), the *pro nobis* is accorded such central importance that soteriology swallows up Christology, and the exposition of the gospel becomes caught within 'the anthropological triangle of law, sin and grace'.[122] What Barth fails to find in Bultmann is a sense that the Christ-event 'possessed an intrinsic significance of its own, and that only because it has that primary significance has it a derived significance here and now'.[123] And, in response to Bultmann's reply to *Rudolph Bultmann*, Barth writes thus:

> I have become increasingly a Zinzendorfian to the extent that in the New Testament only the one central figure as such has begun to occupy me – or each and everything else only in the light and under the sign of this central figure. As I see it, one can and should read all theology in some sense backwards from it: down to anthropology, ethics, and then methodology ... [I]n this light it has become for me a very positive business ... One cannot discuss the fact that 'Jesus lives', as we are both convinced. But one can, as a theologian, either refrain or not refrain from thinking to and from this 'objective' reality. I myself cannot refrain from doing so.[124]

The issue here, as throughout *Dogmatics* IV, is not simply one of the importance assigned to the subjective realm in talking of the work of Christ: on that, both are in some measure agreed (Barth more than is commonly realised). The issue is much more one of the grounds upon which the subjective realm is affirmed. By securing that realm by reference to the 'prophetic' character of Christ's work (rather than by reference to the dynamics of human existence or faith), Barth is denying that there are two realities, the reality of Christ on the one hand and, on the other hand, the quasi-independent reality of human existence in terms of which Christ's reality has to be made meaningful. Any

[122] K. Barth, 'Rudolf Bultmann – An Attempt to Understand Him', in H. W. Barthsch, ed., *Kerygma and Myth. A Theological Debate*, vol. 2 (London, 1962), p. 122.
[123] Ibid., p. 110.
[124] *Letters 1922–1966*, pp. 106f.

such affirmation, Barth has come to propose, is in the end
a form of unbelief, a covert disqualification of the absoluteness of Jesus Christ as the God-man who embraces both
sides of the covenant relation. Over against Bultmann, Barth
presses the point that what matters is not that – in apologetic
fashion – Jesus' history be made meaningful in our history
(as if there were any real human history *extra Christum*), but
the opposite: what matters is our being drawn into his
sphere, which is in truth the sphere in which alone we may
properly be said to exist:

Whatever it may or may not mean for us subjectively; whatever
may be its reflection in our consciousness, the fact that reconciliation is also revelation and Jesus Christ lives and works as Prophet
means that objectively we can no longer be remote from Him in
a private sphere, but that we are drawn into His sphere, into
what takes place in Him.[125]

Barth's protest, then, is that by according such significance
to the existential conditions for the gospel's realisation,
Bultmann fails to see the objective history of Jesus as 'history
in the supreme sense, history in which we have a share
whether we realise it and like it or not, history in which
our own history takes place'.[126] In sum: on the basis of his
doctrine of the hypostatic union, Barth stresses that the
existential realm is 'a minor and conclusion' deduced from
'a given major'.[127]

This 'minor and conclusion', however, is no slight or
dispensable thing. For it is by our participation in the 'most
basic history' of the covenant enacted in Jesus that we truly
become human agents. The same two basic assertions that
we have already indicated are involved here also. First, it
is *only* by virtue of our participation in the covenant through
God's grace in Christ that we become agents. This is a direct
implication of Barth's earlier replacement of the doctrines of
'nature' or 'creation' by doctrines of the vicarious humanity

---

[125] IV/3.1, p. 182.
[126] Ibid., p. 183.
[127] IV/1, p. 286.

of Christ and of union with Christ: being human, acting
humanly, are possibilities grounded in Christ's incarnational
union with us, not in some general *humanum*. In terms of
his account of the human agent, this means that Barth
proposes a fundamental *passivity* as anthropologically basic.
This passivity corresponds to the fact that the human person
is a creature of God's covenant-establishing grace. In a
lengthy exposition of the theology of substitution in paragraph 59.2 ('The Judge Judged in Our Place'), Barth writes
with great power and vividness of 'His activity as our
Representative and Substitute'. Most of all, he presses the
logic of substitution by urging that, in virtue of Christ's
unreserved solidarity with us, there is an identity between
Jesus' history and ours. This identity as it were de-centres
us, locating our true being outside ourselves in a sequence
of events in which Another took our place:

'Jesus Christ for us' means that this one true man Jesus Christ
has taken the place of us men, of many, in all the authority and
omnipotence and competence of the one true God, in order to
act in our name and therefore validly and effectively for us in all
matters of reconciliation with God and therefore of our redemption
and salvation, representing us without any co-operation on our
part.[128]

Such affirmations clearly relativise the significance of our
own acts in our self-definition. Moreover, they suggest (as
we see from the discussion of sin as pride in paragraph 60)
that the image of the self as fashioner of its own identity
through its acts is, simply, wicked and ruinous. 'Wicked',
because it is a direct refusal of God's omnipotent grace;
'ruinous', because it thereby opposes the one true source of
our well-being. Sin as pride is the hopeless delusion that
we can maintain our own cause without grace, the sin of
'the man who does not want to be helpless, who thinks that
he can be his own helper'.[129] As such, sin is simply that

[128] Ibid., p. 230.
[129] Ibid., p. 459.

'absurd act'[130] which contradicts the truth of that being which is ours by virtue of Christ's taking our place as our helper. Accordingly, Barth gives considerable weight to the motif of justification (as it is correlated with the notions of substitution and faith), since *iustificatio imputata* offers another means of locating true human identity outside the stream of human existing and acting. And more: that true identity, hidden in Christ, cannot be made entirely transparent to us in self-reflection or established by a pattern of acting of our devising. The truth about our existence is that we are 'participants in th[e] great drama' of reconciliation rather than shapers of our own selfhood. The history of *God's* gracious act of reconciling us to himself 'is our true history, in an incomparably more direct and intimate way than anything which might present itself as our history in our own subjective experience, than anything we might try to represent as our history in explanation of our own self-understanding ... Compared with it, measured by the reality of it all, the things which we think we know of ourselves – in the unriddling of riddles which are not genuine riddles – are a fairy-tale and a myth.'[131] Because it is that history, and not the history of our own actions and sufferings, which is 'our true and actual today',[132] it is always 'a strange today, although it is ours',[133] since it is the history of 'the effective self-substitution of God for us'.[134] And thus to *iustitia aliena* there corresponds *sola fide*, for as 'wholly and utterly humility',[135] faith 'has to be an empty hand, an empty vessel, a vacuum'.[136]

But can this monumental insistence on *solus Christus* and *sola fide* support a properly covenantal account of the relation of God to the creatures of his grace? Does not the logic of

[130] Ibid., p. 419.
[131] Ibid., p. 547: the contradiction of Bultmann is plain.
[132] Ibid., p. 548.
[133] Ibid., p. 549.
[134] Ibid., p. 550.
[135] Ibid., p. 618.
[136] Ibid., p. 631.

substitution, alien righteousness and the passivity and humility of faith effectively cut out the human agent by throwing our identity onto that of Jesus?

What initially prevents us from such a reading of Barth's doctrine of reconciliation is the weight which he attaches to the doctrines of sanctification and vocation, whose emphasis on the renewal of the human agent forms crucial background to the ethical material with which this volume of the *Dogmatics* closes. In his opening remarks on justification, Barth protests against the false absolutisation of justification as '*the* word of the Gospel' at cost to *sanctificatio* and *vocatio*;[137] the same theme informs his account of sanctification in paragraph 66. Picking up Calvin's notion of *duplex gratia*, Barth pursues the complementarity of justification and sanctification as a correlate of the ordered mutuality of the covenant, an order in which grace precedes precisely in order to evoke the response of dependent partnership. The precedence of grace certainly means that in talking of sanctification we do not move into a sphere in which 'the saints' are the agents of their own sanctity, for 'it is the Holy One who is the active Subject of sanctification'.[138] And, again, there can be no question of jettisoning the theology of substitution which has played so central a role so far: holiness, like righteousness, is 'alien', rooted in our union with Christ and participation in his benefits. Yet the *telos* of grace is the evocation in its human recipients of a new life-act. How is this move – the move from the (*de jure*) reality of what is established for us by Christ's own work and the (*de facto*) reality of our own existence and acts – to be made?

Barth's handling of this question is central to any understanding of his ethics and his entire anthropology. Above all, he refuses to see the move from *de jure* to *de facto* as one in which the 'objective' becomes 'subjectively real'. As in the critique of Bultmann's existential interpretation, so here: what is apparently 'merely' objective *is* the true subjective

[137] Ibid., p. 521.
[138] IV/2, p. 513.

reality of the saints of God – there is 'no separation between Him and them'.[139] Our existence and acts do not interpret or realise the objective reality of Christ's saving work, for it is 'a matter of its own self-interpretation'.[140] Barth negotiates the passage from objective to subjective, not through a theory of spirituality, experience, or morality, but through the doctrines of resurrection and Holy Spirit in which the outgoing, self-realising character of reconciliation is articulated. Reconciliation is not a mere possibility awaiting realisation; it is, as Barth puts it later, 'the only reality' which 'can alone lay claim to the term'.[141] Christian existence and the acts of the Christian life take place within the space of this reality, in 'the age of the Holy Spirit'.[142]

But this 'age' is the time in which our life-in-act is both required of us and made possible for us, as a testimony which corresponds to the truth in which we have been established. Corresponding, then, to the fundamental passivity articulated in the doctrine of justification, there is a no less fundamental activity in the Christian life. 'He willed to have us at His side and in His discipleship in our own free work.'[143] And, in that work, it is 'a matter of the common action of the Lord and His servant which derives from and corresponds to their common being'.[144] Such common action is, of course, irreversibly ordered as 'a differentiated fellowship of action in which Christ is always superior and the Christian subordinate'.[145] There is, indeed, more than a hint of reserve here: Barth is very unwilling so to emphasise the reality of the human acting subject that it becomes detached from its gracious origin and its sustaining energy in the act of God. This is what underlies his choice of terms like 'witness' or 'service' as leading motifs for discussing the active life of the Christian: the modesty of the terms

---

[139] Ibid., p. 521.
[140] Ibid.
[141] IV/3.1, p. 246.
[142] Ibid., p. 435.
[143] Ibid., p. 333.
[144] IV/3.2, p. 651.
[145] Ibid., p. 598.

expresses the fact that the Christian's acts are not self-creation, but 'free action' in which the Christian 'accompanies his sovereign Lord in His action, assisting, seconding and helping Him'.[146]

Such, then, is the broad background of the ethics of reconciliation, shorn of its detailed discussions. Barth has set out an account of 'the place and meaning and inner structure of this sphere of ours, or the existence and situation of man in relation to the conditions valid and effective within it'.[147] All ethical reflection has implicit or explicit within it an anthropology and an ontology of history – a construal of the moral agent and of the field in which the moral agent acts. What is most striking about Barth's account (as well as what separates it from nearly all contemporary accounts) is its undeflected attention to one set of historical incidents as ontologically, noetically, and morally fundamental. That sequence, Barth insists, can only be seen as fundamental to our moral projects if we strenuously resist two temptations: the temptation to see God's act in Jesus Christ as self-enclosed and incommunicable, and the temptation to see it as a mere possibility awaiting our moral actualisation. Theomonism and anthropomonism, Barth will say at the beginning of his doctrine of baptism, are equally to be rejected, for both abstract from the history of the Royal Man, the progress of whose life is God with us and, therefore, grace restoring to us our human reality. Of that reality we must say neither too little (absorbing it within the reality of God's self-positing) nor too much (proposing it as a self-subsistent realm of being and activity). Rather, we are to say, with all astonishment, that to God's grace there does, indeed, correspond our own act. That is why 'the concept which forces itself upon us is that which says neither too much nor too little, the concept of analogy'.[148] The ethics of reconciliation is an exploration of the shape of existence in analogy to Jesus.

---

[146] Ibid., p. 602.
[147] IV/3.1, p. 346.
[148] IV/1, p. 769.

CHAPTER THREE

The moral field

The ethics of reconciliation in *Church Dogmatics* paragraph 74 begins with a recapitulation and refinement of some of the primary axioms of Christian ethics which Barth has developed earlier in the *Dogmatics*: that Christian ethics is specifically *theological* in character, that it is disciplined reflection on God's command issued to God's covenant partner, that good human action is essentially obedience to that command. Though much of what he has to say in the opening pages of *The Christian Life* is familiar from other treatments, it is important to be clear about what Barth is here seeking to accomplish. He is orienting the subsequent discussion by drawing a map of the moral field, delineating the space in which the human moral agent exists and acts as recipient of, and respondent to, the grace of God in Jesus Christ. By orienting what he has to say in this way, Barth betrays a set of preoccupations and a manner of approach very different from those styles of Christian ethics, for example, in which the boundaries between the respective tasks of the Christian ethicist and the moral philosopher are very fluid, and in which there is a transferability of content and method from one discipline to another. Such styles of ethical analysis usually attend only with reluctance to those aspects of Christianity which sustain a distinctively *Christian* ethos. Barth, by contrast, is writing unashamedly *positive* ethics, thereby distinguishing (some would say, isolating) himself from other modes of ethical inquiry. A description of this 'positive' character is not a description of the external casing of some essence of morality available under a number of different forms. For Christian ethics, the world is a different place, and part of a Christian theory of morality is a careful delineation of that difference.

The distinctiveness of Barth's procedure is heightened, moreover, by his refusal to allow deliberative moral consciousness to dominate his construal of ethics. Certainly Barth's ethics of reconciliation is what he calls 'special' ethics, concerned not only with the command of God (which is the theme of 'general ethics') but with human response to that command. Yet his interest in the 'subjective' side of the ethical relation between God and humanity is not focussed on the self as moral consciousness, but on the self as agent. A recent English textbook opens with the sentence: 'Moral philosophy is the attempt to understand the kind of thinking normally called moral judgment.'[1] Barth takes a radically different approach: describing the moral field is not a matter of analysing judgments made, but of portraying the encounter of God with humanity with as much density as possible.

THE CENTRAL PROBLEM OF SPECIAL ETHICS

'Ethics', Barth writes, 'is an attempt to answer theoretically the question of what may be called *good* human action'.[2] Lest Christian ethics be thought simply a determinate version of a generic discipline, however, Barth immediately adds a qualifier: 'Theological ethics such as is attempted here finds both this question and its answer in God's Word.'[3] Not, note, simply the *answer* to the question, but the question itself, is first formulated in the sphere of revelation. Accordingly, 'theological ethics can be understood only as an integral element of dogmatics'.[4] Theological ethics is pursued within the sphere of the church's obedient hearing and teaching of the Word of God, and the critical testing of its

[1] W. D. Hudson, *A Century of Moral Philosophy* (London, 1980), p. vii.
[2] *ChrL*, p. 3.
[3] Ibid.
[4] Ibid.

hearing and teaching by dogmatic science. Like all Christian reflection, theological ethics does not operate 'in the empty space above the churches',[5] or in isolation from the 'cumbersome symbolic language of theology'.[6] Christian ethics is a positive science.

More closely, the ethics of reconciliation finds its organising centre in a personal history – the history of the encounter between God and his human partners:

God's command, and what it means for man as claim, decision, and judgment, is not the timeless truth of a general principle, or a collection of such truths, but the specific content of what is always a special event between God and man in its historical reality. Where and when it goes forth and finds an answer in man's obedience or disobedience, it is a precise and filled-out direction and not, therefore, an empty form that still needs filling out and preciseness. Special ethics, then, must resist the temptation to become legalistic and casuistic ethics. Its task is to point to that event between God and man, to its uncontrollable content.[7]

Moreover, the participants in this history are not 'unwritten pages or unknown quantities'. They are describable:

Who the commanding God is and who responsible man is – God in the mystery of his commanding and man in the mystery of his obedience or disobedience – is not hidden from us but is revealed and may be known in the one Jesus Christ: God *and* man, if not in their essence, at least in their work and therefore in their manner; God *and* man, accessible to human apprehension, if not expressible in human words, at least describable and attestable.[8]

And so reference to this history can be more than indefinite: though never exhaustive, it can be a matter of 'formed and contoured reference'.[9]

Most of the rest of paragraph 74 is given over to describing the contours of the ethical history of God and humanity. But, before looking in more detail at what Barth has to

[5] K. Barth, 'Fate and idea in theology', in H.-M. Rumscheidt, ed., *The Way of Theology in Karl Barth* (Allison Park, 1988), p. 26.
[6] Ibid., p. 30.
[7] *ChrL*, pp. 4f.
[8] Ibid., p. 5.
[9] Ibid., p. 6.

say, it is important to guard against a misunderstanding. Barth is not saying that Christian ethics is one kind of ethical reflection alongside others, one of a number of self-sufficient and possibly incommensurable worlds of moral meaning, to be grasped 'intrasystematically' rather than by comparison or assimilation to a larger class. As we have already seen, if Barth is no correlationist, neither is he a relativist or a pluralist. His insistence on the history of Jesus and the covenant fulfilled in him as that which gives specificity to Christian ethics is not simply a matter of insisting on the particularities of a local province of meaning. Jesus' history, and the covenant history which takes place in him, is in its specificity unimaginably comprehensive, catholic in scope; in it, 'we have to do with the centre, core and origin of the totality as such'.[10]

In terms of ethics, this means that Christian ethics retains a claim to universal validity, even though that claim is not unavailable under any other description than that which it takes in the sphere of the Christian confession. Earlier in the *Church Dogmatics*, Barth asked:

Is God's revelation revelation of the truth, or is it only the source of certain religious ideas and obligations, alongside which there are very different ones in other spheres? Outside and alongside the kingdom of Jesus Christ are there other respectable kingdoms? Can and should theology of all things be content to speak, not with universal validity, but only esoterically?[11]

The reference there to Christ's kingdom makes the point: Barth's refusal of the general is not born of recognition of a plurality and contingency of modes of ethical engagement, but out of a sense that the energies of God find their concretion in the history of Jesus, 'the centre, the source of all the reality and revelation of God and man'.[12]

This obstinate preoccupation with the second article raises the issue to which the ethics of reconciliation returns again

---

[10] Ibid., p. 10.
[11] II/2, p. 526.
[12] *ChrL*, p. 9.

and again, the relation of our acts to the act of God in Christ, in which their ultimate origin lies. In short, the argument runs thus: Christocentricity, construed according to the Chalcedonian model of the unity in differentiation of divinity and humanity in Jesus Christ, excludes Christomonism. For:

The Word of God with which dogmatics (and consequently theological ethics) is concerned at every point as the basis, object, content, and norm of true church proclamation, is, however, Jesus Christ in the divine–human unity of his being and work. In God's Word, then, we are dealing both with God and with man: with God acting in relation to man and with man acting in relation to God; or, to put it in terms of the ethical problem, with the sure and certain goodness of the divine action and with the problematical goodness of the human action. At every point in true church proclamation it must and will be a matter of both.[13]

The next section of paragraph 74 is given over to an initial sketch of the God who commands and the responding human agent.

THE GRACIOUS GOD AS THE COMMANDING GOD

In the context of the doctrine of reconciliation, special ethics serves to demonstrate how far the command of the one God is centrally the command of the Lord of the covenant, in which the action of sinful man is determined, ordered, and limited by the free grace of the faithful God manifested and operative in Jesus Christ.[14]

Barth focusses his exposition of the thesis by examining four related issues: the character of the commanding God; the character of the human creature who is responsible to God; the situation in which God and humanity encounter each other; and the nature of the command and the appropriate response of obedience. We look at each stage of the argument in turn.

[13] Ibid., p. 3.
[14] Ibid.

First, who is the God whose command is the matter of
Christian ethical reflection? Barth's answer has to be seen
in the light of a primary conviction which undergirds the
whole *Church Dogmatics*: God is particular. The question of
the divine identity is 'an answered question in Jesus Christ,
exclusively in him, but in him clearly, solidly, exhaustively,
and definitively'.[15] In terms of the construction of theological
ethics, this means that, for Barth, God's command cannot
be understood as an abstract imperative, but only in the
context of the history of Jesus Christ, in which 'among and
with and for and to men he acts and speaks as himself
man'.[16] In sum: 'God commands as he, Jesus Christ, commands.'[17] One result here is that Barth begins his exposition
by stripping the notion of 'command' of any connotations
which might detract from the sheer graciousness and goodness of the one who commands. Thus talk of God's commanding rule is talk of 'a definitely shaped and qualified
action', for God's

> powerful action is the great and active Yes of his free and gracious
> address to the world created by him, and to man who is at the
> heart of it. God reigns unequivocally by pronouncing this Yes
> and putting it into action in the instituting, upholding, executing,
> and fulfilling of his covenant with man. This takes place with
> right and power, but also with the concrete mind and purpose of
> him who is Lord of man, but also man's Father and Brother.[18]

This means, for example, that the establishment of God's
Kingdom is for the benefit of its human subject; 'it does
not strive against him but for him'.[19] God rules precisely in
order to establish himself as humanity's *friend*, so that the
God who commands is none other than the God who 'reconciles man to himself'.[20] Or again, talk of God's judgment

[15] Ibid., p. 13.
[16] Ibid.
[17] Ibid.
[18] Ibid., p. 15.
[19] Ibid.
[20] Ibid., p. 16.

is not talk of an act of divine hostility, but of the establishment of righteousness in which humanity can flourish:

His righteousness revealed in the gospel (Rom. 1.17) is not the empty distributive justice of a world judge scrutinising, assessing, rewarding, and punishing people from a distance. Rather, it consists of his own work in the establishment of his divine right and therefore in assisting, protecting, and helping the right of mankind against all his near and distant enemies, and primarily against the nearest of them all, namely, himself.[21]

And so 'the God who rules in Jesus Christ, the gracious God, is the God who commands'.[22] To act under obligation to *this* God is thus to act in the field of grace.

Second, in turning to the character of the human person responsible to this gracious commanding God, Barth again refuses any abstract notion of humanity, for 'man is no more, and no less, no other than what he is through and with and for Jesus Christ', since 'in Christ he is constituted as man by God'.[23] What Barth emphasises, therefore, is not a given human capacity for obedience to God which precedes being in Christ, nor, by contrast, the ruin of human life and work brought about by sin. Humanity is defined neither by a natural tendency to God nor by sinful disinclination from God. Rather, to be human is already to be 'in' grace, existing within the sphere of reconciliation to God by virtue of our inclusion in the scope of the history of Jesus Christ. To exist as a responsible agent is not to exist, therefore, as one who must anxiously establish himself or herself by works of merit; rather, 'the man who is responsible to the gracious God is the man who is affirmed and loved and elected by God'.[24] At this point, Barth appeals to what we have already seen to be a major motif in earlier treatments of anthropology in the *Church Dogmatics*, that of humanity as the covenant-partner of God:

[21] Ibid., p. 17.
[22] Ibid., p. 16.
[23] Ibid., p. 19.
[24] Ibid., p. 22.

He [Jesus Christ], or God through him, makes man a partner in this covenant. Together with him, as one whom God has set at his side and exalted to be his brother, man is this partner of God. He is so in order to serve God by serving Jesus Christ. In his history God acts exemplarily and fruitfully on and to all men. So each man as such – not just the man who knows him but also the man who scarcely knows him or knows him not at all – has a part in his history and without it would have no history of his own. He could not know his own history as human (in distinction from purely natural) history apart from his share in the history of Jesus Christ.[25]

It is important to notice that the covenant theme is here introduced not in order to emphasise mutuality and reciprocity of agency between God and humanity (that use of the motif will surface later). Rather, its deployment here is to secure a fundamental direction to Christian anthropology, one in which 'all are what they are or are not in a circle around him [Jesus Christ]'.[26] Barth's concern, then, at this early stage in his map of the moral field is, once again, with covenant as *grace*.

Third, however, when he moves on to discuss the situation in which the covenant partners encounter each other, the question of mutuality immediately surfaces:

Let it be asserted ... that God and man are two subjects in genuine encounter. God and man do in fact confront one another: two partners of different kinds, acting differently, so that they cannot be exchanged or equated. God cannot be compared, confused or intermingled with man, nor man with God. They are totally unlike and remain so not only in their relationship as Creator and creature but also, with specifically sharp contours, in the relationship which now concerns us, their relationship in the covenant of grace and its basis in the action whereby God reconciled the world to himself. God is gracious to man, not man to God. And man is responsible and indebted to God, not God to man. Any reversal or obscuring of the distinction between the two is impossible ... Even in their unity in Jesus Christ himself, God does not cease to be God nor man to be man. Their distinction

---

[25] Ibid., p. 20.
[26] Ibid.

even in their unity in Jesus Christ typifies the qualitative and definitive distinction between God and every other man.[27]

Barth's point here is a good example of what George Hunsinger identifies as the 'Chalcedonian pattern', through which Barth handles the question of 'the event of double agency', human and divine.[28] In the various contexts in which they occur, Barth's appeals to the unity-in-distinction motif make a twofold claim. First, the grounding of humanity in Jesus Christ's fulfilment of the covenant disallows the absolute autonomy of human acts, since those acts have their substance in so far as they mysteriously co-inhere in God's own act in Jesus Christ (this is the 'unity' motif). Second, the unity of God and human agency is a differentiated unity (the 'distinction' motif) which disallows the complete absorption of the human agent into God. God and humanity are, therefore, not to be confused, both to safeguard the priority of grace and also to protect the reality of responsible human agency. We may not envisage the 'togetherness of God and man as any other than one of distance and distinction', for 'what would responsibility mean if the one who is responsible to God did not truly and genuinely stand *over against* him?'[29] Without the proper distinction between God and humanity, the divine command would find no corresponding responsible human action. Yet, again, that human action may not be so emphasised that God and humanity are no longer fundamentally bound to each other in the unity of the God-man, Jesus Christ. 'In the covenant of grace they are distinct partners, but precisely in their distinction they are partners who are inseparably bound to one another.'[30]

In place of either theomonism or anthropomonism, Barth tries to articulate an account of the distinction between God and humanity in which there is a specific ordering of their relationship:

[27] Ibid., pp. 27f.
[28] G. Hunsinger, *How To Read Karl Barth* (Oxford, 1991).
[29] *ChrL*, p. 28.
[30] Ibid.

The fellowship of God with man ... is fellowship in a specific and irreversible order of before and after, above and below. God unconditionally precedes and man can only follow. The free God elects and wills. The free man must elect and will what God elects and wills. God is the giver and man the recipient. Man is an active, not an inactive recipient, yet even in his activity he is still a recipient.[31]

In that order of priority, the human partner is by no means otiose, but 'an active, not an inactive, recipient'.[32] Nevertheless, our perspective on human acts is considerably shifted. Human responsibility to act is not such that we are obliged to maintain the covenant, establishing ourselves by obedient response. Yet if Barth thereby removes from human action a weight of responsibility, he does so not in order to diminish its significance, but in order as it were to set human beings free in relation to their acts. In an important passage, Barth suggests that human acts are properly born of neither hubris nor anxiety about self-maintenance. Rather, they flow from achieved status which issues in free action:

To be sure, a yoke is laid on them ... and a burden must be carried. Yet this does not make his labour and load heavier; it does not make them infinite as an obligation to serve that lofty God who looks out for his own interests. Instead, when the man who labours and is heavy laden is summoned to obedience, it creates for him ἀναπαυσις sabbath refreshment, rest.[33]

So far, Barth has sketched an understanding of the grace of the commanding God in which human action is neither a superfluous appendix to the work of God, nor a struggle to somehow establish or guarantee our standing before God. Rather, it is 'the work of his εὐχαριστια corresponding to the χαρις of God shown to him'.[34] In the context of this ordering of divine and human work, what, fourth, is God's command and what response is required?

---

[31] Ibid., p. 29.
[32] Ibid.
[33] Ibid., p. 31; cf. IV/2, p. 594.
[34] Ibid., p. 31.

As part of the answer to this question, there surfaces Barth's restructuring of the relationship between law and gospel.[35] In his controversial 1935 paper on 'Gospel and Law', and in his treatment of the topic in the ethical section of the doctrine of God, Barth has already expounded the law as 'nothing else than the necessary form of the Gospel, whose content is grace. It is just this content that enforces this form, the form which calls for a like form, the form of law.'[36] Hence:

The Law is completely enclosed in the Gospel. It is not a second thing alongside and beyond the Gospel. It is not a foreign element which precedes or only follows it. It is the claim which is addressed to us by the Gospel itself and as such, the Gospel in so far as it has the form of a claim addressed to us, the Gospel which we cannot really hear except as we obey it.[37]

Barth's confrontation with one of the fundamental principles of Lutheran soteriology and theological ethics is not intended to qualify the radically unconditional character of divine grace. It is at heart motivated by a desire to register a place for human action in response to God. The law is 'the work of God which makes room for the Gospel in our

---

[35] See the 1935 paper 'Gospel and law', in *God, Grace and Gospel* (Edinburgh, 1959), pp. 1–27, with III/2, pp. 509–630 and IV/3, pp. 370f. From the very considerable discussion which followed, see P. Althaus, *The Divine Command* (Philadelphia, 1966); and 'Durch das Gesetz kommt Erkenntnis der Sünde', in *Um die Wahrheit des Evangeliums* (Stuttgart, 1962), pp. 168–80; W. Elert, *Law and Gospel* (Philadelphia, 1967); H. Gollwitzer, 'Zur Einheit von Gesetz und Evangelium', in *Antwort. Karl Barth zum 70. Geburtstag* (Zurich, 1956), pp. 287–309; W. Joest, *Gesetz und Freiheit* (Göttingen, 1957); E. Jüngel, 'Gospel and law', in *Karl Barth. A Theological Legacy* (Philadelphia, 1986), pp. 105–26; B. Klappert, *Promissio und Bund* (Göttingen, 1976); W. Krötke, *Das Problem "Gesetz und Evangelium" bei W. Elert und P. Althaus* (Zurich, 1965); E. Schlink, 'Gesetz und Paraklese', in *Antwort*, pp. 323–35; and 'Law and gospel as a controversial theological problem', in *The Coming Christ and the Coming Church* (Edinburgh, 1967), pp. 144–85; H. Thielicke, *Theological Ethics* I (London, 1968), pp. 98–117; G. Wingren, 'Evangelium und Gesetz', in *Antwort*, pp. 310–22; and *Creation and Law* (Edinburgh, 1961). See also the collection *Gesetz und Evangelium. Beiträge zur gegenwärtigen theologischen Diskussion* (Darmstadt, 1968). There is a useful English-language survey in G. O. Forde, *The Law–Gospel Debate* (Minneapolis, 1969). See further S. H. Rae, 'Law, gospel and freedom in the theological ethics of Karl Barth', *Scottish Journal of Theology* 25 (1972), 412–22.

[36] K. Barth, 'Gospel and law', p. 10.

[37] II/2, p. 557.

human room and that makes room for us men in the Gospel'.[38] Grace, precisely because it has 'the form of law, commandment, demand, claim',[39] carries an 'impetus'; grace 'excites'.[40]

Ultimately, then, the issue is anthropological: Barth seeks to underscore a conviction that the human person under grace remain an agent. This involves him in sharp divergence from Luther's anthropology, where the primary passivity of the human recipient of grace dominates.[41] Because God in Christ is electing God and elect human partner, divine action is complemented, not by an absence of human agency, but by corresponding human action. 'What we have to establish', Barth writes, 'is that the being and essence and activity of God as the Lord of the covenant between himself and man include a relationship to the being and essence and activity of man. It is as He makes Himself responsible for man that God makes man, too, responsible. Ruling grace is commanding grace.'[42] As Jüngel comments, 'Barth's version of the relationship of law and gospel is, in the final analysis, concerned with this correspondence, this analogy between God and humanity, an *already* ontological correspondence between the existence of God as pure act and the existence of the human person who is self-defined in action.'[43]

From this vantage-point, those who find in Barth some kind of monism are rather wide of the mark. Thielicke, for example, claims that, on Barth's account, 'the event of salvation is reduced to a monologue which he holds with himself in his character as Father and Son, as representative of deity and representative of humanity'.[44] But Barth's emphasis on the law as the form of the gospel – especially when that emphasis is seen as a corollary of a Chalcedonian

---

[38] 'Gospel and law', p. 11.
[39] Ibid., p. 15.
[40] Ibid., p. 9.
[41] See here E. Jüngel, 'Gospel and law', pp. 123f.
[42] II/2, p. 511.
[43] 'Gospel and law', p. 124.
[44] H. Thielicke, *Theological Ethics* I, p. 112.

unity-in-distinction model of the relation of divine and human agency – is intended to avoid precisely the weakness with which Thielicke charges him. Or again, H. Richard Niebuhr's sophisticated critique of legal imagery in ethics does not read Barth very accurately at this point. Niebuhr suggests that Barth 'has to transform the law into a form of the gospel and the commandment into permission in order to reconcile the peculiarity of the gospel ethos with deontological thinking'.[45] But Barth's account of gospel and law is not directed by an abstract 'legal symbol',[46] but by the mutuality of God and creature as reciprocal agents, much along the lines of Niebuhr's own definition of responsibility as 'an agent's action in response to an action upon him in accordance with the interpretation of the latter action and with his expectation of response to his response; and all of this in a continuing community of agents'.[47]

Such is the background to Barth's discussion here in the ethics of reconciliation of God's command as the law of the *gospel*. Setting law within the context of election to the covenant, its role is redefined: no longer primarily accusatory, no longer a source of hostility to drive the sinner to repentance, the law incorporates into the relation of God and humanity that imperatival aspect which makes humanity under grace more than simply a beneficiary:

The commandment of God may always be recognized as such because, as the command of Jesus Christ, the one Mediator between God and man, it encounters man in the form of grace: not as the exponent of man's own fantasies, wishes, and desires, nor as the dictate of an unknown deity coming upon him as an alien or enemy, but as the direction of him, who, apart from and even in opposition to man's own acts and merits, loved him from all eternity, who understands him better than man does himself, who intends better for him than he does for himself, who with this better knowledge and intention, for his salvation, reminds him of his freedom, takes him seriously in this freedom, and

---

[45] H. R. Niebuhr, *The Responsible Self* (New York, 1963), p. 66.
[46] Ibid., p. 130.
[47] Ibid., p. 65. Barth would probably disagree with the phrase 'in accordance with his interpretation of the latter action'.

summons him to make the only possible use of it. The command of God will infallibly make itself known as the law of the gospel.[48]

The command, we might say, is a gift, to be 'clearly distinguished from man's own insights or the suggestions of other spirits and forces'.[49] Obligation is received at the hands of the gracious God; it is not created or used to consolidate the self through moral achievement. Moreover, what is given in the command is human freedom, detaching the human agent from 'fantasies, wishes, and desires', from the whole spectre of self-wrought human ruination, and setting human acts in a proper relation to God: 'God's requirements of man can be no other than the sharply contoured imperatives of the love that is freely addressed to him, that freely affirms him, and that freely wills and accomplishes his salvation.'[50]

The command is the *gracious* command; yet it remains a command. Even in the gospel of grace, there is law and there is form, 'the law of the gospel, the form of grace'.[51] The gospel, that is, is more (though never less) than indicative: it is imperative. And grace has a form, a *Gestalt*, to which there corresponds a perceptible form of human life, 'the shaping [*Gestaltung*] of our lives as Christians'.[52] As in the earlier debates on gospel and law, Barth is here canvassing an understanding of the gospel of grace as not simply the offer of achieved status, but as a summons to internalise a given role and the attendant moral dispositions – in sum, as that which evokes the project of the Christian life. And so as he goes on from here to review and reject several rubrics under which we might set this form of life, it becomes clear that he is searching for a material concept for Christian existence, one which does not merely state in a formal way the relationship of human morality to its anterior enabling by God's grace, but which specifies the *shape* of the Christian life. 'What we want', he writes, in rejecting conversion or

[48] *ChrL*, p. 35.
[49] Ibid.
[50] Ibid., p. 36.
[51] Ibid.
[52] Ibid., p. 44.

decision as possible rubrics, 'is not just a formally clear concept, but also one that is filled out materially, one that tells us *what* is the conversion that is according to God's will, *what* is the decision to which man is summoned by it'.[53] Along with repentance and decision, freedom, faith, thanksgiving, and faithfulness are all rejected, and he finally lights upon 'the invocation of God', *Anrufung Gottes*.

We are speaking of the humble and resolute, the frightened and joyful *invocation* of the gracious God in gratitude, praise, and above all petition. In the sphere of the covenant, this is the normal action corresponding to the fulfilment of the covenant in Jesus Christ. Man is empowered for this, and obligated to it, by God's grace. In it man in his whole humanity takes his proper place over against God. In it he does the central thing that precedes, accompanies and follows all else he does. In it he acts as the one who is referred wholly to God and has absolute need of him. In it he ventures the turning to God for which no worthiness qualifies him. He does it in fearless hope on the basis that God has turned to him and summoned him to this venture. We thus understand calling upon God – in all the richness of the action included in it – as the one thing in the many that the God who has reconciled the world to himself in Jesus Christ demands of man as he permits it to him. It is therefore the general key with which we may enter upon the task that is before us.[54]

Barth settles on the rubric of 'invocation' because of all the various options it best fills out the precise relationship of grace and responsive human action which is at issue in the ethics of reconciliation, as can be seen if we tease the notion apart a little. To say that the human person invokes 'the gracious God in gratitude, praise, and above all petition' is immediately to envisage humanity's relationship to God as one of subsequence, of dependence upon a gracious initiative. Invocation is, therefore, 'the normal action corresponding to the fulfilment of the covenant in Jesus Christ'; the human person is 'empowered for this . . . by God's grace'; in it 'he acts as the one who is referred wholly to God and has

[53] Ibid., p. 38.
[54] Ibid., p. 43.

absolute need of him'. Yet the gracious God so invoked is
not the inhibition of action or the removal of its necessity,
for 'God has turned to him and summoned him to this
venture', so that in invocation 'man in his whole humanity
takes his proper place over against God'. And so invocation
is both 'humble and resolute', both 'frightened [*erschrokkenen*]
and joyful' action in response to God's grace, which is a
source of both empowering and obligation.

In sum: the moral field is 'the circle of the covenant of
grace',[55] the location and the event of the encounter between
God and humanity, an encounter whose focal point is petitionary prayer. In tying together prayer and ethics, Barth
explores a moral ontology and a moral anthropology in
which dependence is not diminishment and resolute action
is not self-assertion. His insistent style may lead us to miss
the delicacy of his thought here. Both the 'unity-in-
distinction' motif and the careful delineation of the relation
of law and gospel, as well as the rubric of invocation of
God, are easily misunderstood if, with a slight tilt of the
balance, one or other affirmation – the priority of God or
the reality of the human agent – is allowed to gain the
upper hand. Reading Barth, here as elsewhere, demands
stringent attention to the range and subtlety of his dialectic.

The next two chapters will explore in greater detail how
Barth fills out the sketch of the relation of God and
humanity, as well as the kinds of critiques which it has
evoked. In a perceptive essay on Barth's anthropology, F.
W. Graf argues that the whole of the *Church Dogmatics* is
'pure *theo-logy* in the strongest and narrowest sense of the
word';[56] even Barth's Christological concentration is, in the
end, a concentration on the self-positing of God, so that
'the Christological construction of particular *loci* serves as
part of the presentation of the absolute subjectivity of God'.[57]

---

[55] Ibid., p. 32
[56] F. W. Graf, 'Die Freiheit der Entsprechung Gottes. Bemerkungen zum theozentrischen Ansatz der Anthropologie Karl Barths', in T. Rendtorff, ed., *Die
Realisierung der Freiheit* (Gütersloh, 1975), p. 76.
[57] Ibid., p. 78.

Accordingly, for Barth human actions are only material for the dogmatic corpus because God's path to perfection includes God's assumption of humanity: it is *'for the sake of God* that the doctrine of creation is anthropology'.[58] Graf very acutely perceives the set of issues with which Barth is preoccupied in these last writings, and presses home the question as to whether, even here, Barth's ethics is undergirded by a conception of a self-affirming and ultimately self-sufficient divine being of whom alone agency may properly be predicated. 'We know only of acts, supremely and finally of religious acts, but not of the act of all acts, the purest act', Barth told his audience in his first dogmatics lectures in Göttingen in 1924–5.[59] Or later in Münster:

The action required of us is obviously not only action in the reverence that is proper to the creature who has no reality without God, but action in the humility of the creature whose reality has fallen through its guilt and which has received again the time that it has, not now as an attribute of its creaturely reality, but as a pure gift of grace, a gift to which it has no right in the framework of creaturely claims. Relevant here is the biblical description of man as a servant of God in the sharp sense of a slave, of one who no longer owns himself but is owned by another. Human action is now good when it takes place within this bondage.[60]

But with the ethics of reconciliation we have come far from Barth's early negations of 'contingent, secondary, non-causative causes'[61] – cultural, political, economic or personal – and from the almost exclusive identification of action with divine action. As Barth expounds for the last time the doctrine of Christian baptism and then the opening petitions of the Lord's Prayer, we can see how those great negations made it possible for him to give renewed attention to the reality of human deeds.

---

[58] Ibid., p. 81.
[59] K. Barth, *The Göttingen Dogmatics. Instruction in the Christian Religion* 1 (Grand Rapids, 1991), p. 403.
[60] K. Barth, *Ethics* (Edinburgh, 1981), pp. 404f.
[61] K. Barth, 'The problem of ethics today', p. 138.

CHAPTER FOUR

Baptism with the Holy Spirit

[T]he sacraments are nothing whatever but response, the response not only of the candidate for baptism but also of the congregation. What takes place in baptism, communion and proclamation is all response. There are these remarkable relics . . . of the idea that by our own actions – whether in proclamation or in the sacraments – we could, as it were, set the divine allocation in motion. That is something we are totally unable to do. All we can do is witness how God speaks. Witness, however, is response. The whole life of the church from top to bottom is nothing but response to the Word of God. The Church lives under the promise and the hope that in this response, this echo of God's Word (whether in the form of preaching, the sacraments, or religious instruction), God's Word itself will become audible.[1]

I regard baptism, in brief, as an act, a confession, a prayer of faith, or of the obedience of faith – not as a 'means' of grace and salvation, not as a 'sacrament'.[2]

Church Dogmatics IV/4 offers a Christological and ethical, rather than a salvific or sacramental, interpretation of Christian baptism. Its concern is with how Jesus Christ's saving work, present and effective in baptism with the Holy Spirit, finds a human ethical echo in the Christian life, of which baptism with water is the first great act of obedience. Implicit within Barth's final account of the topic are two

---

[1] K. Barth, 'An outing to the Bruderholz', in *Fragments Grave and Gay* (London, 1971), p. 88.
[2] Letter to H. Bizer 29 March 1963, in K. Barth, *Letters 1961–8* (Edinburgh, 1981), p. 96.

fundamental criteria for a correct theology of baptism. First, no account of baptism is adequate if it allows creaturely action (whether of the candidate or the community) to trespass upon the unique, finished work of Jesus Christ the reconciler, or upon the self-communication of that work through the Holy Spirit. Second, no account of baptism is adequate if it allows the human act of water-baptism to be absorbed, overwhelmed or excluded by the divine act of baptism with the Holy Spirit. At first sight these two criteria appear to pull in contrary directions – the first laying emphasis upon the action of God in Jesus Christ as proper to him alone and therefore incommunicable, the second laying emphasis on an equally non-transferable human action. As the exposition proceeds, however, it becomes clear that for Barth these two criteria reflect two fundamental themes in the *Dogmatics*: first, that to the action of God there corresponds a genuinely human action; second, that the divine and the human action are neither to be confused nor separated. In terms of Christian baptism, Barth proposes, baptism with the Holy Spirit is the exclusive divine act in which the Christological character of baptism is displayed; baptism with water is the human act which manifests the beginning of the Christian ethical life. Baptism is, therefore, to be understood against the background of an understanding of an ordered correspondence between a prevenient, causative divine act of saving grace, and a subsequent human act of confession, thanksgiving, and obedience.

These criteria for an adequate theology of baptism are deeply instructive for an understanding of the *Dogmatics* as a whole.[3] In one sense, paragraph 75 of the *Dogmatics* is a test case for our reading of the entire argument.[4] If the key to understanding IV/4 is the question of whether there is a

---

[3] On this point, see E. Jüngel, 'Thesen zu Karl Barths Lehre von der Taufe', in *Barth-Studien* (Gütersloh, 1982), p. 294, thesis 1.1, and the excellent essay by D. Schellong, 'Der Ort der Tauflehre in der Theologie Karl Barths', in D. Schellong, ed., *Warum Christen ihre Kinder nicht mehr taufen lassen* (Frankfurt/M, 1969), pp. 108–42.

[4] See E. Jüngel, 'Karl Barths Lehre von der Taufe', pp. 286f.

'second, other subject alongside or outside God',[5] then our judgment about its coherence with the overall design of the *Dogmatics* will depend upon how we construe Barth's answer to that question in the rest of the work. Earlier chapters have sketched one reading of that answer; the present and following chapters offer an interpretation of paragraph 75 with an eye to the larger purpose of the *Church Dogmatics* as 'the-anthropology', as an extended description of the history of the covenant between God Creator, Redeemer, and Reconciler, and the human creature and partner.

BARTH ON SACRAMENTS

'Relative mediation'

Barth's various writings on sacramental theology from the early 1920s to the end of his career frequently return to a central theme of the Augustinian sacramental tradition: how does God's action relate to human, ecclesial action? Plotting the shifts in his thinking on this issue will help set the context for his late doctrine of baptism.

Church Dogmatics IV/4 contains Barth's well-known denials of the sacramental status of baptism with water and of the propriety of infant candidature. The position which Barth finally put into print in IV/4 (transcripts of the lectures had had fairly wide prior circulation)[6] represents a shift from his earlier (somewhat uneasy) espousal of the classical Reformed understanding of sacraments in general and of baptism in particular, according to which the sacraments, like preaching, constitute 'definite signs' of the objectivity of revelation.[7] These signs are 'a divine act', such that a sacrament is to be construed as 'the moving of an instrument in the hand of God'.[8] Or, as Barth puts it elsewhere, a sacrament is 'an

---

[5] T. Rendtorff, 'Der ethische Sinn der Dogmatik. Zur Reformulierung des Verhältnisses von Dogmatik und Ethik bei Karl Barth', in T. Rendtorff, ed., *Die Realisierung der Freiheit* (Gütersloh, 1975), p. 125.

[6] See IV/4, p. ix.

[7] I/2, p. 223.

[8] Ibid., p. 227.

action in which God acts and man serves, his service taking
the form of the execution of a divine precept. In accordance
with this precept and by means of the definite concrete
media witness is borne to God's grace and through this
men's faith is awakened, purified and advanced.'[9] What
Barth at this earlier stage calls 'the gift of baptism'[10] is a
sign 'put at the beginning of the Christian life as an objective
testimony pronounced upon us'.[11] In his earlier work, then,
Barth shows no unqualified hostility to the principle of
sacramental mediation or representation (provided it is properly construed via the uniqueness and primacy of divine
action), and he lays emphasis on the *passivity* of the recipient
of baptism. 'We did not (fortunately) experience our baptism', he remarked in the Göttingen dogmatics cycle, 'yet
we *are* baptized'.[12]

However, the question of mediation needs further probing,
for what Barth has to say on this issue contains the seeds
of his later rejection of the classical Reformed theory of
sacraments. In the earlier sections of the *Dogmatics*, Barth
makes a twofold affirmation about creaturely mediation.
First, revelation is represented to us in creaturely or 'sacramental' form:

God gives Himself to be known ... in an objectivity different
from His own, in a creaturely objectivity. He unveils Himself as
the One He is by veiling Himself in a form in which He Himself
is not. He uses this form distinct from Himself, He uses its work
and sign, in order to be objective in, with and under this form,
and therefore to give Himself to us to be known. Revelation means
the giving of signs. We can say quite simply that revelation means
sacrament, i.e., the self-witness of God, the representation of His
truth, and therefore of the truth in which He knows Himself, in
the form of creaturely objectivity and therefore in a form which
is adopted to our creaturely knowledge.[13]

---

[9] K. Barth, *The Knowledge of God and the Service of God* (London, 1938), p. 192.
[10] K. Barth, *Ethics* (Edinburgh, 1981), p. 105.
[11] I/2, p. 232.
[12] K. Barth, *The Göttingen Dogmatics I*, p. 68.
[13] II/1, p. 52.

Second, however, the 'basic form' of this creaturely or sacramental objectivity of revelation is the humanity of Jesus:

> The basic reality and substance of the creatureliness which He
> has commissioned and empowered to speak of Him, the basic
> reality and substance of the sacramental reality of His revelation,
> is the existence of the human nature of Jesus Christ. *Gratia unionis*,
> i.e., on the ground of and through its union with the eternal
> Word of God, this creature is the supreme and outstanding work
> and sign of God ... The humanity of Jesus as such is the first
> sacrament, the foundation of everything that God instituted and
> used in His revelation as a secondary objectivity both before and
> after the epiphany of Jesus Christ. And, as this first sacrament,
> the humanity of Jesus Christ is at the same time the basic reality
> and substance of the highest possibility of the creature as such.
> Not of itself and by itself, but of and by God's appointment and
> grace, the creature can be the temple, instrument and sign of
> God Himself. The man Jesus is the first to rise out of the series
> of creatures which are not this. But the fact that He does so is
> a promise for the rest of God's creation. He and no other creature
> is taken up into unity with God. Here we have something which
> cannot be repeated. But the existence of this creature in his unity
> with God does mean the promise that other creatures may attest
> in their objectivity to what is real only in this creature, that is
> to say, God's own objectivity – so that to that extent they are
> the temple, instrument and sign of God as He is.[14]

This second, Christological, affirmation is at one and the
same time a grounding and a relativising of sacramental
mediation by reference to the humanity of Jesus. His human
nature is both a promise, a gift of possibility to other
creatures, and also a prohibition, a limit to creaturely 'repetition' of what he uniquely is as the 'first sacrament'. In
later work, the prohibition will press upon Barth very
strongly: he will no longer affirm that 'the existence of the
man Jesus is a beginning of which there are continuations',[15]
and this rejection of 'sacramental continuity'[16] will lead in

[14] Ibid., pp. 53f.
[15] Ibid., p. 54.
[16] Ibid.

IV/4 to the final dismantling of his 'modified Augustinian Catholic position' found here in II/1.[17]

At this earlier stage, however, Barth is generally content to lay the two affirmations alongside each other. On the one side, he insists repeatedly that a theology of sacraments must be firmly grounded in a theology of grace.[18] Thus there can be no *necessary* connection between the sign and the thing signified: it is 'not of and by itself, but of and by God's appointment and grace' that creaturely reality signifies God.[19] This is above all because the knowledge of God which the sacrament mediates still stands under the fundamental rule: 'God is known through God and through God alone.'[20] Consequently, Barth underlines the freedom and unavailability of God even in God's creaturely objectivity: 'His unveiling in His works and signs always means for us His veiling too . . . His revelation always means His hiddenness.'[21] Similar critical reserve surfaces at many points in Barth's earlier work. It can be seen in his objection that Luther's doctrine of the eucharist threatens the glory of God 'in the acceptance of a definite given object of contingent revelation'.[22] Again, an early essay on 'Church and theology' notes that even in talking of the sacraments as *res coelestis et terrestris* and of *manducatio oralis et spiritualis*,[23] the *et* must not be taken to refer to a comprehensive combination of the two elements: there remains 'the infinite qualitative distinction' which is overcome only 'in the act of the divine

---

[17] C. C. West, 'Baptism in the reformed tradition', in R. T. Bender and A. P. F Sell, eds., *Baptism, Peace and the State in the Reformed and Mennonite Traditions* (Waterloo, 1991), p. 23.

[18] On this point in the earlier work of Barth, see U. Kühn, *Sakramente* (Gütersloh, 1985), pp. 174–82; Kühn rightly lays emphasis on Barth's incipient Christological critique of the notion of sacrament in the early sections of the *CD*.

[19] II/1, p. 54.

[20] Ibid., p. 44.

[21] Ibid., p. 50; cf. p. 315.

[22] K. Barth, 'Luther's doctrine of the eucharist. Its basis and purpose', in *Theology and Church. Shorter Writings 1920–1928* (London, 1962), p. 108.

[23] K. Barth, 'Church and theology', in *Theology and Church*, p. 300.

Word and Spirit'.[24] Similarly, in the homiletics seminar of 1932–3, Barth notes that 'the relation between the Word of God and the human word' cannot be named in a single, synthetic statement: any such synthesis would be 'an attack on the honour of God'.[25] All these remarks signal that, even in his alliance with Reformed sacramental theology, Barth takes some considerable pains to root the sacramental character of the church's acts in Christology, in a way which will eventually subvert the very affirmation he is making.[26]

On the other hand, Barth argues that, despite such critical reserves, there *is* a continuity between Jesus' humanity and creaturely mediation of God's revelation: even the new Christian economy of revelation in Christ 'does not amount to the removal or abolition of sign-giving as such'.[27] And so in a 1928 lecture on 'Roman Catholicism: a question to the Protestant church', Barth argues that the Reformers' insistence on 'the absolute unrepeatability of [Christ's] work' does not entail the 'obliteration of the idea of mediation, of the concept of the church service, of the insight that the Church is the House of God'.[28] Rather, the thrust of the Reformation protest is to emphasise 'that the reality of the mediation must again be understood as *act*, as the act of God himself, instead of as an institution under the control of men'.[29] There remains, therefore, 'the possibility and necessity of a *relative* mediation, of a *relative* service of God, which though relative must be taken seriously'.[30] In terms of Christian baptism, the consequence is clear: baptism is 'a sign of this true and supreme power of God's Word. As a real act on man, as an act of sovereign disposition, it proclaims for its part that man belongs to the sphere of

---

[24] Ibid., p. 301.

[25] K. Barth, *Homiletics* (Louisville, 1991), p. 45.

[26] On this, see the very helpful account of Barth's earlier ecclesiology in W. Greive, *Die Kirche als Ort der Wahrheit. Das Verständnis der Kirche in der Theologie Karl Barths* (Göttingen, 1991), pp. 302–23.

[27] I/2, p. 226.

[28] K. Barth, 'Roman Catholicism: a question to the Protestant church', in *Theology and Church*, p. 318.

[29] Ibid.

[30] Ibid., p. 319.

Christ's lordship prior to all his experiences and decisions. Even before he can take up an attitude to God, God has taken up an attitude to him.'[31]

The Teaching of the Church Regarding Baptism

Something of a shift has occurred by the 1943 lecture on *The Teaching of the Church Regarding Baptism*. Barth continues to be at home with the language of sacrament as representation (*Abbild, Darstellung*), claiming that 'there is no teaching about Christian baptism which would directly contest the view that water baptism itself is also, and indeed primarily, to be understood as a symbol, that is as a type [*Entsprechung*] and a representation [*Darstellung*] . . . of that other divine–human reality which it attests'.[32] Certainly, like all Christian symbolic activity, baptism is 'plainly a human act'.[33] Its capacity to mediate a divine reality is therefore wholly derivative:

If in fact [baptism] has the potency of a living and expressive representation, able to represent and denote man, then it owes this to the fact that it is, together with all the other parts of the Church's proclamation, in itself and in its complete humanity, still indirectly and mediately a free word and act of Jesus Christ Himself. It is this which gives life to all parts of the Church's proclamation and to baptism along with the others. The Church stands under the government of her Lord, an instrument at her disposal.[34]

Or, more tersely: 'The potency of baptism depends upon Christ who is the chief actor in it.'[35] Yet baptism, precisely because of its divine acting subject, is indeed *potent*. In the fifth section of the lecture, where Barth turns to consider the efficacy of baptism, there are some remarkably strong statements concerning the 'absolute efficacy' of baptism.[36]

[31] I/I, p. 154.
[32] K. Barth, *The Teaching of the Church Regarding Baptism* (London, 1948), pp. 13f.
[33] Ibid., p. 16.
[34] Ibid., pp. 16f.
[35] Ibid., p. 19.
[36] Ibid., p. 59.

Baptism 'operates irresistibly';[37] and 'because of its nature, its power and its meaning' baptism 'laughs at any *obex*'.[38] Nor can the abuse of baptism undermine its efficacy:

> What baptism effects, can manifestly, in the nature of the case, not be dependent – so far as it takes and concerns the candidate – either on the quantity of piety or impiety with which he receives the sacrament, or on the Christian perfection or imperfection with which he afterwards, as receiver of the sacrament, sets to work and proves himself.[39]

Such assertions sit rather uneasily alongside a new theme in Barth's sacramental theology which finds expression in the lecture. Barth is keen to stress that in baptism the candidate is 'not only dealt with', but 'finds himself taking an active part',[40] so that one of the founding principles for the proper ordering of baptism is 'the responsible willingness of the baptized person to receive the promise of the grace directed towards him and to be party to the pledge of allegiance concerning the grateful service demanded of him'.[41] Hence baptism must 'avoid the character of an act of violence'.[42] 'Neither by exegesis nor from the nature of the case can it be established that the baptized person can be a merely passive instrument [*Behandelter*]. Rather, it may be shown ... that in this action the baptized is an active partner [*Behandelnder*].'[43] In 1943, then, Barth is already moving in a rudimentary way towards the twofold analysis of baptism in terms of divine grace and human response. He already considers that baptism involves 'a summons to the believing man, engaging him to respond to this reality in his own being and to become obedient to the Holy Spirit according to the gift that is his'.[44] Hence in a crucial passage, Barth argues:

[37] Ibid., p. 58.
[38] Ibid., p. 59.
[39] Ibid., p. 57.
[40] Ibid., p. 14.
[41] Ibid., p. 40.
[42] Ibid., p. 47.
[43] Ibid., p. 41.
[44] Ibid., p. 28.

The word and work of Jesus Christ is not only powerful in itself; it is that which attracts our apperception by its powerful representation of itself. Whilst it alone is the generative cause of salvation, it desires to be seen, heard, perceived, savoured, understood, considered, and obeyed, by the man who is saved and believes in his salvation.[45]

This apperception is, moreover, a matter of *obedience*; that is, an *ethical*, and not simply a cognitive, response is also required:

With divine authority there is pronounced over the candidate . . . his pledge of allegiance regarding the grateful service demanded of him. It is said to him that, by virtue of the death and resurrection of Jesus Christ, which happened on his account, he is no longer his own; that he is under obligation to his Deliverer; that as one who has been certainly and completely freed, he has equally certainly and completely been bound; that he has been set on a path from which henceforth he cannot any more deviate, weak, erring, foolish, wicked though he still is and will be. He has received a Lord.[46]

And so if Barth distances himself from infant baptism in the 1943 lecture, it is not only because he fears a notion of baptismal efficacy *ex opere operato*,[47] but also because he is already tying together generative divine action and the notion of moral obligation.

The doctrine of reconciliation

Over the course of writing the doctrine of reconciliation, Barth became increasingly unsettled about classical Reformed sacramental theology in general, and baptismal theology in particular. By the time he began lecturing on the ethics of reconciliation in the winter semester 1959–60, Barth was very clear: the so-called 'sacraments'

are not events, institutions, mediations, or revelations of salvation. They are not representations and actualizations, emanations,

[45] Ibid.
[46] Ibid., p. 33.
[47] Ibid., p. 40.

repetitions, or extensions, nor indeed guarantees and seals of the work and word of God; nor are they instruments, vehicles, channels, or means of God's reconciling grace. They are not what they have been called since the second century, namely, mysteries or sacraments.[48]

Rather, they are

actions of human obedience for which Jesus Christ makes his people free and responsible. They refer themselves to God's own work and word, and they correspond to his grace and commands. In so doing they have the promise of the divine good pleasure and they are well done as holy, meaningful, fruitful, human actions, radiant in the shining of the one true light in which they may take place and which they have to indicate in their own place and manner as free and responsible human action.[49]

What pushed Barth in this direction? There are three focal issues in Barth's discussions of sacramental theology in the doctrine of reconciliation: the nature of sacramental mediation; the place of religion; and the reality of human action in response to divine grace.

First, sacramental mediation. Barth became convinced over the course of the 1950s that liberal Protestant theology, represented by Bultmann and having its roots in Schleiermacher and in the younger Luther, and also classical Roman Catholic and even Reformed sacramental theology, had seriously mishandled the question of how the objectivity of Jesus Christ and his salvation becomes subjectively real to the Christian believer.[50] These schools of thought and practice, Barth came to believe, envisaged the transition from the *extra nos* to the *in nobis* to be accomplished by the mediation of creaturely agencies. In the case of classical Roman Catholic thought, for example, the mediation is located in the sacramental being and activities of the

---

[48] *ChrL*, p. 46.
[49] Ibid.
[50] Barth's linking of the liberal Protestant tradition and Roman Catholic thought over the issue of pneumatology can be found much earlier, however: see the 1929 lecture on *The Holy Ghost and the Christian Life* (London, 1938), pp. 11–8, 28–39.

church.[51] In the case of theological liberalism or existentialism, mediation occurs through moral or experiential 'realisation' in which the reality of Jesus *in nobis* is understood
through the dynamics of faith or Christian existence. Both,
Barth believed, accorded the wrong kind of significance to
creaturely action, by envisaging it as *repraesentatio* in which
'the history of Jesus Christ' becomes 'coincidental with that
of the believer': 'What is Bultmann's conception but an
existentialist translation of the sacramentalist teaching of
the Roman Church, according to which, at the climax of
the mass, with the transubstantiation of the elements – in
metaphysical identity with what took place there and then –
there is a "bloodless repetition" of the sacrifice of Christ
on Golgotha?'[52]

As Barth pursued this train of thought, he began to leave
behind some of his own earlier affiliation with Reformed
sacramental doctrine. Where he had at one time spoken of
a continuity between Jesus Christ as the 'first sacrament'
and creaturely signs (with the important safeguard that the
hiddenness of God is such that there can be no *necessary*
connection between the *signum* and the *res significata*), Barth
now moves to a significantly different affirmation: Jesus
Christ is not the first but the only sacrament. As the doctrine
of reconciliation unfolds, it becomes clear that what other
theologies seek to achieve through ecclesiology or through
analysis of faith as a form of human existence – that is, an
account of the subjective realisation of God's saving work –
Barth seeks to achieve through the doctrines of Christ and
the Holy Spirit.

In terms of Christology, this means that the perfection of
Jesus Christ's work is such that it stands in need of no
human or created mediation. Christ's work is characterised

---

[51] For an analysis of this issue which relies heavily on Barth, see E. Jüngel, 'The
church as sacrament?', in *Theological Essays* (Edinburgh, 1989), pp. 189–213.
See further C. Schwöbel, 'The creature of the Word: recovering the ecclesiology
of the reformers', in C. Gunton and D. Hardy, eds., *On Being the Church. Essays
on the Christian Community* (Edinburgh, 1989), pp. 110–55, especially on the
proper distinction between *opus dei* and *opus hominum*.
[52] IV/1, p. 767.

by what might be called 'inclusive perfection': its complete-
ness is not only its 'being finished', but its effective power
in renewing human life by bringing about human response
to itself. Consequently, the relation of 'objective' and 'subjective' shifts. The objective is not a complete realm, separate
from the subjective and, therefore, standing in need of 'translation' into the subjective. Rather, the objective includes the
subjective within itself, and is efficacious without reliance
on a quasi-independent realm of mediating created agencies.
The notion of 'sacramental continuity' between the human
Jesus and created signs is replaced, therefore, by that of
attestation. As he puts it in IV/I:

> The confession of Christians, their suffering, their repentance,
> their prayer, their humility, their works, baptism, too, and the
> Lord's Supper can and should attest this event but only attest it.
> The event itself, the event of the death of man, is that of the
> death of Jesus Christ on Golgotha: no other event, no earlier and
> no later, no event which simply prepares the way for it, no event
> which has to give to it the character of an actual event. This is
> the one *mysterium*, the one sacrament, and the one existential fact
> before and beside and after which there is no room, for any other
> of the same rank.[53]

Jesus Christ is the one sacrament of the church, therefore,
in the sense that the perfection of his work *includes* its
effectiveness in human history, rendering superfluous any
human mediations, experiential or ecclesial or sacramental.
As Jüngel puts the point in an early essay, 'The being of
Jesus Christ, which *ex opere operato* effects salvation, is as
such the one *sacramentum fidei*.'[54] The ultimate root for this
is the resurrection of Jesus. As the risen one, Jesus Christ
lives as *Word*, lives in an ongoing activity of self-
communication, a self-communication whose dynamism
requires no intermediate agencies for its actualisation.

---

[53] IV/I, p. 296.
[54] E. Jüngel, 'Das Sakrament – was ist das?', in E. Jüngel and K. Rahner, *Was
ist ein Sakrament?* (Freiburg, 1971), p. 37. Cf. 'Thesen zu Karl Barths Lehre von
der Taufe', p. 292, thesis 2.12.

'Barth's basic thesis, which supports everything else, is that Jesus Christ is equally the one saving work of God and the one saving word of God.'[55] In this sense, Jesus' 'history takes place in every age'.[56] The effect of this on the theology of baptism is clear: 'The understanding of the being of Jesus Christ as a history which has accomplished and revealed the reconciliation of all people and the world to God, which grounds Barth's doctrine of reconciliation, destroys the traditional theological concept of baptism as a sacrament.'[57]

Barth appeals to the doctrine of the Holy Spirit to make much the same point about the *effectiveness* of Jesus Christ's perfect work:

The real presentation [*repraesentatio*] of the history of Jesus Christ is that which He Himself accomplishes in the work of His Holy Spirit when He makes Himself the object and origin of faith. Christian faith takes note of this, and clings to it and responds to it, without itself being the thing which accomplishes it, without any identity between the redemptive act of God and faith as the free act of man. Jesus Christ and His death and resurrection do not cease to be its object and origin.[58]

As with his theology of resurrection, so with his theology of the Holy Spirit: Barth seeks to secure a theology of Christian existence and ecclesial action against forgetfulness of the primacy of divine agency. His appeal to language about the Holy Spirit is in effect a denial of the communicability of the perfect work of Jesus Christ by agents other than Jesus himself, who is the agent of his own realisation and attestation in the human world: 'God sets among men a fact which speaks for itself.'[59]

---

[55] W. Kreck, 'Karl Barths Tauflehre', in F. Viering, ed., *Zu Karl Barths Lehre von der Taufe* (Gütersloh, 1971), p. 18.

[56] IV/2, p. 107.

[57] Jüngel, 'Thesen zu Karl Barths Lehre von der Taufe', p. 291, thesis 2.1. See also 'Zur Kritik des sakramentalen Verständnisses der Taufe', in *Barth-Studien*, pp. 313f.

[58] IV/1, p. 767.

[59] IV/3, p. 221.

Second, Barth's critique of sacramental mediation is a late flowering of his critique of religion.[60] Barth's earlier critique of religion (so much more nuanced than it is usually read to be) is best understood as a corollary of his primary commitment to the non-relative character of divine revelation. It is undergirded by a proposal deep within the *Dogmatics* that both the self-giving of God *and* its reception by human persons are grounded only in God: 'Not only the objective but also the subjective element in revelation, not only its actuality but also its potentiality, is the being and action of the self-revealing God alone.'[61] Barth's critique of the notion of sacrament and the associated ecclesial practice is an expression of the same principle. Sacramental acts, like religion, can become a means of setting aside God's immediate activity in self-communication by tying our encounter with God to the existence and operation of some natural factor. Barth, therefore, reads both sacraments and religion as almost inevitably trespassing upon divine sovereignty in the area of the application of the benefits of Christ's saving work.

Furthermore, Barth is very hostile to any idea that the Christian community and the civil community are co-extensive by virtue of a civil religion in which the baptism of infants plays a basic initiatory role. He protests that 'the absurd result' of this initiatory theology and practice is that 'in this way (via infant baptism) whole populations of whole countries have automatically been made and can automatically be made the holy community'.[62] The word 'automatically' is important there. For not only is such civil religion a form of social ideology;[63] it is also increasingly seen by

---

[60] Cf. here R. Weth, 'Taufe in den Tod Jesu Christi als Anfang eines neuen Lebens', in H. Deuser et al., ed., *Gottes Zukunft – Zukunft der Welt* (Munich, 1986), p. 149.

[61] I/2, p. 280.

[62] IV/1, p. 696.

[63] Cf. H. Mottu, 'Les sacrements selon Karl Barth et Eberhard Jüngel', *Foi et Vie* 88 (1989), 33–55. See also M. Murrmann-Kahl, 'Ein Prophet des wahren Sozialismus? Zur Rezeption Karl Barths in der ehemaligen DDR', *Zeitschrift für die neuere Theologiegeschichte* 1 (1994), 141f.

Barth as suppressing the sense of personal responsibility which emerged in the 1943 baptism lecture and plays a prominent role in the argument of the doctrine of reconciliation.

This leads, third, to Barth's insistence that Christian baptism cannot be understood in isolation from its ethical significance as the first act of Christian obedience. It is important that Barth's rejection of the concept of sacramental representation should not be read as a diminution of the reality of human agency. Villette argues, for example, that Barth's sacramental theology rests on a principled opposition of nature and grace, which leads to an assertion of 'the impossibility of positive human action vis-à-vis God'.[64] But quite the opposite is the case: Barth rejects human instrumentality precisely to safeguard the genuineness of human action as just that – *human* action. Once again, the way in which he develops his theology of baptism in IV/4 is profoundly shaped by his desire to remain true to the fundamental theme of the *Dogmatics*: the covenant relation between God and humanity. The overarching theme of the ethics of reconciliation is 'God and man' as 'two subjects in genuine encounter'.[65] Portraying that encounter demands that the distinction-in-relation of God and humanity be attended to with great care, for '[t]he crux of a correct answer to the meaning of baptism lies in a strict correlation and a no less strict distinction between the human action as such and the divine action from which it springs, on whose basis it is possible, and towards which it moves'.[66] This distinction and correlation informs the whole structure of IV/4, with its bipartite treatment of baptism with the Holy Spirit as the exclusive divine act, to which there corresponds baptism with water as the first human act of faithfulness to the covenant. And so '[t]he "praise of baptism" cannot be exhausted by a reference to the divine basis and the divine

---

[64] L. Villette, *Foi et Sacrement 2: De Saint Thomas à Karl Barth* (Paris, 1964), p. 302.
[65] *ChrL*, p. 27.
[66] IV/4, p. 134.

goal of this human action. Baptism has to be seen and understood and praised also in the true and distinctive thing which characterises it as a human action.'[67]

In effect, then, Barth's doctrine of baptism in *Church Dogmatics* IV/4 replaces his earlier modest theory of sacramental mediation with an understanding of baptism as consisting of a generative divine act and a responsive human action. On the earlier account, the inferior human action was a representation of and instrument for the communication of the superior operation of God. Now Barth separates these two operations into distinct spheres of agency, and the prevenient grace of God is not so much effective through creaturely mediation as evocative of a properly human ethical analogy to itself. Barth's rejection of the sacramental character of baptism with water is also made, therefore, for *ethical* reasons: the clear distinction between divine and human agency is not an invalidation of human action, but its liberation to be truly human, responsive to, and not absorbed within or instrumental to, an overruling act of God. The rest of the present chapter gives particular attention to the work of the Holy Spirit as the immediate, generative act of God; but it will be important to bear in mind that Barth's protest is not only against the psychologism or moralism of modern pneumatology, but also against 'the conjuring away' of human response.[68]

BAPTISM WITH THE HOLY SPIRIT

What Barth has to say about the Holy Spirit usually has to be approached through what he has to say about other topics, such as revelation, reconciliation, or the Christian life. Whatever path be taken, many of the same affirmations are made along the way: the rootedness of what is said about the Spirit's person and work in what is said about Jesus Christ; the affirmation, in particular, that the Spirit

---

[67] Ibid., p. 101.
[68] Ibid., p. 106.

is the awakening power of the risen Jesus in the lives of specific persons; a corollary denial of any independent creaturely capacity for God; a firm linking of Spirit to ecclesiology, ethics, and eschatology. The treatment of baptism with the Holy Spirit in *Church Dogmatics* IV/4 shares this indirectness, for it is said as part of the ethics of reconciliation. The ethics of reconciliation seeks to describe what takes place when God the Reconciler issues his command, thereby summoning the human covenant-partner to responsible action. What Barth has to say about baptism with the Holy Spirit in paragraph 75.1 concerns the fundamental ground from which the divine command derives its force and validity in human life, concerns, that is, how 'man himself becomes the subject' of the event of the Christian life as response to God's command.[69] It therefore concerns the Holy Spirit as that personal divine act through which the transition from objective to subjective is accomplished, and through which human life is (to use a phrase from IV/2) 'given direction', that is, shown to be what it is (indication), separated from what it is not (correction), and summoned to particular acts of obedience (instruction).[70] The second part of paragraph 75 and the subsequent fragments of paragraphs 76–8 focus on the aspect of instruction; paragraph 75.1 focusses on indication, on the Holy Spirit as the effective accomplishment of our transition into the new reality constituted by the risen Jesus himself.

Barth announces early on in paragraph 75 the twofold theme of what will follow: 'The mystery and miracle of the event of which we speak consists in the fact that man himself is the free subject of this event on the basis of a possibility which is present only with God.'[71] The theme is that of the free subjectivity of the human covenant partner, a free subjectivity whose condition of possibility is God himself. Paragraph 75.1 inquires into the second half of the theme – the divine possibility. Nevertheless, what is said about this

[69] Ibid., p. 4.
[70] See IV/2, pp. 362–77
[71] IV/4, p. 5.

theme must not obscure Barth's equally firm insistence upon the reality of human agency, in his discussion of baptism with water in paragraph 75.2. Grasping this point will lead to a very different reading of Barth from that which has become established in much of the secondary literature on his pneumatology. In a work which has become a benchmark for much criticism of Barth's doctrine of the Spirit, P. J. Rosato argues that Barth's pneumatology fails in two basic areas. First, by tying Spirit and Son so closely together, Barth is pushed to think of the trinity as 'a closed triangle in a timeless realm',[72] in which God 'is not conceived as open to a reality outside himself'.[73] Second, because Barth collapses *Spiritus Creator* into *Spiritus Redemptor* he eclipses the 'pneumatic conception of man', and so finds acute difficulties in stating that the human person 'is free to stand before God as a true partner in the drama of history'.[74] But on the contrary: Barth's doctrine of the Holy Spirit in his ethics of reconciliation is essentially concerned with the dignity, stature, and inalienable freedom of God's human covenant partners; and that concern is not a *qualifying* of the Spirit as Christ's self-attestation, but its inescapable *consequence*. Barth's doctrine of the Holy Spirit, as Tom Smail puts it, 'is . . . designed to affirm . . . human freedom and to give a theological explanation of its actuality and possibility'.[75] How does Barth make this argument?

'We ask', Barth writes, 'concerning the origin, beginning and initiation of the faithfulness of man which replies and corresponds to the faithfulness of God'.[76] Paragraph 75 thus opens with 'the astonished question' concerning the fact that there really is a form of human life lived in response to God, a state of affairs before which one stands 'with helpless

---

[72] P. J. Rosato, *The Spirit as Lord. The Pneumatology of Karl Barth* (Edinburgh, 1981), p. 135.
[73] Ibid., p. 136.
[74] Ibid., p. 143.
[75] T. A. Smail, 'The doctrine of the Holy Spirit', in J. Thompson, ed., *Theology Beyond Christendom* (Allison Park, 1986), p. 89.
[76] IV/4, p. 3.

astonishment'.[77] Very simply, Barth's answer to the question which this fact evokes is that God the Holy Spirit is the origin of human faithfulness. But, at the very beginning of this answer, two delimitations are to be noted.

First, docetism is ruled out. 'We have to be clear that the faithfulness to God here at issue must be understood as a human act, the Christian life as the life of a man.'[78] No adequate answer to the question of the origin of human faithfulness can 'evade the fact that man himself is at issue' – otherwise, Barth asks, 'how can one claim man seriously . . . as one who for his part is a faithful partner in the covenant of grace?'[79] Second, Barth denies that there is any basis for the occurrence of the Christian life other than God alone:

We do not know what we are talking about if in this matter of the awakening and origin of a human faithfulness corresponding to God's faithfulness, in this matter of the foundation of the Christian life, we count upon some other possibility than that which is with God alone because it is subject only to His control. So great is the mystery and dignity of this event![80]

Over against any grounding of the Christian life in innate human capacities, Barth is very firm in asserting the mysterious character of its beginning, the fact that '[t]he Christian life begins with a change which cannot be understood or described radically enough, which God has the possibility of effecting in a man's life in a way which is decisive and basic for his whole being and action, and which He has in fact accomplished in the life of the man who becomes a Christian'.[81]

These initial direction-setting moves are very instructive. They show that the field in which Barth is developing a doctrine of the Holy Spirit is in one sense 'anthropological',

[77] Ibid.
[78] Ibid., p. 4.
[79] Ibid.
[80] Ibid.; cf. *Credo* (London, 1936), pp. 130–2.
[81] IV/4, p. 9.

perhaps even 'existential'.[82] However, the field of human or Christian existence does not constitute a larger context within which language about the Holy Spirit can demonstrate its validity and authenticity in relation to certain given anthropological states of affairs. Language about the Holy Spirit does not merely render Christianly thematic what is available under other depictions; nor is Christian life in the Spirit a member of a class of possible realities. This is why Barth underscores the incomparability of the 'new birth' over against what he calls 'liberalism', which he dismisses as

so much scattered surmising, comparing and questioning whether that which, with so many others, the Christian also seeks and thinks he has may not be found and enjoyed equally well or even better, more radically, in a way which is more satisfying and liberating, in a way which gives greater happiness, with greater depth or height, or simply, perhaps, more practicably, in some other form.[83]

All such 'surmising, comparing and questioning' presupposes that there is 'a general deity',[84] whereas for Barth the ground of possibility for human faithfulness lies elsewhere: in the utterly specific, non-translatable, 'unsubstitutable' action of God in Christ. The Christian life is thus grounded in 'the freedom of which He, the God of Abraham, Isaac and Jacob, has made use in supreme majesty and condescension in the history of Jesus Christ'.[85] Thus: 'Jesus Christ, His history, became and is the foundation of Christian existence, this and this alone.'[86] 'Many human events and developments may have other origins and beginnings; the Christian life, faithfulness to God as the free act and attitude of a man, begins with that which in the days of Augustus and Tiberius, on the way from the manger of Bethlehem to the

[82] E. Jüngel, 'Karl Barths Lehre von der Taufe', pp. 273f and n. 74.
[83] IV/4, p. 11.
[84] Ibid., p. 12.
[85] Ibid., p. 13.
[86] Ibid., p. 14.

cross of Golgotha, was actualised as that which is possible παρα θεου, with God.'[87]

To sum up Barth's initial orientation of the argument: the question of the origin of the Christian life cannot be answered by reference to antecedent human potential, or by reference to some general sphere of possibility of which Christian language about the Spirit is merely illustrative. It is to be answered by direct, immediate reference to the person and work of Jesus Christ, and it is in this Christological – rather than purely anthropological or experimental – context that language about the Spirit is generated. Barth's next move, accordingly, is to specify the Christology which underlies his account of the Spirit and the Christian life.

The late writings of Barth frequently show how alert he was to the difficulty thought by many to vitiate his work, namely a Christological totalitarianism in which the reality of God in Jesus Christ simultaneously grounds and absorbs all other realities, at best leaving their ontological status ambiguous, at worst rendering them superfluous. And so in the present context, he asks:

Does . . . the unavoidable and unequivocal statement of the New Testament that the divine change effected in the history of Jesus Christ is the origin and beginning of the Christian life, simply bring us back to the highly unsatisfactory view that this change does not affect the man himself, who is not Jesus Christ and whose history is not His history, that it necessarily remains alien and external to him, that it neither is nor can be his own change from disobedience to obedience?[88]

The question takes on added urgency, because Barth's covenantal understanding of the relation between God and humanity commits him to rejecting any assertions about divine agency which deny that 'the founding of the Christian life is an event of genuine intercourse between God and man as two different partners'.[89] Barth is thus led to reject

[87] Ibid., p. 17.
[88] Ibid., p. 18.
[89] Ibid., p. 19.

('liberal' or 'anthropomonist') 'subjectivism from below',[90] in which Jesus' history 'is regarded as a mere predicate or instrument, cipher or symbol, of that which truly and properly took place only *in nobis*'.[91] But he also rejects 'subjectivism from above', or what he calls the 'Christomonist solution',[92] in which

the *in nobis*, the liberation of man himself, is a mere appendage, a mere reflection, of the act of liberation accomplished by Jesus Christ in His history, and hence *extra nos*. Jesus Christ, then, is fundamentally alone as the only subject truly at work.[93]

Once we proceed along this route, Barth argues, '[t]he question of a human activity corresponding to the divine activity, the ethical problem of the genesis of the Christian life, is answered by its dismissal as irrelevant'.[94]

Barth prevents himself from being pulled in this direction, not by casting around for other than Christological resources to add substance to the reality of human response (resources such as a natural anthropology or ethics), but by 'a true Christocentricity',[95] in which Jesus' history is not simply substitutionary, but also and as such 'fruitful', evocative, and generative of other histories. For that history is 'from the very first a particular story with a universal goal and bias. In its very limitation it reaches beyond itself.'[96] And more:

[I]t comes with revolutionary force into the life of each and every man. As this individual history it is thus cosmic in origin and goal. As such it is not sterile. It is a fruitful history which newly shapes every human life. Having taken place *extra nos,* it also works *in nobis,* introducing a new being of every man. It certainly took place *extra nos.* Yet it took place, not for its own sake, but *pro nobis.*[97]

---

[90] Ibid., p. 20.
[91] Ibid., p. 19.
[92] Ibid.
[93] Ibid.
[94] Ibid.
[95] Ibid.
[96] Ibid., p. 21.
[97] Ibid.

And so, in a crucial passage, Barth proposes:

[The] change which God has made is in truth man's liberation. It comes upon him wholly from without, from God. Nevertheless, it is his liberation. The point is that here, as everywhere, the omnicausality of God must not be construed as His sole causality. The divine change in whose accomplishment a man becomes a Christian is an event of true intercourse between God and man. If it undoubtedly has its origin in God's initiative, no less indisputably man is not ignored or passed over in it. He is taken seriously as an independent creature of God. He is not run down or overpowered, but set on his own feet. He is not put under tutelage, but addressed and treated as an adult. The history of Jesus Christ, then, does not destroy a man's own history.[98]

Barth's point here has already received ample exposition earlier in the doctrine of reconciliation, most of all in his recovery and reinterpretation of the *munus propheticum* and in his interpretation of the risen presence of Christ. In paragraph 75.1, Barth recapitulates two emphases from these earlier discussions.

First, Jesus is risen; as such, he is not locked in an external sphere, objective and unavailable. Rather, he is present and effective *for us*. For in his resurrection, Jesus' history 'showed itself in its totality to be, not past and transient history, but history which, because it happened once-for-all, is present to all later times and indeed to all earlier times, cosmically effective and significant history'.[99] As the risen one, Jesus is 'the Revealer, Proclaimer, Prophet and Apostle of the salvation history of all men accomplished in His death',[100] demonstrating that his history is not only *extra nos*, but *pro nobis*.

Second, '[i]n the work of the Holy Spirit the history manifested to all men in the resurrection of Jesus Christ is manifest and present to a specific man as his own salvation history'.[101] The Holy Spirit is that divine agent through

---

[98] Ibid., pp. 22f.
[99] Ibid., p. 24.
[100] Ibid., p. 25.
[101] Ibid., p. 27.

which the effective history of Jesus Christ *pro nobis* comes to be *in nobis*, thus inaugurating the divine change. By virtue of the resurrection of Jesus, 'a power is at work' which 'enables, permits and orders' certain people 'to become responsible subjects of their own human history'.[102] This power is the power of the Holy Spirit, through which that which took place *illic et tunc* in Jesus reaches its goal in the *hic et nunc* of the personal history of a specific human being.[103] Crucially, this notion of the Holy Spirit as the 'outstretched arm'[104] of the risen Jesus is the *beginning* of responsible human action, not its cessation. For:

Intercourse between God and man does not cease in the work of the Holy Spirit. In this work it begins to be genuine intercourse in which the human partner, far from confusing himself with the divine partner or trying to take His place, occupies the place which is appropriate in relation to Him. The work of the Holy Spirit, then, does not entail the paralysing dismissal or absence of the human spirit, mind, knowledge and will.[105]

To sum up so far: 'baptism of the Holy Spirit' is 'the power of the divine change in which the event of the foundation of the Christian life of specific men takes place'.[106] Here, as throughout the *Dogmatics,* Barth expounds the doctrine of the Holy Spirit as a means of articulating how the world of grace comes to appropriate to itself certain persons, thereby establishing them in their humanness. The question at the beginning of paragraph 12 of the *Dogmatics* – 'How do men come to say this [Jesus is Lord]?'[107] – and that at the beginning of paragraph 16 – 'In what freedom of man's is it real that God's revelation reaches him?'[108] – is asked again in an ethical form at the beginning of paragraph 75: 'How does . . . man come to accept this alien thing, the

---

[102] Ibid., p. 26.
[103] For a much fuller account of this aspect of the activity of the Holy Spirit, see IV/2, pp. 125–34, 318–23.
[104] IV/2, p. 323.
[105] IV/4, p. 28.
[106] Ibid., p. 30.
[107] I/1, p. 448.
[108] I/2, p. 204.

Kingdom of God, with such actuality?'[109] And the answer is the same: *Credo in Spiritum Sanctum.*

What more is said in paragraph 75.1 of the church's confession of the Holy Spirit? Five points are to be noted.

First, Barth reiterates that the work of the Holy Spirit in founding the Christian life is not detachable from Jesus Christ's perfect work; it is an internal component of that perfection, not a subsequent activity of an entirely separate divine agent. In the work of the Holy Spirit, Jesus, 'He alone, acts as the author.'[110] Because of this, the Holy Spirit is not to be identified with activities of the church community or with individual acts or decisions (even the decision to offer oneself for water-baptism). 'Jesus Christ Himself, and He alone, makes a man a Christian' by baptising with the Holy Spirit.[111]

Second, baptism with the Holy Spirit is effective grace, 'a form of the grace of God which actually reconciles the world to Him – the form of this grace in which it is addressed to a specific man'.[112] The reason for this is not hard to find: the Holy Spirit is what Barth has earlier called the 'direct and immediate presence' of Jesus Christ.[113] Consequently, Barth betrays no embarrassment in predicating direct causality of the Holy Spirit and denying saving causality to ecclesial acts:

The baptism of the Holy Spirit is more than a reference and indication through image and symbol. It is more than an offer and opportunity. Expressions which are undoubtedly inappropriate with reference to human decision, and more particularly with reference to water baptism, are quite in order and indeed necessary here. Baptism with the Holy Spirit is effective, causative, even creative action on man and in man. Here, if anywhere, one might speak of a sacramental happening in the current sense of the term.[114]

---

[109] IV/4, p. 3.
[110] Ibid., p. 31.
[111] Ibid., p. 33.
[112] Ibid.
[113] IV/3, p. 350.
[114] Ibid., p. 34.

The further nuancing of Barth's dissatisfaction with the Reformed tradition of sacramental doctrine is to be noted. Calvin also makes a distinction between Spirit and sacrament, and echoes some of Barth's anxieties about insufficiently restricted claims for sacramental efficacy:

I make such a division between Spirit and sacraments that the power to act rests with the former, and the ministry alone is left to the latter – a ministry empty and trifling, apart from the action of the Spirit, but charged with great effect when the Spirit works within and manifests his power.[115]

But, where Calvin envisages the Spirit as operative 'within', Barth envisages the Spirit as active *prior to* the church's agency in its ordinances, whose function is then redefined as one of confessing and attesting, rather than realising or rendering effectual. And so it is only baptism with the Holy Spirit, and not the answering act of water-baptism, that we are entitled to describe as 'the active and actualising grace of God'.[116]

Third, as 'the divine change' which quickens its human recipient, baptism with the Holy Spirit 'deserves and demands full, unreserved and unconditional gratitude'.[117] The work of the Holy Spirit, once again, has an *ethical* dimension:

As an act of omnipotently penetrating and endowing grace, and therefore as the self-attestation and self-impartation of Jesus Christ which changes man radically and effectively, it is both man's baptism with the Holy Ghost and also as such the command of God directly given to man. In it man effectively acquires his Lord and Master. As it comes to him, obedience is effectively demanded of him. The problem of ethics is thus raised for him, or, more exactly, the problem of the ethos corresponding to it, of the response of his own being, action and conduct.[118]

---

[115] J. Calvin, *Institutes of the Christian Religion* IV.xiv.9, ed. J. T. McNeill (London, 1961) vol. 2, p. 1284.
[116] IV/4, p. 34.
[117] Ibid., p. 35.
[118] Ibid.

The ethical field which the Spirit opens up is not to be construed as an independent area for human operations, in which grace excites to moral endeavour, but does not constitute the innermost substance of the agent. Certainly it cannot be that 'God's act on and in man' makes of the agent a mere 'cog set in motion'; certainly there is even a proper sense in which the creature is 'autonomous'.[119] But such autonomy is not to be considered as in competition with divine determination. For the regenerative coming of the Holy Spirit abolishes the counterfeit freedom of indeterminate choice or unrestricted scope of action, precisely by bestowing on the subject of the divine change the freedom to be *this* person, ordained and called by God to act *thus*.

Above all, he cannot seek refuge in a separate freedom of choice and control respecting his own being, action and conduct which still remains to him alongside the choice and control for which he is empowered and to which he is also invited and ordered by God, for a choice and control other than that for which he is freed and to which he is referred by God does not even enter into the question for him, for the man who has become new and different through God's act, through his baptism with the Holy Ghost. God has truly 'beset him behind and before'.[120]

Barth's point remains obscure if read with the assumption that grace and morality, heteronomy and autonomy, are necessarily in conflict. Barth's ethics as a whole denies the conflict, ultimately by denying its ontological basis – by denying, that is, the claim that the world of human 'autonomy' or 'freedom' has substance apart from the creative and redemptive activity of God in Christ. Once human reality is understood as *essentially* that which God constitutes in Jesus, and once life in grace is seen as originally and properly human (not as an accidental modification of some larger category of human being), then human freedom is no longer a sphere from which we may observe God's

[119] Ibid.
[120] Ibid., p. 36.

command and choose to obey or disobey. 'Freedom' is allegiance to what by the Holy Spirit the human person inescapably *is*. It is in this precise sense that the Christian life involves the Christian in 'a walking genuinely on his own feet as he is beset by God'.[121]

Fourth, the beginning of the Christian life in the baptism of the Holy Spirit has an ecclesial dimension, since it is 'the beginning of [the Christian's] life in a distinctive fellow-humanity', in which the Christian 'unavoidably discovers himself to be the companion, fellow and brother of these others, bound to them for better or for worse'.[122] As in the discussions of ecclesiology in paragraphs 62, 67, and 72, so here: the activity of the Holy Spirit creates 'special, Christian fellow-humanity',[123] in which is reinforced Barth's earlier anthropological dictum: *si quis dixerit hominem esse solitarium, anathema sit.*[124]

Fifth, baptism with the Holy Spirit has an eschatological dimension. From the beginning of the *Dogmatics*, Barth emphasised that 'everything that is to be said about the man who receives the Holy Spirit and is constrained and filled by the Holy Spirit is an eschatological statement'.[125] Here in iv/4, the point remains firm: baptism with the Holy Spirit 'is and remains a real beginning', 'a commencement which points forward to the future', 'a take-off for the leap towards what is not yet present'.[126] This is to be read not only as Barth's familiar insistence that the Christian life is a process of continuous conversion, in which the believer does not progress by the acquisition of skills, but simply exists in the miraculous fact that his or her Christian life is 'always and everywhere a wholly new thing'.[127] Barth is also making the point that, through the work of the Holy Spirit, the Christian is set in relation to the 'absolute future',

[121] Ibid.
[122] iv/4, p. 37.
[123] Ibid.
[124] iii/2, p. 319.
[125] i/1, p. 464.
[126] iv/4, p. 38.
[127] Ibid., p. 39.

the full revelation of Jesus Christ in which 'He shall manifest Himself as the Pantokrator of all life',[128] and in anticipation of which Christian existence now is 'one long Advent season'.[129]

In summary: the Holy Spirit is that personal activity of God whereby the risen Lord Jesus imparts himself to particular persons and makes them new. As the sealing of the eternal covenant between God and these persons, the Holy Spirit is present with imperative as well as indicative force. This is why paragraph 75.1 is immediately followed by a discussion of human agency – in exactly the same way, for instance, that the earlier discussion of the divinity of the Spirit in paragraph 16 is followed in paragraph 18 by ethical considerations under the rubric of 'The Life of the Children of God'. Any idea that language about the Holy Spirit precludes inquiry into human subjectivity is firmly ruled out; indeed, any subordination of the subjective to the objective is forbidden, since it would 'indirectly call into question the *homoousia* of the Holy Spirit'.[130]

It is this which makes Barth's relation to Schleiermacher – so complex, nuanced, and restless, and therefore so easy to misrepresent – at once so close and so distant in these matters. Barth was very keenly aware that in Schleiermacher's theology there existed potential for a 'pure theology of the Holy Spirit', that is, for 'the teaching of man brought face to face with God by God, of man granted grace by grace'.[131] But he was no less keenly aware that

---

[128] Ibid., p. 40.

[129] Ibid. This eschatological orientation explains why Barth regards baptism with the Holy Spirit as both the *basis* and the *goal* of baptism with water. In the same way that in the baptism of Jesus the Spirit's descent signifies 'the divine appreciation, acknowledgment, approval and affirmation' (ibid., p. 66), so also Christian baptism with water has a 'teleological character' (ibid., p. 71), pointing beyond itself to 'its fulfilment in the future baptism with the Holy Spirit' (ibid.). Water baptism is thus 'a human work which derives from and hastens towards the work of God' (ibid., p. 73).

[130] I/2, p. 208.

[131] K. Barth, *Protestant Theology in the Nineteenth Century* (London, 1963), p. 460. This more positive appreciation of Schleiermacher in the area of pneumatology is well traced by A. Collins 'Barth's relationship to Schleiermacher: a reassessment', *Studies in Religion/Sciences Religieuses* 17 (1988), 213–24, who argues with

Schleiermacher exposed himself to the danger of dissolving the divinity of the Spirit by making the priority of God over humanity in faith potentially reversible,[132] thereby failing to state how the Spirit of God is – as Barth put in his 'little song of praise to Schleiermacher' – 'an absolutely *particular* and specific spirit, which not only distinguishes itself again and again from all other spirits, but which is seriously to be called "holy"'.[133] It is this flaw – incipient in Schleiermacher, more boldly present in theological existentialism and certain forms of sacramental teaching – that Barth seeks to avoid in his pneumatology.

Barth did not believe that Christian theology requires a supplementary theory of how the objective is mediated to the human historical existence – whether the theory be an anthropology, a phenomenology of sacramental signs, or a philosophical hermeneutics. He denies the necessity of such strategies, on the grounds that Jesus Christ himself, the living Word of God, is immediately present and active in his Holy Spirit. Language about the Spirit constitutes for Barth not only a necessary, but also a sufficient, explanation of how it is that the Christian life comes to be. Talking of the realisation of the benefits of Christ does not require us to step out of the sphere of the *Credo*. To put the point in trinitarian terms, because God *extra nos* is God *pro nobis*, and because God *pro nobis* is present *in nobis*, 'the "perfect" truth of revelation already includes the concept of its existence for us'.[134] The work of the Holy Spirit is a repetition, impress, and reinforcement of the objective in such a way that our subjective reality comes to exist in correspondence to its grace, such that 'our blind eyes are opened and . . . thankfully and in thankful surrender we recognise and acknowledge that it is so: Amen'.[135] But that 'Amen' is not

some success that, in Barth's later work, 'it is through pneumatology that a viable and valid anthropocentrism is able to emerge' (p. 221).

[132] Cf. Barth, *Protestant Theology in the Nineteenth Century*, p. 460.

[133] K. Barth, 'Concluding unscientific postscript on Schleiermacher', in *The Theology of Schleiermacher* (Edinburgh, 1982), p. 276.

[134] 1/2, p. 238.

[135] Ibid., p. 239.

passive acquiescence; it is ethical allegiance, the beginning of the work of humanity reconciled and renewed. And to talk further of that, Barth moves on from baptism with the Holy Spirit to baptism with water:

[I]n the one event of the foundation of the Christian life we have the wholly different action of two inalienably distinct subjects. On the one side is the action of God in His address to man, and on the other, made possible and demanded thereby, the action of man in his turning towards God. On the one side is the Word and command of God expressed in His gift, on the other man's obedience of faith required of him and to be rendered by him as a recipient of the divine gift. Without this unity of the two in their distinction there could be no Christian ethics.[136]

---

[136] IV/4, p. 41.

CHAPTER FIVE

Baptism with water

Luther once remarked that '[t]he whole world was, and still
is, full of baptism and of the grace of God'.[1] By this he
meant that God has pronounced a verdict of futility upon
'our own anxious works':[2] the radically creative nature of
God's action in baptism orients the Christian life in its
entirety to the divine *extra nos*. As we have seen in the
previous chapter, for Barth, too, baptism with the Holy
Spirit means that the Christian life is what he calls a
'mystery and miracle', a matter for astonishment at the new
thing which God does.[3] But this 'mystery and miracle' is
not simply a matter of God alone at work; rather, it 'consists
in the fact that man himself is the free subject of this event
on the basis of a possibility which is present only with
God'.[4] Barth's discussion of baptism with water in paragraph
75.2 moves from discussion of the divine possibility to
description of the free human subject.

That this is Barth's concern is very clear from his initial
orientation of the question at the beginning of paragraph
75.2. 'Christian baptism', he proposes, 'is the first form of
the human decision which in the foundation of the Christian
life corresponds to the divine change'.[5] Brought into being

[1] M. Luther, 'The holy and blessed sacrament of baptism', in *Luther's Works*, vol.
35 (Philadelphia, 1960), p. 42. On this theme in Luther, see L. Grane, 'Luther,
baptism and Christian formation', in E. Gritsch, ed., *Encounters with Luther*, vol.
2 (Gettysburg, 1982), pp. 189–98.
[2] Ibid.
[3] IV/4, p. 3.
[4] Ibid., p. 5.
[5] Ibid., p. 44.

by, following after, and shaped by the divine action of
baptism with the Holy Spirit, there is genuinely 'human
work, action and conduct'.[6] Barth lays considerable stress
upon the fact that at the beginning of the Christian life
there stands neither speculation nor contemplation nor even
speech, but 'the Yes of his [the baptizand's] human work':[7]

[T]he foundation of the Christian life belongs to the ready doing
of this work, the immediate first step in the new life-act for which
man is empowered and to which he is summoned by the divine
change. The genuineness of the faith in which he receives and
takes to heart the pledge and promise given to him must and
will prove itself at once in action which corresponds to this pledge
and promise.[8]

Of course, as the word 'empowered' there suggests, the new
life-act is not in any way self-generated; its root is not in
the Christian's 'own free will and action, nor a matter of
his own caprice'.[9] On the contrary: this new life-act is
required by the nature of reality as it truly is in Jesus
Christ. It is, therefore, what Barth calls an 'obedient' action.
That is to say, it is an action in which the Christian disposes
of him- or herself in conformity with the order of reality as
it is established in Christ and made known in the gospel.
This first act of obedience is therefore 'prefigured, pre-
scribed, ordered and commanded of him by that in which
he believes, the reconciliation of the world to God as the
divine change which comes over him'.[10] At the beginning
of his discussion of baptism with water, then, Barth
announces his characteristic twofold theme: the human
action which, as obedient action, is enclosed within the
prevenient action of God. The new Christian

---

[6] Ibid., p. 42.
[7] Ibid.
[8] Ibid. It is here at this initial stage that Macken's critique of Barth goes awry.
Macken claims that Barth's later theology of baptism is dominated by noetic
issues or by 'formal word categories' (*The Autonomy Theme*, p. 85), and that
Barth 'concentrates on knowledge as the point of mediation between God and
man' (ibid., p. 83). Barth's understanding of baptism as the foundation of the
Christian *ethos* clearly points in a quite different direction.
[9] IV/4, p. 43.
[10] Ibid.

freely asks to be baptized. Of his own resolve he is baptized. Yet this is no capricious act. He does it because he is invited and commanded to do it by the grace of God which has come upon him, by the history of Jesus Christ which has taken place for him, by the manifestation of this history which has occurred for him in the resurrection from the dead, by the work of the Holy Spirit in which that history and manifestation become an event in his own life, in short, by Jesus Christ Himself.[11]

And hence Barth establishes the following basic principle for his interpretation of water-baptism:

That a man has himself baptized is something which, according to the presentation in the New Testament, he owes wholly and utterly to the free resolve of the divine word and work of salvation which has or will come upon him; he owes it to this just as certainly as it is the free act of his own resolve and work for which he is liberated and to which he is summoned by that divine resolve.[12]

This theme – the ordered relation of divine and human action – is the central preoccupation of Barth's exposition of baptism with water, which divides into three main blocks of material: the basis of baptism, the goal of baptism, and the meaning of baptism.

THE BASIS OF BAPTISM

[O]n what basis and for what reason is baptism the first step of the human decision which follows the divine change, the first concrete form of a new life-act of man corresponding to the faithfulness of God, faithful to it in return, and hence obedient? Why is baptism, secondarily but indispensably, part of the foundation of the Christian life?[13]

Barth's answers to his own questions here are very instructive. Rather than looking for a basis for baptism in the baptismal command in Matthew 28, Barth proposes that baptism is properly rooted in Jesus' own baptism by John,

[11] Ibid., pp. 43f.
[12] Ibid., p. 48.
[13] Ibid., p. 50.

remarking (not without a certain wryness) that 'the story
of the baptism of Jesus contains the aetiological "cult-
legend" which creatively indicates the origin of Christian
baptism'.[14] Crucially, Jesus' own baptism is understood
under the aspect of *vocation*: the event in the Jordan is,
Barth writes, 'the point of intersection of the divine change
and the human decision',[15] and (more pointedly) Jesus' 'free
subjection to the will of God, His free association with men,
His free entry upon the service of God and men'.[16] Elaborating on this, Barth identifies Jesus' baptism as the point at
which Jesus enters into his office as Messiah, Saviour, and
Mediator 'in an act of unconditional and irrevocable submission to the will of His Father'.[17] Allegiance to the divine
will is central here: at his baptism, Jesus demonstrates 'the
required readiness'; he 'submits to' and 'gives recognition
to' the coming act of God which John announces.[18] In so
doing, he enters into solidarity with sinners, and takes up
his mediatorial functions. All of this, furthermore, demands
that we read the story of Jesus' baptism bearing in mind
the clear distinction between Jesus' self-offering for baptism
with water by John ('what Jesus and John do') and the
descent of the Spirit ('the work and word of God').[19]

Essentially, then, the story of Jesus' baptism by John in
the Jordan is read by Barth as a call narrative, a story of
vocation and responsive obedience which is paradigmatic
for the first great act of Christian obedience. In the same
way that Jesus enters into his mission at his baptism, so
per analogiam the Christian enters into the moral role of
disciple at his or her water-baptism, which is accordingly
seen as an act of submission, allegiance, and commitment
to the divine will. In some respects, Barth here anticipates
what has become a primary theme in much recent theology

14 Ibid., p. 52.
15 Ibid., p. 53.
16 Ibid., p. 54.
17 Ibid.
18 Ibid., p. 55.
19 Ibid., p. 65.

of Christian initiation, namely the interconnectedness of baptism and the life of responsible discipleship. In so far as it has been shaped by the converging influences of the liturgical and ecumenical movements, much contemporary theology of baptism and many recent texts of Christian initiation give high profile to the covenantal obligations which are essential to Christian baptism properly understood. Such obligations not only make adults the normative (though in practice by no means the only) candidates for baptism in many major Christian traditions; they also provide the shape for the ongoing life of the follower of Jesus Christ, and are regularly rehearsed at the 'renewal of the baptismal covenant' in public worship and Christian living. Barth differs from these more recent developments in his insistence that to talk of baptism under its ethical and vocational aspect is to exclude any notion of water-baptism as a sacrament: the covenantal obligations are established for the disciple not in some sacramental rite, but in the immediate regenerative operation of God the Holy Spirit. Nevertheless, Barth poses much the same question as more recent writers on Christian initiation:

The point at issue is whether ... the practice of administering baptism at a considerable interval in time apparently before even the beginnings of repentance and faith and the assumption of moral responsibility does such violence to the relation between the divine initiative and human response in the work of salvation that such baptism ceases to be an embodiment of the gospel.[20]

The ethical orientation of Barth's interpretation of water-baptism helps explain why he says little about the relation of baptism to the remission of sin. Certainly in the opening pages of IV/4 he sees baptism in terms of the sinner's radical

---

[20] G. Wainwright, *Christian Initiation* (London, 1969), p. 50. For an older treatment of the same theme, see N. Clark, 'The theology of baptism', in A. Gilmore, ed., *Christian Baptism* (London, 1959), pp. 306–26. On recent ecumenical developments, see G. Wagner, 'Baptism from Accra to Lima', in M. Thurian, ed., *Ecumenical Perspectives on Baptism, Eucharist and Ministry* (Geneva, 1983), pp. 12–32, and L. S. Mudge, 'Convergence on baptism', in ibid., pp. 33–45. A useful account of some New Testament background can be found in N. Gäumann, *Taufe und Ethik* (Munich, 1967).

passage from death to life. Yet that passage has already been effected in Christ; 'conversion' takes place on Good Friday and Easter Day, and the Christian's coming to faith is an attestation, not a realisation, of the fact that sin and death have already been cast away by the divine 'No'. Water-baptism, moreover, does not 'effect' remission of sins or regeneration, nor even mediate the effects of Christ's saving work, for it is the work of the Holy Spirit (and not some ecclesial work) effectively to represent to us the setting aside of sin. Water-baptism is therefore best seen not as the point at which cleansing from sin takes place, but as the beginning of life-long obedience to the situation in which the candidate has been placed by the effective work of Christ and its self-presentation. In sum: once remission of sins is located in the work of Christ whose merits are distributed by the Holy Spirit, water-baptism is most naturally associated with vocation.

THE GOAL OF BAPTISM

What does the Christian community have in view when, because its Lord, the origin, theme and content of its faith, was first willing to be, and was, baptised by John, it administers the same act of washing with water to those who with it confess faith in Him and therewith declare that they are willing and ready to join Him, and so to join it, too, as the people of His witnesses?[21]

Barth's very question begs other questions of course: *Is* Christian baptism 'the same act of washing' as Jesus' own baptism by John? *Is* Christian baptism primarily an act of confession of faith and a mark of adherence to the community of witnesses? But, those points aside, it is important to grasp that water-baptism 'looks beyond itself', since '[i]ts *telos* is transcendent, not immanent'.[22] Like the baptism of John, which 'sought only to look and stretch forward to the coming act of God',[23] so the human act of baptism with

---

[21] IV/4, pp. 68f.
[22] Ibid., p. 69.
[23] Ibid., p. 70.

water is 'in no sense a self-sufficient act which is in some way divinely fulfilled or self-fulfilling within itself. Its goal does not lie in its administration.'[24] As baptism εἰς, baptism has a 'teleological character', since it is 'directed to seek its divine, creative fulfilment in that which it cannot be or achieve or bring about or mediate of itself, but which it can only seek and intend and hasten towards'.[25] This divine fulfilment is what Barth calls 'the future baptism with the Holy Spirit'.[26] This account of the matter is, no doubt, in need of some terminological clarification: 'baptism with the Holy Spirit' is used to refer both to the generative divine act ('the divine change'[27]) which *precedes* baptism with water, and to a *future* act of God to which the Christian is committed by baptism with water. But the general sense is clear: Christian baptism is 'a human work which derives from and hastens towards the work of God'.[28]

Confession is the essence of this human work. 'Christian baptism is the human work of basic confession.'[29] Like some other terms which Barth uses very heavily in the doctrine of reconciliation, the term 'confession' is best explicated in terms of the understanding of the relation of divine and human work which it presupposes. Because water-baptism 'confesses' the divine action, it is not to be construed as in some fashion the *instrument* of a divine work:

The dignity, seriousness, power and glory of this baptism is that it stands or falls with the fact that, unlike the baptising of John and the baptism of Jesus Himself, it takes place with a view to God's word and work as a pure and sincerely humble act of obedience which looks forward to the divine act of salvation and revelation, doing so in modest resolution and with resolute modesty, prepared from the very outset to renounce any attempt to represent – or misrepresent – itself as divine speech or action ... The more certainly Christianity will deceive itself and the world

[24] Ibid., p. 71.
[25] Ibid. See further Barth's exegetical elucidations, pp. 90–100.
[26] Ibid.
[27] Ibid., p. 72.
[28] Ibid., p. 73.
[29] Ibid.

if it pretends that its baptism accomplishes something which is more and better than a human answer, and at the same time a human question, in face of God's grace and revelation.[30]

On the other hand, to 'confess' is indeed to act, humanly and responsibly, to adopt a role as well as to acknowledge a benefit:

What God does in Jesus Christ through the Holy Spirit is exclusively His action. Similarly, what man can and should do in face of the divine action is wholly his own human action. Let us be grateful that there is a necessary and firm connection between God's action and ours, between ours and His! Let us be grateful that we are liberated and summoned by the divine change to make the corresponding and ensuing human decision! Let us do this in the gratitude of obedience, not with the arrogant opinion that we have to effect the divine change along with God, that in, with and under our work – the work of faith, hope and love, the work of our service – we have to do the work of God Himself! Our human work has to acknowledge the work of God, to bear witness to it, to confess it, to respond to it, to honour, praise and magnify it. This is befitting for us. It is enough that we are allowed to do it.[31]

In sum: baptism with water is confession of the work and word of God in Jesus Christ, As such, it 'is the first concrete step of the human decision of faith and obedience corresponding thereto in so far as it is resolutely and exclusively movement to Him, and thus the true baptism of conversion'.[32] It is in this way – and not by any sacramental *concursus* of divine causality and mediating human agency – that 'there is a necessary and firm connection between God's action and ours, between ours and His'.

THE MEANING OF BAPTISM

Having established the basis and goal of baptism with water, Barth moves on to a much lengthier treatment of

[30] Ibid.
[31] Ibid., p. 72.
[32] Ibid., p. 90.

the meaning of baptism, in what is in effect the central section of the baptismal fragment. His starting-point is this:

The 'praise of baptism' cannot be exhausted by reference to the divine basis and the divine goal of this human action. Baptism has to be seen and understood and praised also in the true and distinctive thing which characterises it as a human action proceeding from that basis and hastening to that goal.[33]

At this point, the connection between Barth's ethical concern and his repudiation of the sacramental status of baptism with water becomes very explicit. To fail to grasp the character of baptism with water as a human work is to confuse divine and human action by envisaging the real meaning of water-baptism as some 'immanent divine work'.[34] And to do this is either to swallow up 'that which men will and do' in a divine work, or to make water-baptism itself into the accomplishment of the divine work in a way which in effect renders the latter superfluous. 'Either way, Christian baptism is treated docetically',[35] because its character as the act of human moral agents is obscured and undermined. It is on these – moral – grounds that Barth opposes 'in principle and *ab ovo*' an entire theological and ecclesiastical tradition which, in a variety of ways, has made use of the notion of sacramental mediation, according to which 'the meaning of baptism is to be sought and found in a divine action which is concealed in the administration by men and which makes use of this'.[36] If this tradition is to be rejected, it is because it obscures the reality of 'the human action which corresponds to the divine action in the founding of the Christian life'.[37] For Barth, this is not to deny that God is the '*auctor primarius* of all creaturely occurrence';[38] but it is to say that God's

---

[33] Ibid., p. 101.
[34] Ibid.
[35] Ibid., p. 102.
[36] Ibid., p. 105. See further the discussion of the application to baptism of the term μυστήριον, p. 109.
[37] Ibid., p. 105.
[38] Ibid.

action within and on them, His presence, work and revelation in their whole action, and therewith in their baptism, does not supplant or suppress their action. It does not rob it of significance. On the contrary, it establishes and demands it as their own action which is obedient to Him, which hopes in Him, which does not encroach but is responsible to Him, which in its genuine humanity bears witness freely to Him.[39]

Hence: 'Our objection to the sacramental interpretation of baptism is directed against this conjuring away of the free man whom God liberates and summons to his own free and responsible action.'[40]

Barth's intention, then, is plain: to establish 'the ethical meaning of baptism'.[41] A lengthy excursus seeks to make the case exegetically. He divides the relevant data into four groups of passages. First, in looking at Acts 22.16, Hebrews 10.22, Ephesians 5.25f, and Titus 3.5, passages which appear to speak of baptism in vividly realistic terms, Barth proposes that the texts are best read, not through the lens of water-baptism as a means of grace, but rather as referring to the efficacious work and word of God, to which water-baptism is a responsive act of obedience. In brief, Barth argues that a 'non-sacramental exposition' of such passages, whilst not incontestable, is much to be preferred.[42] A second group of passages (Galatians 3.27, Romans 6.3f, Colossians 2.12, and John 3.5) speaks of Christian baptism in connection with the unity of Christ and the believer. Once again, Barth's account of these texts seeks to protect them from any attribution of saving causality to baptism, by locating the saving activity in 'the divine act and revelation in Jesus Christ' made present by the Holy Spirit.[43] Moreover, Barth is at pains to argue that, in view of the unique and efficacious nature of God's saving act in Christ, water-baptism has in these passages only 'a subsidiary character'.[44] In this light,

[39] Ibid., pp. 105f.
[40] Ibid., p. 106.
[41] Ibid., p. 107.
[42] Ibid., p. 114.
[43] Ibid., p. 116.
[44] Ibid., p. 117.

a passage such as Galatians 3.27 ('As many of you as were baptized into Christ have clothed yourselves with Christ') is best interpreted as

> looking back to the divine change, to the putting on of Christ which in Christ Jesus Himself has been effected objectively and subjectively for the recipients of the epistle by His Holy Spirit, and that baptism is recalled as the concrete moment in their own life in which they for their part confirmed, recognised and accepted their investing with Christ from above, their ontic relationship to Him, not only in gratitude and hope, but also in readiness and vigilance.[45]

Third, Barth looks at two passages which seem to ascribe a saving function to baptism: Mark 16.16 and 1 Peter 3.21. Here Barth interprets σωτηρία not as a divine action but as 'an action and mode of life in which they [human agents] are to set forth and declare in practice, to work out ... the σωτηρία divinely promised and present to them, their salvation'.[46] Thus: 'Baptism saves because, like faith and with it, it is an element in the action which God has entrusted to and enjoined upon those who will be saved by God and who are saved already in hope in Him. It is a human work which is, like faith, wholly appropriate and indispensable proper to their position.'[47] Finally, Barth examines two Johannine passages (1 John 5.5–8 and John 19.33–37) whose linking together of 'water and blood' has furnished a classical exegetical warrant for a sacramental interpretation of water-baptism. Once again, his interpretation turns upon the centrality of God's action in Christ: water and blood refer not to any ecclesial actions or elements, but to Jesus' 'history, to His having come in the flesh'.[48]

Having sought to make a case on exegetical grounds that, since water-baptism is not a sacrament, its meaning 'is to be sought in its character as a true and genuine human

[45] Ibid., p. 116.
[46] Ibid., p. 122.
[47] Ibid.
[48] Ibid., p. 123.

action which responds to the divine act and word',[49] Barth gives over the rest of the section to an exposition of the positive content of baptism with water. Two statements indicate the heart of his argument:

The crux of a correct answer to the question of the meaning of baptism lies in a strict correlation and a no less strict distinction between the human action as such and the divine action from which it springs, on whose basis it is possible, and towards which it moves.[50]

[T]he fact that the choice, will and action of the participants are at issue in the baptismal act constitutes the meaning of baptism.[51]

Baptism is best described as a human act of obedience and hope; and obedience and hope are both embraced by the concept of conversion. Baptism is therefore about 'the conversion of all who have a part in it'.[52] Some discriminations are in order at this point. To say that baptism is about the participants' 'choice, will and action' is once again not to make baptism into an act of moral self-constitution. For all that baptism with water is an ethical act, it is as such wholly referred to its transcendent basis and goal. Conversion is neither 'moral rearmament' nor commitment to some Christian ideology. It is essentially theocentric moral action, in the sense that the candidate for baptism is not choosing from a range of possible goods and thereby establishing value, but making a choice to acknowledge the inescapable truth that he or she is faced with and claimed by the will of God. Baptism is therefore a matter of the candidate 'deciding to let God be God, to let Him be his God, and his precisely'.[53] But such a decision is 'a distinctly human action':

That it is God's gift and grace to be awakened, summoned and empowered to do this, that man cannot start to justify God except in the freedom which is given him by God – that is one thing.

[49] Ibid., p. 128.
[50] Ibid., p. 134.
[51] Ibid., p. 135.
[52] Ibid., p. 138.
[53] Ibid., p. 142.

What he does, however, when he starts to do this, the movement which he executes in conversion, is not superhuman or supernatural. It is genuinely and truly human correspondence to the legal claim which God asserts over against him in His work and word. One has even to say that all pseudo-human masks fall away, and truly human action is evident, when a man is reduced to justifying God, when his action becomes that desire, when it is one long hungering and thirsting after righteousness. In the fact that man's conversion is the most human thing he can do is to be found also its dignity and honour. Since it is effected in human knowledge, thought, resolve and will, it is, of course, 'only' human. It is not divine. It is human action which simply responds to divine action. Nevertheless it does so in an appropriate way. It reflects this action. It is thus a pre-eminent human action.[54]

Appropriately, then, Barth turns to a more extensive description of the obedience and hope which together constitute the conversion which lies at the heart of baptism with water. Such an account can, indeed *must*, be given, for what takes place in baptism is not 'a mystery which is either to be interpreted capriciously or to be surrounded by reverent silence', but 'free and responsible human action, a happening which can be imagined and portrayed'.[55]

Obedience

Obedience is neither slavish submission nor some purely arbitrary directing of the will. Rather, Barth notes, in this as in every aspect of Christian ethics, 'obedience is freedom and freedom is obedience'.[56] To be baptised and thus to take the first step of the Christian life is inescapably required, for the Christian is one who has come to see that the world is as the gospel proclaims it to be. To bind oneself to that reality is to render that 'obedience which alone is possible in the discipleship of Jesus and the school of the Holy Spirit'.[57] This free obedience involves a renunciation and a

[54] Ibid., p. 143.
[55] Ibid., p. 153.
[56] Ibid., p. 154.
[57] Ibid., p. 155.

pledge. Baptism as renunciation flows from the divine 'No' in which the candidate's old life has been set aside, and so it is

a confession of the sin and guilt which in the crucifixion of Jesus Christ man may know to be forgiven sin, pardoned guilt and remitted condemnation, but which, since Jesus Christ took his place there, he must also recognise as his own sin, guilt and condemnation, from which, looking to Jesus Christ, he is separated, from which he must now remain separated, whose continuation and increase are quite unthinkable, especially in the form of further efforts at self-justification and self-cleansing. In baptism, the candidate confesses with the community that all this has been rendered impossible by what Jesus Christ has done and is for him.[58]

But baptism as pledge flows from the divine 'Yes' in which the new life of the Christian is established by God. In baptism, candidate and community

say Yes to this Yes. How can their Yes, spoken to God's Yes, be an idle Yes? They set to work energetically to respond to this Yes. They join forces and swear together to do so, i.e., to render the service which quite undeservedly is entrusted to them and laid upon them by the divine Yes. Baptism is the oath which is taken by them in concert.[59]

Again, the care with which Barth describes the idea of moral decision is instructive. Hans Urs von Balthasar notes that Barth has what he calls 'a noticeably Augustinian concept of freedom', by which von Balthasar means that

freedom is primarily a life lived in the intimacy of God's freedom. This freedom . . . cannot be defined negatively, as merely a neutral stance toward God, as if freedom were merely presented with a 'menu' of options from which the *liberum arbitrium* would make its selection. On the contrary, when freedom is authentic, it is a form of living within that mysterious realm where self-determination and obedience, independence and discipleship, mutually act upon and clarify each other.[60]

---

[58] Ibid., p. 159.
[59] Ibid., p. 161.
[60] H. U. von Balthasar, *The Theology of Karl Barth* (San Francisco, 1992), p. 129.

Von Balthasar catches Barth's point here exactly: the human decision given perceptible form in baptism is not, like the decision of Hercules before the crossroads, a matter of 'a choice between a number of possibilities available to him'.[61] Rather, the Christian 'chooses that which alone is actual and possible, and therewith he rejects *eo ipso* that which is absolutely impossible in the light of what is alone actual and possible'.[62] The ontological force of what Barth is saying here is critically important: real human deciding or choosing is not arbitrary, but deciding for and choosing 'the one true reality'.[63] And yet reality is so characterised that it evokes (rather than supplants or suppresses) responsive action from those who are grasped by its sheerly necessary character. Why? Because 'the one true reality' is God in Jesus Christ reconciled to the people of the covenant, who are 'taken seriously as God's partners':[64]

Even, and indeed precisely, in that which takes place in the sphere of the covenant of grace, we find dialogue and dealings between two who stand in clear encounter, God on the one side and man on the other, God and all the men concerned, so that, while these men can only follow what God says and does, they are all active subjects for their part, and they can and should follow with their own speech and action on the basis of their own responsible decision. Matters are not decided over their heads. They are not just objects who are discussed, moved and pushed around. Precisely in the covenant of grace, the house of the Father, the kingdom of Jesus Christ and the Holy Ghost, there can be no talk of divine omnicausality. One is attacking this house and kingdom at the very foundations if one fails to see that, even if in total subjection to the rule of Him who alone can rule here, there is given to men, to all the men concerned, not merely a place of their own and freedom of movement, but also the freedom of decision, with the commission to exercise it.[65]

The strength of Barth's language there is striking. Its root lies in his serious opposition to the way in which the practice

---

[61] IV/4, p. 162.
[62] Ibid.
[63] Ibid.
[64] Ibid., p. 163.
[65] Ibid.

of infant baptism militates against the ethical understanding of baptism by reducing the baptismal candidate to 'an object of the community's action', subjected to a rite in which 'he has no function, no active part'.[66] What drives Barth's objection to infant baptism, then, is his insistence that the life of Christian discipleship 'cannot be inherited'.[67] For, if baptism signifies the renunciation and pledge which are the centre of conversion, then the candidates for baptism represent themselves, entering by responsible action into a life of continuing responsible action. 'No Christian environment . . . can transfer this life to those who are in this environment. For these, too, the Christian life will and can begin only on the basis of their own liberation by God, their own decision.'[68] From this perspective, it is significant that, in looking at the dogmatic issues surrounding the baptism of infants, Barth identifies the matter of 'relating baptism on the one side to the faith of those baptized on the other side' as 'the one great dogmatic problem of the doctrine of baptism'.[69] Linking faith to the previously developed concepts of renunciation and pledge, Barth presses that a proper Christian theology of baptism can have no room for vicarious faith, for such a notion would in the end mean that 'grace . . . works automatically'.[70] Infant baptism therefore stands for Barth as 'profoundly irregular', 'an ancient ecclesiastical error' in which 'the character of baptism as both obedience and response is so obscured as to be virtually unrecognizable'.[71] And so: 'Enough of this tiresome matter!'[72]

Hope

Baptism is an act of hope because it is oriented to the goal of the final and definitive manifestation of Jesus Christ. Baptism, Barth argues, 'takes place in orientation to the

[66] Ibid., p. 165.
[67] Ibid., p. 184.
[68] Ibid.
[69] Ibid., p. 185.
[70] Ibid., p. 190.
[71] Ibid., pp. 194f.
[72] Ibid., p. 194.

reality of the covenant between [God] and man which is established, fulfilled and faithfully kept by God – to the eschaton of the revealed reality of the reconciliation between God and man which has been accomplished in Him, of His free grace which in Him is ascribed and directed to all men, which judges all men, which helps them all to their right, but which also claims them all for God's right'.[73] But if baptism is thus eschatologically oriented, it is no less ethically oriented, for 'the life of Christians as a life in this hope begins with the decision made in their baptism. The whole of the further progress on the way which they plainly enter here can consist only in further responses to the word of God which they accepted here, and hence in mere repetitions and variations of the grasping and exercising of this hope.'[74] In this movement into the future, the baptised exercise a 'prophetic' ministry, making known the gospel to the unbaptised. Much of what Barth has to say here anticipates what is discussed in greater detail in *The Christian Life*. One urgent question hangs over both discussions: the question of the sheer fragility of human action. '[W]hat a venture baptism is for all concerned when the only future truly open to them is this one [which] lays on them so many and so great demands!'[75] And yet by human judgment, what follows from baptism is declension and failure which hardly does justice to the greatness of the venture upon which the baptised have entered. What makes baptism different from any other human intention? 'Is not Christian baptism itself compromised and denied, and not just confirmed, by what follows?'[76]

The question weighs very heavily for Barth because baptism has been so clearly associated with Christian ethics. His answer, given briefly here in IV/4 and developed with considerable nuance over the course of *The Christian Life*, is both to reaffirm the reference of human ethical agency to

---

[73] Ibid., p. 195.
[74] Ibid., p. 198.
[75] Ibid., p. 203.
[76] Ibid., p. 204.

the sustaining grace of God, and to insist that divine grace is not an absolution from the necessity of moral action, but a limiting or relativising of its reach. Baptism is hope in Jesus Christ, 'not the quite untenable hope in the goodness of their own action subsequent to baptism'.[77] And, since this is the case, human declension, like the human decision which it corrodes, is not an absolute factor. At baptism, both candidate and community

cleave and orientate themselves to the fact that from the very outset, in the whole sphere which opens up after baptism, they will not merely find their own weakness, corruption, failure and declension. As the Lord of their time, and hence of their future, Jesus Christ is on this way, waiting for them and moving towards them. The Christian life which begins with baptism can thus be a life in which they are not alone and left to their own devices with all the very dubious things which are certainly to be expected on their side. It is a life in which, whether they realise and experience it or not, He is with them and among them every day and every hour.[78]

But, if eschatology relativises human action, it also excites to activity. In baptism, '[w]hat is really at issue . . . is the hope of these men in Him and their own action in this hope.'[79] And such hope is 'not an inactive hope', but 'active in prayer',[80] for prayer is that active turning to, reliance upon, and acting out of the grace of God in Jesus Christ; as such, it is (as *The Christian Life* will reinforce) the fundamental human ethical action:

Where there is prayer, man's relationship to God is corrected and it is in order. Because and to the degree that baptism is prayer, the participants act in this order. They are free both from any calculating manipulation of God's grace and also from any uncertainty as to its being given. They let God be God, but they let Him be their God, who has called them and to whom they may call in return, who hears them and who is heard as they may hear Him, and, hearing, obey Him. Because and to the degree

[77] Ibid., p. 206.
[78] Ibid., pp. 206f.
[79] Ibid., p. 207.
[80] Ibid., p. 209.

that baptism is prayer, it is at once a very humble and a very bold action, free from all illusions and profoundly sober, yet bold and heaven-storming.[81]

It is from this point that Barth moves into his exposition of the Lord's Prayer as a framework for the Christian ethical life: *lex orandi, lex agendi*.

REFLECTIONS

What is the permanent value of the baptismal fragment of *Church Dogmatics* IV/4?

At one level, the text is an important exercise in 'negative ecclesiology'.[82] The consistency with which Barth adheres to the exclusiveness of the history of Jesus as *the* sacrament of the church is a protest against the ease with which the sacramental activity of the church can come to put itself on a par with, or can even supplant, the being and activity of Jesus Christ himself. If we are made ill at ease by the sharpness of Barth's protest, it may be that a certain style of ecumenical theology has elided some of the distinctions which Barth believed to be fundamentally necessary for a consistent exposition of the gospel: distinctions between *opus dei* and *opus hominem*, between the Holy Spirit and the human spirit, between the divine act of salvation and the ecclesial and religious world in which its benefits are appropriated. Setting baptism within a vision of the Christian life in which faith, hope, and obedience constitute the shape of human life in response to Jesus' presence in the power of the Spirit, Barth extracts baptism from its historical identification with the ecclesial representation of grace, and in effect 'secularises' it by giving it a radically vocational or ethical interpretation, thereby leaving behind the last traces of the idea of the church as *mediatrix*.

As we shall see in looking at *The Christian Life* in the next chapter, there is a political aspect to this vocational

---

[81] Ibid., p. 210.
[82] The phrase is that of E. Schillebeeckx, *Church. The Human Story of God* (New York, 1990), p. xix.

interpretation of baptism. Barth associates infant baptism
with civil religion, seeing it as part of the easy pact between
church and state in which authentic Christian witness cannot
flourish, and through which the church ceases to be 'an
essentially missionary and mature' church.[83] There is, therefore, an inner connection between what Barth says about
Christian baptism in iv/4 and what he says about rebellion
in *The Christian Life*: to be baptised is to enter into a situation
in which there can be no truce with the *status quo*, since
baptism is the beginning of a life lived in the light of God's
establishment of a different order of reality: the reality of
God's Kingdom and righteousness.

But most important for our present purpose, however, is
the significance of the baptismal fragment for the construction of Christian ethics. Barth's late doctrine of baptism is
best read as an answer to such questions as: why is the
Christian an agent rather than simply a recipient? What is
the imperative force of the ongoing history of Jesus? Why is
faith always obedience? For Barth, theologically responsible
answers to those questions take their rise in a distinction
which informs the whole discussion: that between divine
omnicausality and divine sole causality.[84] Barth's sharp separation of Spirit-baptism from water-baptism clearly rests
on this distinction, and is made, as we have seen, in order
to enable him to develop an account of the human person
as agent. Such agency is neither identical with, nor in
competition with, the action of God, but in correspondence
with God's activity, subordinate to that activity and in that
very subordination enjoying its genuine substance. As Jüngel
puts it:

Once again the old theologian of Basel impresses upon his readers
the realisation with which the pastor of Safenwil had at one time
startled theology and the church: God is God and humanity is
humanity. Now, however, this statement is not something at
which to be startled, but something to trust. It expounds, according to the Christological starting point of the *Church Dogmatics*,

[83] iv/4, p. xi.
[84] Cf. iv/4, p. 22.

the proposition that in Jesus Christ, God became human. And that God became human, that this man Jesus was in the form of God, does not make the early distinction between God and humanity untrue, but makes it all the more true ... For the distinction is not understood as a saving distinction within the saving connection which makes the distinction possible at all ... The distinction between God and humanity is therefore the good ordering of being which corresponds to the blessing of salvation.[85]

The next chapter will look in more detail at how Barth uses this motif of correspondence to talk of the shape of the human life in response to God's gracious initiative. However, before leaving IV/4, it is important to probe a little more into some of the issues in sacramental theology which it raises, since some of the difficulties into which Barth's text undoubtedly falls in this regard alert us to aspects of the deeper ethical intention of the fragment.

Criticism of the baptismal fragment tends to gravitate towards its exegetical basis, as well as towards some basic dogmatic questions. Two lines of exegetical critique are particularly important.[86] The first concerns Barth's assertion that the core of the New Testament's teaching about Christian baptism is to be found in the material concerning Jesus' own baptism by John in the Jordan. Whilst this assertion is clearly consistent, as we have seen, with Barth's interpretation of baptism with water as a responsive act of allegiance, it is nevertheless striking that the New Testament does not elsewhere refer back to Jesus' own baptism in its discussions of the beginning of the Christian life. Barth's own explanation for this fact – that for the New Testament the matter was so self-evident as to require no explicitation[87] – is hardly convincing. A second critique argues that Barth's exegesis of the material is governed by dogmatic considerations which make it very difficult for him to acknowledge the plain sense

---

[85] E. Jüngel, 'Karl Barths Lehre von der Taufe', pp. 255f.
[86] The exegetical objections are most thoroughly summarised by E. Dinkler in 'Die Taufaussagen des Neuen Testaments. Neu untersucht im Hinblick auf Karl Barths Tauflehre', in F. Viering, ed., *Zu Karl Barths Lehre von der Taufe*, pp. 60–153.
[87] See IV/4, p. 68.

of the biblical texts. This is particularly the case when Barth prefaces his exegesis by insisting that, 'when the New Testament speaks directly or indirectly about baptism, a distinction has always to be made. Does what is said about it really refer to the action as such, or does it refer ... to what we have called its basis on the one side and its goal on the other, i.e., to the divine act of salvation and revelation which is the basis and the intention of the action and which is reflected, though only reflected, in it?'[88] Especially when applied to passages such as Ephesians 5.25f., Titus 3.5, Galatians 3.27, and Romans 6.3f., the sharpness of the distinction is very difficult to maintain.

In terms of dogmatic issues, two clusters of problems can be identified. First, does Barth have too 'individualistic' a notion of personal decision and of the life-world in which decisions are made?[89] Does the urgency with which Barth seeks to secure the inalienable character of human action lead him to lift the individual's act at the beginning of the Christian life from its embeddedness in the social realities of common discipleship? Mottu asks, for example: 'Are we always this subject which inaugurates and begins on its own? Are we not also made and constructed by a corporate totality which precedes us? Does the Ego ever exist without being incorporated from its birth into a social and cultural whole?'[90] At one level, the objection is rather hard to sustain: both in his earlier anthropology and ecclesiology and in his treatment of baptism here in paragraph 75, Barth makes constant reference to the corporate character of human being: 'At its very beginning, which is at issue in baptism, the Christian life, without detriment to its individual particularity, is a participation in the life of the Christian community.'[91] Barth is unwilling to surrender 'individual

---

[88] Ibid., p. 111.
[89] Cf. T. Rendtorff, *Ethics*, vol., 2 (Minneapolis, 1989), p. 118.
[90] H. Mottu, 'Les sacrements selon Karl Barth et Eberhard Jüngel', p. 51.
[91] IV/4, p. 131. This aspect of Barth is given considerable weight by N. Biggar in *The Hastening that Waits*, who seeks to establish the – admittedly controversial – point that Barth assigns to the church the role of being 'a school for the formation of Christian character' (p. 127). Though Biggar is correct to

particularity', however, over the question of the non-transferable character of faith, above all in the baptism of infants. Ultimately this is because for him faith is to be understood not simply in terms of its embodiment in social roles or its historical location in the tradition of a community, but in terms of its immediacy and directness as obedience to God. Barth's 'individualism' is not, therefore, a denial of sociality, nor some vestigial moral Cartesianism, but a conviction that growth into Christian moral selfhood involves personal acts of allegiance. Nevertheless, Barth's account of the corporate dimensions of Christian belief and behaviour will be thought by some to be decidedly thin; such critics may conclude that Barth is to some degree docetic in this regard, allowing his distaste for mere inherited Christianity to deflect his attention away from Christianity as a mode of social belonging.

A second question concerns the relation of divine to human action. Barth's rejection of sacramental mediation is made, as has been shown, in order to retain the proper mutuality of the covenant relation between God and humanity – in order, as Mottu puts it, to secure an understanding of the relationship between God and humanity as one of 'differentiated partnership'.[92] On this basis, he distinguishes God's action in baptism with the Holy Spirit from the human action of baptism with water. For many interpreters, Barth falls into a kind of dualism at this point,[93] 'spiritualising' baptism by undervaluing its worldly element, denying any capacity to creaturely action to participate in God, and disallowing that *a* sacrament can reflect *the* sacrament without replacing it.[94] From what has been said so

observe that Barth is not irreconcilably opposed to the idea of a continuous moral subject (such as is required by the notion of moral 'character'), he does not take sufficient account of Barth's hostility to the way in which the shaping influence of the *ecclesia* may eclipse the activity of God. Once again, Barth's 'negative ecclesiology' is ethically significant.

[92] Mottu, p. 42.

[93] Cf. T. F. Torrance, 'The one baptism common to Christ and his church', in *Theology in Reconciliation* (London, 1975), p. 99.

[94] C. C. West, 'Baptism in the Reformed tradition', p. 25. Cf. J. Macken, *The Autonomy Theme*, pp. 83–5.

far, and from the discussion of the relation of divine and
human action in *The Christian Life*, it soon becomes clear
that many of these anxieties are misplaced and may stem
from an inadequate appreciation of Barth's ethical intention.
T. F. Torrance's criticism of Barth's later baptismal theology
is a good example. Torrance regards the treatment of baptism in the ethics of reconciliation as a return to a 'sacramental dualism ... in which the meaning of baptism is not
found in a direct act of God but in an ethical act on the
part of man made by way of response to what God has
already done on his behalf'.[95] Such a development Torrance
holds to be 'deeply inconsistent' with Barth's doctrines of
the trinity and the incarnation.[96] His unease stems from his
own very powerful stress upon the vicarious humanity of
Christ, according to which 'Jesus's human agency in vicarious response to the Father overlaps with our response,
gathers it up in its embrace, sanctifying, affirming and
upholding it in himself, so that it is established in spite of
all our frailty as our free and faithful response to the Father
in him.'[97] Though at many points Barth will say similar
things, his real divergence from Torrance concerns the
covenantal character of the relation between God and
humanity, which Barth sees as ethically fundamental (in
that it affirms the inalienable difference-in-relation of God
and humanity), but which is obscured in Torrance's exclusive stress upon the vicarious character of Jesus' being and
act in relation to humanity. In Torrance's account of the
matter, Jesus' humanity threatens to absorb that of others;
in Barth's account, Jesus' humanity graciously evokes corresponding patterns of being and doing on the part of those
whom it constitutes.[98]

To charge Barth with 'dualism' here is to press the logic
of his account of the relation of God to humanity in ways

---

[95] T. F. Torrance, 'The one baptism', p. 99.
[96] Ibid.
[97] Ibid., p. 102.
[98] Further on Torrance here, see *The Mediation of Christ* (Exeter, 1983), pp. 83–
108; *The Trinitarian Faith* (Edinburgh, 1988), pp. 146–90.

which Barth – if what he says elsewhere is to be taken
seriously – would himself disallow. It is only when the texts
are read without an eye to their larger ethical intent that
they seem to be promoting a 'contrastive' account of divine
and human action.[99] However, Barth's separation of Spirit-
baptism from water-baptism may still be made unnecessarily
sharply (though, even here, Macken's judgment that Barth
'adopts an axiomatic disjunction between God's act and
man's' is much too strong).[100] It would not be impossible
to construct an account of Spirit-baptism and water-baptism
as a differentiated unity without threatening either the
uniqueness and incommunicability of the work of Jesus
Christ or the full reality of the human response. A carefully
phrased notion of sacramental mediation could allay Barth's
fears about overinflation of ecclesial activity and, at the
same time, avoid the overschematic separation of divine and
human work which afflicts his exegesis. Indeed, Barth's
pre-war writings on sacraments elaborate just such a notion
of mediation, insisting, with the classical Reformed tradition,
upon the rooting of any consideration of sacrament in Christology and pneumatology. What makes Barth lose confidence
in the cogency of such an account, it would seem, is partly
the use to which it can be put when pressed into the service
of a particular view of the church's relation to the civil
community. Yet the language of sacrament as 'means' or
'instrument' is not necessarily ruined by its association with
the abuses of indiscriminate baptism, and may still furnish
a reliable way of avoiding what Barth wishes to avoid
without sustaining his losses. Nor would such an account
exclude Barth's entirely appropriate insistence on the ethical
dimensions of Christian baptism, any more than the indica-
tives of Paul's theology of baptism (Romans 6.3–11) exclude
the consequential imperatives (Romans 6.12–23). At the
very last, the 'Chalcedonian' pattern is under some strain in
the baptismal fragment, as Barth's insistence upon 'without

---

[99] Cf. K. Tanner, *God and Creation in Christian Theology. Tyranny or Empowerment?*
(Oxford, 1988), p. 46.
[100] J. Macken, *The Autonomy Theme*, p. 80.

confusion' is not always explicitly balanced by appreciation of 'without separation'. Having lost heart about the way in which 'without separation' has been stated in the theology and – above all – the practice of the Reformed tradition, Barth leaves himself exposed to the charge of having broken away from the delicate pattern through which human history and action are savingly incorporated into the work of God. If Barth presses for a sharp distinction, it may be because, fearful of intolerable losses in the ethical realm, he too narrowly restricts the options, reads the theology of sacramental initiation through the practices of civil religion, and so makes the moral consequences of Christian baptism into its material content.

CHAPTER SIX

The Christian Life

In the summer of 1926, Barth gave two Bible studies on Romans 12.1f. to German SCM students, transcripts of which were later published and translated under the title *The Christian Life*.[1] At a number of points, his exposition prefigures what he will say much later in the ethics of reconciliation lectures translated under the same title. The transition from indicative to imperative, the move to exhortation, is, Barth stressed, 'a perilous step';[2] 'the recognition of the immense peril of the undertaking must be allowed to work upon us'.[3] Why? Because, when we raise the question of 'our own human activity as Christians',[4] 'we are only too readily inclined to turn things upside down . . . and to answer the question about the Christian life in a way that views the matter equilaterally: God has done something for us, now it is up to us to do something for him'.[5] Barth's sketch of the Christian life is, in other words, shaped by a strong assertion that 'the two sides in the relationship are not on [sic] an equality'.[6] But alongside this there is another affirmation: our non-equality to God does not signify our obliteration. And so 'the question about

[1] K. Barth, *The Christian Life* (London, 1930). For parallel material from around the same period, see the 1929 lectures *The Holy Ghost and the Christian Life* (London, 1938), and somewhat later *The Knowledge of God and the Service of God* (London, 1938), pp. 113–47, especially pp. 136–47.
[2] *The Christian Life* (1930), p. 16.
[3] Ibid., p. 17.
[4] Ibid., p. 24.
[5] Ibid., p. 26.
[6] Ibid.

the Christian life as a question about what happens to us, about our little Ego, is a special one that very well deserves to be asked! In raising this question we are loyal and true.'[7] And why is the question important? Because the Christian life has an eschatological setting, standing between achieved reconciliation and expected redemption:

The Apostle Paul ... did not speak to the perfect and the redeemed, but to the reconciled, to men who have heard the word of faith but who, dwelling in this temporal state, have not yet taken down the tent, who still await the habitation which is in heaven. This is the situation in which we are also! And when we pass over into the position in which we are exhorted and in which we allow ourselves to be exhorted, this transition, far from meaning that we have a conceit of ourselves, could rather mean that we honestly understand that God is only on the way with us.[8]

These three themes – the asymmetrical relation of divine and human agency, the significance, nevertheless, of discussion of human action, and the eschatological frame of the Christian life – all recur in Barth's last dogmatics lectures as he reflects on the introductory invocation and the first two petitions of the Lord's Prayer, which provide the structure for paragraphs 76–8 of the *Church Dogmatics*.

'A LIFE IN THIS VOCATIVE'

Barth begins his exposition of paragraph 76 with a remarkable series of short meditations on one word: *'Vater!'* 'Father!' As the meditations proceed, he unfolds his intention of showing how the *lex orandi* implies a *lex credendi*, which in turn we see to contain a *lex agendi*:

The Lord's Prayer is, in the words of Tertullian, a breviary of the whole gospel. It invites us in a unique fashion to apply the old adage that the law of prayer is the law of faith. We shall here accept this invitation by understanding the law of faith that is implicit in the law of prayer, and is to be taken from it, as a

---

[7] Ibid., pp. 20f.
[8] Ibid., pp. 19f.

law of life, a criterion by which to answer our question concerning the obedience required of Christians.[9]

'*Father!*' Why is this vocative of such singular significance to Barth? When used in Christian thought and speech as a term for God, the word 'Father' is always to be employed and understood in the same sense that it has here in the introit to the Lord's Prayer, namely, as a vocative. This can and must be called the fundamental rule of its Christian use and understanding ... If the word is to have a Christian meaning and content, even in third-person statements it must be used in such a way that the function of the nominative as a *locum tenens* for the vocative is kept in mind and is indeed brought out in the nearer or more distant context of the statements concerned. If it is a matter of God, then seriously, properly, and strictly Christians cannot speak *about* the Father but only *to* him.[10]

Barth's point could be read as the rather bland one that the meaning of terms is context-dependent. But he is not, however, simply observing linguistic behaviour; rather, he is securing a theological conviction, that the specific *modus loquendi theologicus* is not mere linguistic eccentricity, but the form which language takes under compulsion from the divine realities which it articulates. A helpful parallel to Barth may be found in Luther's remarks on 'a new and theological grammar' of certain terms about human agency, made in the course of the lectures on Galatians first published in 1535. In his exposition of chapter 3, Luther comments that words such as 'working' or 'doing' perform a different function in different worlds of discourse:

'[D]oing' is one thing in nature, another in philosophy, and another in theology ... We have to rise higher in theology with the word 'doing' so that it becomes altogether new. For just as it becomes something different when it is taken from the natural area into the moral, so it becomes something much more different when it is transferred from the Law into theology. Thus it has a completely new meaning; it does indeed require right reason and a good will, but in a theological sense, not in a moral sense,

[9] *ChrL*, p. 50.
[10] Ibid., p. 51.

which means that through the Word of the Gospel I know and believe that God sent his Son into the world to redeem us from sin and death. Here 'doing' is a new thing, unknown to reason, to the philosophers, to the legalists, and to all men; for it is a 'wisdom hidden in a mystery' (I Cor. 2:7). In theology, therefore, 'doing' necessarily requires faith itself as a precondition.[11]

What makes Christian language distinctive is, however, a difference not simply of *use*, but of *reference*. There is for Luther a specifically 'theological grammar' of 'working' or 'doing', different from the 'moral grammar' of the same terms by virtue of its reference to the acts of faith. And so 'in theology they become completely new words and acquire a new meaning'.[12] The dogmatic groundwork of such a theological semantics is that, construed according to their 'theological grammar', words such as 'doing' or 'working' refer to the *invisibilia* of faith, not to the visible works of human agents: the theological grammar retains the priority of divine agency and thereby accords with and expresses a specific moral ontology. And so with Barth: the vocative 'Father!' is fundamental to the theological grammar of the word 'doing', since its case specifies both the priority of God as subject, and human subsequence in relation to him. In that Christian language about God is primordially vocative, it retains reference to the antecedent subjectivity of God. Invocation of God, then, is 'invocation of the self-acting Subject-Father'.[13] Vocative address of God brings to expression the priority of his active selfhood over the selves of those who invoke him in this way.

As Barth's meditation spirals around the word '*Vater!*' in its specifically Christian, vocative usage, he attempts to give language about divine paternity a very particular content not to be derived from its more familiar deployment in both religious and non-religious contexts. It refers to that which

---

[11] M. Luther, *Lectures on Galatians 1535. Chapters 1–4*, in *Luther's Works* vol. 26 (St. Louis, 1963), p. 262.

[12] Ibid., p. 267. Further on Luther here, see I. U. Dalferth, 'The visible and the invisible: Luther's legacy of a theological theology', in S. W. Sykes, ed., *England and Germany. Studies in Theological Diplomacy* (Frankfurt/M, 1982), pp. 15–44.

[13] *ChrL*, p. 53.

is absolutely singular, to a defining property of God as a self-subsistent being, and so in Christian usage gains a sense 'supremely transcending the most immediate sense of the term'.[14] The God who is invoked as Father may be so invoked because he *is* such. Divine paternity is not a postulate for Barth, a consoling or threatening projection. It is that 'which he *is*'.[15] Once again, Barth's morphology of Christian speech examines language as it were from the other end – from the controls set upon it by that to which it refers. Here is the root of what some would see as Barth's confidence, others as his *naïveté*, in handling a tradition of Christian language which, more than any other, has been criticised as thoroughly androcentric, and, in its ethical deployment, as encoding 'the morality of victimization'.[16]

For Barth, the concept of divine paternity is not necessarily hostile to human morality if we attend to its proper Christian usage and the origin of that usage in the divine self-naming. This argument is familiar from other places in his work, where he proposes that 'Father' is not to be construed as human naming, but as a predicate identifying that which properly (not merely by attribution or metaphorical transfer) belongs to God. Barth secures the point in a number of closely connected moves.

To begin with, he rejects any idea that 'Father' is 'a title, a label pasted on God',[17] since this is 'nominalism, that is, an attitude of man that allows him to dispose of God. From human experience we know what a father is and we apply this title to God.'[18] More closely, he refuses to concede that Christian language about God is generated by the projective and expressive activities of human speakers. Christian language about God derives rather from God's self-articulation.

[14] Ibid., p. 56.
[15] Ibid., p. 59.
[16] M. Daly, *Beyond God the Father. Toward a Philosophy of Women's Liberation* (Boston, 1985), p. 105.
[17] K. Barth, *The Faith of the Church. A Commentary on the Apostles' Creed according to Calvin's Catechism* (London, 1960), p. 36.
[18] Ibid., p. 37.

[I]t must not be said that the name 'Father' for God is a transference to God, figurative and not to be taken literally, of a human creaturely relationship, whereas God's essential being as God *per se* is not touched nor characterised by this name, nay, He is infinitely above being Father to us, indeed, is something different altogether. But what is figurative and not literal is that we characterise and imagine we know fatherhood in our human creaturely sphere.[19]

What Barth suggests here is a good example of what George Hunsinger identifies as Barth's rejection of 'expressivism', in which the origin and use of anthropomorphic language about God is *at our discretion*:

Expressivism thought of God's attributes as something to be postulated; Barth as something to be acknowledged. Anthropomorphic metaphors applied to God by scripture were for expressivism objectifications of emotive experience; for Barth they were depictions of an agent ... In short, for expressivism which metaphors and concepts to use was largely discretionary, emotively based and fraught with the corresponding uncertainty; for Barth which to use was largely obligatory, scripturally based and secured with corresponding confidence.[20]

Barth views Christian speech about God, that is, as a matter of 'God's self-analogization'.[21] Thus: the crucible for language about God is not its cultural or religious *use* nor willed or unconscious acts of *projection*, but *revelation*. The propriety of naming God by certain terms is warranted by God's revelation in Jesus Christ of his antecedent reality: 'God presents himself to me as the Father of this Son.'[22]

---

[19] K. Barth, *Credo* (London, 1936), pp. 23f. For a more extended account, see I/1, pp. 390–8. In a well-known essay, Pannenberg correctly notes that in Barth's understanding of analogical language about God 'the motive power is always transmitted from above to below', so that analogy is grounded 'both ontologically and noetically from God's side': 'Analogy and doxology', in *Basic Questions in Theology* vol. 1 (Philadelphia, 1970), p. 214 and n. 3.

[20] G. Hunsinger, 'Beyond literalism and expressivism: Karl Barth's hermeneutical realism', *Modern Theology* 3:3 (1987), 214f.

[21] Ibid., p. 215. See further E. Jüngel, 'Anthropomorphism: a fundamental problem in modern hermeneutics', in *Theological Essays* (Edinburgh, 1989), pp. 72–94.

[22] K. Barth, *Learning Jesus Christ through the Heidelberg Catechism* (Grand Rapids, 1981), p. 60.

This is why 'Jesus Christ is the source and warrant for the divine Fatherhood and our sonship.'[23]

Barth works with a highly 'realist' understanding of language of God as Father: 'when God the "Father" is called "our Father", we are thereby saying something about God that is valid, that is true, and true, moreover, in the deepest depths of his nature, true unto all eternity.'[24] This realism, however, depends partly upon resistance to filling out the term with content derived from other contexts, but most of all upon a confidence in the sufficiency of revelation: 'God expresses and represents himself adequately.'[25] Instead of human language reaching after its object, that is, revelation 'commandeers' language, *making* it into a fit instrument for God's self-articulation.[26]

On such a basis, *The Christian Life* proposes that the New Testament statements about God as Father describe

not the work of an unknown Almighty who can be pictured at will, but that of a very definite Almighty, whose work has a concrete character, the work of the father who wills to be and can be invoked, not in fear but in respect, that is, in a fear of God which is not frightened of him but honors him, in the authentic fear of trust in God. God is the Father who is the 'Father in Heaven' not merely as the living Lord of everything and all things but also as the one who is this with a specific intention, disposition, and purpose in relation to his household.[27]

As such, God is the 'dear Father', the one whose Fatherhood is made known as 'free Fatherly goodness'.[28] Again: behind the predicate lies the divine Subject; and

---

[23] K. Barth, *Prayer and Preaching* (London, 1964), p. 26. See also *Credo*, p. 20: 'according to the passages in scripture where the conception "Father" gets its most pregnant meaning, the revelation of God the Father is the revelation of God in His Son Jesus Christ through the Holy Spirit. Scripture explicitly calls it the *sole* revelation of the Father. Therefore it is exclusively in this place that we shall have to seek to understand decisively and finally the conception "Father".'

[24] K. Barth, *Dogmatics in Outline* (London, 1949), p. 43.

[25] *The Faith of the Church*, p. 37.

[26] See here Barth's treatment of the *vestigium trinitatis*, I/I, pp. 333–47, with E. Jüngel, *The Doctrine of the Trinity* (Edinburgh, 1975), pp. 5–15, and G. Hunsinger, 'Beyond literalism and expressivism', 216f.

[27] *ChrL*, p. 58.

[28] Ibid., p. 59.

the decision regarding the nature and existence of the Subject upon whom Christians call as Father cannot be their own affair – the affair of their own courage or concern – their own problem. This decision lies behind them: not as one they had to make, nor as one which they had to win through either casual resolution or more or less severe intellectual and moral battles and traumas, nor as a commitment that might later be reconsidered, that would indeed have to be reconsidered like all the human decisions we make. Rather, it is a decision that has been made irrevocably at a very different place . . .[29]

Invocation of God as Father is thus neither an arbitrary nor a self-willed human venture, but that which is permitted and commanded by God in Christ. Christians therefore 'come from the decision which is taken in him [Christ] with divine authority concerning the existence of the Subject, God the Father, when, without fear of looking in the wrong directions or even in the void, they venture to cry, "Abba, Father" '.[30]

What is the significance of this *lex orandi* for the *lex agendi*? Is the language of divine paternity necessarily hostile to morality? To grasp Barth's answer, we need to attend carefully to the full range of what he has to say.

On the one hand, Barth insists that the Christian life, whose determining motif and primary form is invocation of God as Father, is all along the line taken up with God the 'self-acting Subject', and only secondarily with human subjectivity and action. This insistence is particularly forceful in the second part of paragraph 76 (*The Christian Life*, pp. 69–85), where Barth turns from 'the Father' to consider 'the children of the Father'. The section offers an extended reflection upon the gracious character of the relation of God's children to the Father:

The freedom of the children of God to do what they are commanded to do is purely and simply the work and gift of the grace that is addressed to them and recognized by them. Because it is grace, the freedom cannot be one that is inherited or won. On any other basis and with any other origin it would be a pretended

---

[29] Ibid., p. 62.
[30] Ibid.

and false freedom, a secret and even an open non-freedom. Grace is the presence, event, and revelation of what man cannot think or do or reach or attain or grasp, but of what is, in virtue of its coming from God, the most simple, true, and real of all things for those to whom it is addressed and who recognize it.[31]

In line with earlier discussions of freedom, Barth insists upon a 'true freedom grounded in the grace of God',[32] *toto caelo* different from 'the counterfeit freedom originating in an intrinsic or achieved human worthiness'.[33] The freedom to invoke God as Father, and thus the moral freedom to dispose of oneself in obedience to God, is given, a possibility for human persons only on the basis of Christ's incarnational union with humanity:

In him they [those who invoke God] have all acquired a Brother, who even though he was and is in this great distinction, still was and is so – what a promise is this! – as the Son of God who for their sake became and was and is the Son of Man. Their Brother, who did what he did and was what he was, not for himself alone but also for them! He did it and was it in their place . . . Divine sonship, and with it . . . the freedom to call upon God as Father, became and was in him a present event for all men of all times and places.[34]

The authorisation and entitlement to call upon God is 'In him! Not outside him! Not without him!';[35] here, at the root of human agency, we have to do with 'the inconceivable and uncontrollable grace of God and its gift'.[36]

But, on the other hand, it would be a mistake to think that, by deploying the notion of the Word's assumption of humanity in this way, Barth disrupts the sense of the substantiality of human persons as historical subjects and agents which, in the end, he is seeking to maintain. It would be possible to read what Barth says here about divine subjectivity and grace as standing in contrast with the lan-

[31] Ibid., pp. 71f.
[32] Ibid., p. 72.
[33] Ibid., pp. 72f.
[34] Ibid., p. 75.
[35] Ibid.
[36] Ibid.

guage of action and responsibility in the earlier doctrine of baptism. Or, again, it would be possible to consider that Barth's refusal of any but the most restricted sense of human continuity ('That they have God as their Father and may be his children is not an ongoing history in the same way as the relationship between people is, for it can be an ongoing history only in pure miracles')[37] as taking him perilously close to moral atomism or occasionalism. Or again: there is a series of statements in which Barth presses the logic of divine grace to a point where he seems to undermine any sense of human maturity, apparently using the language of paternity to reinforce regression into helpless moral passivity:

[T]hose who through God's grace . . . have the freedom to call upon God as their Father will never once . . . encounter God except as those who are inept, inexperienced, unskilled, and immature, as little children in this sense too – little children who are totally unprepared for it.[38]

All human errors and aberrations can be compensated for and made good, but not the inordinate desire of one who in calling upon God wants to meet him, and thinks he can meet him, in more imposing fashion than as a newly registered pupil.[39]

The glory, splendour, truth, and power of divine sonship, and of the freedom to invoke God as father, and therefore the use of this freedom – the Christian ethos in big and little things alike – depends at every time and in every situation on whether or not Christians come before God as *beginners*.[40]

[A]s these people who are inept, inexperienced, unskilled, and immature, as these newborn babes (1 Pet. 2.2), they *are* dear children of the dear Father.[41]

In the sphere of the fulfilment of the covenant the decisive people are not the tested masters but the unproved pupils.[42]

[37] Ibid., p. 78.
[38] Ibid., p. 79.
[39] Ibid.
[40] Ibid., p. 80.
[41] Ibid.
[42] Ibid., p. 81.

In his review of the original Swiss edition of *The Christian Life*, C. C. Dickinson objected with some exasperation that

> Barth's injunction to be 'childish' and indeed 'infantile', especially when stated so undialectically, just as easily and fatally falls into the hands of just such authoritarian Christians who would and do use it to keep other Christians from a Christian *sapere aude!*, from making free, unfettered, and autonomous use of their own independent reason. Such injunction flies directly into the face of such passages as Gal. 4.1–7, Rom. 8.14–17, and Heb. 5.12–14, 6.1, and is absolutely fatal to any attempt, pastoral or otherwise, to nurture or even sanction a Christian or any other form of what is absolutely essential to healthy life, namely maturity.[43]

The mistake here is the suggestion that Barth is 'undialectical': indeed, everything hangs on a just appreciation of the dialectic of Barth's argument. For Barth does, in fact, succeed in combining his unqualified insistence upon dependence on grace and his assertion that the covenant is 'a covenant which God did not just establish between himself and man but in which man was called and impelled to play his own free and active part.'[44] And his ability to do this is a function of the complexity and flexibility of his Christology. The entire meditation on the vocative structure of Christian ethics is undergirded, not by a single insistence on 'Christ in our place', but by two interlocking Christological–anthropological affirmations. First, there is an account of Christ's relationship to humanity whose guiding motif is that of the vicarious humanity of Christ. Christians are enabled to call upon God as Father by virtue of their

---

[43] C. C. Dickinson, 'Church Dogmatics IV/4', in H.-M. Rumscheidt, ed., *Karl Barth in Re-View* (Pittsburgh, 1981), p. 51. Rather curiously, Dickinson suggests that Barth's language of immaturity, which rests on a notion of God as paternal despot, could have been corrected had J. Jeremias' interpretation of 'Abba' been available to him (see J. Jeremias, 'Abba', in *The Prayers of Jesus* (London, 1967), pp. 11–65; the original appeared in 1966). Jeremias certainly argues that to regard 'Abba' as 'the chatter of a small child' is 'a piece of inadmissible naivety' (ibid., p. 62). But no less than Barth, he insists on human dependence on Christ for the entitlement to address God in this way: 'the cry of "Abba" is beyond all human capabilities, and it is only possible within the new relationship with God given by the Son' (ibid., p. 65).

[44] *ChrL*, p. 74.

election as children in the Son, in the benefits of whose assumption of humanity they share. The vocative 'Father!', and the moral acts which correspond to it, thus point beyond the action of the one who invokes, not only to the antecedent subjectivity of God, but also to Jesus Christ's own invocation of the Father, in which the covenant obligations are fulfilled in our stead.

Alongside this vicarious humanity model, however, there is a complementary account of Christ's relationship to humanity as *generative* and *exemplary*. Thus Barth can write that Jesus Christ 'founded calling on God the Father – and made it binding on his people – by doing it first himself, and in so doing giving a prior example of what he demanded of them, or rather, demanding it of them by himself doing it. He took them up into the movement of his own prayer.'[45] Here the two models are brought together: Christ's invocation is both vicarious ('he took them up into the movement') and that which enables and elicits further invocation ('demanding it of them by himself doing it'). At several points in the discussion, the same feature surfaces. Jesus Christ is one who 'enables, invites, and summons' invocation of the Father; Christians pray 'according to the permission, command, and order of Jesus Christ'.[46] Again, the Christian life is spoken of as 'fulfilling this movement [of Christ's own prayer] after him and with him'; Jesus Christ 'not only was but is here and today the man who exists in that movement to the Father, calling upon the Father in the place and at the head of all men'.[47] The expansive phrasing ('enables, invites, and summons', etc.) are not simply examples of Barth's frequent use of reduplication as an emphatic device; rather, they are a means of identifying the range of ways in which we are to conceive of the relationship of Christ's humanity to our own. Barth's Christology, we may now see, is considerably more diverse than is often assumed.

[45] Ibid., p. 64.
[46] Ibid., p. 63.
[47] Ibid., p. 64.

On the whole, the weight tends to fall on the vicarious humanity model in the earlier sections of paragraph 76, so that what Barth calls 'the evangelical imperative' ('Pray then like this') tends to be subsumed under the indicative of our participation in the invocation of Christ who is in our stead. Nevertheless, as he moves on to consider invocation as human action in paragraph 76.3, the complementary empha-sis registers more strongly.[48] We have already noted Barth's insistence upon prayer as human action: both Barth's dis-cussions of prayer in the doctrine of creation return rather frequently to the point,[49] most especially to the mysterious, indeed, miraculous reciprocity between God and humanity to which petitionary prayer testifies: 'the Christian is able to ask'.[50] Once, that is, we admit the propriety of 'asking' in our relationship to God, we already presuppose a duality of agency and disqualify any notion of divine sole causality. And, moreover, asking is rooted not in fear but in freedom:

Christian petition ... is simply the taking and receiving of the divine gift and answer which is already present and near to hand in Jesus Christ. In this gift and answer we have to do with the will of God not only over but with the creature. We have to do with His covenant with man. We have to do with His grace directed towards man as an autonomous being distinct from him-self. We have to do with His work, which in man has an animate and not an inanimate subject. We have to do with His Word, which man can hear and answer. In short, we have to do with the freedom in which man himself can live. In this freedom the Christian takes and receives that which God is and does for him, that which God offers him. In this freedom the Christian asks.[51]

As Barth takes up the theme of invocation in *The Christian Life*, the same theme surfaces again:

[48] The same feature can be seen in the latter sections of paragraphs 77 and 78. Barth nearly always tends to structure his arguments in this field by making first a statement about grace and only then a statement about human action (most obviously in the overall structure of paragraph 75, in which the treatment of Spirit-baptism precedes that of water-baptism).

[49] III/3, pp. 265–88; III/4, pp. 87–115. On this theme, see O. Herlyn, *Religion oder Gebet?* (Neukirchen, 1979).

[50] III/3, p. 269.

[51] Ibid., p. 274.

What God the Father wills with and for us to his own glory and
our salvation is more than a solid but stationary relation or a
firm but passive connection. He is the living Father of his living
children. What he wills with and for these children is, therefore,
history, intercourse, and living dealings between himself and them,
between them and himself. They too have to enter into these
dealings on their side. They have to actualize the partnership in
this history. They have to express in word and deed his fatherhood
and their sonship. This is why he calls upon them and commands
them to call upon him.[52]

Many of the strands of the earlier discussion of human
agency in the context of baptism with water recur in Barth's
account of invocation as a human act. Of these, perhaps
the most important is that of the community of agency
between God and humanity. Because invocation 'aims at
the renewal, or rather, the dynamic actualization, of what
has become a static, stagnant, and frozen relationship',[53] it
expresses the fact that the history of God and humanity is
a history with two subjects and agents. Alongside the Son's
calling upon the Father in our stead, there is also 'the
invocation of God by his children', an action which is 'an
integral part of the history of the covenant between God
and men'.[54] The agency of Christ is not, therefore, inhibitive
of all other agency. There is something 'beyond what he
has done and does for all men in him – which is 'the human
factor and element in this history'.[55] Consequently, 'the grace
of God is the liberation of these specific people for free,
spontaneous, and responsible co-operation in this history':[56]

[T]he God who is known as 'our Father' in Jesus Christ is not this
supreme being who is self-enclosed, who cannot be codetermined
from outside, who is condemned to work alone. He is a God who
in overflowing grace has chosen and is free to have authentic and
not just apparent dealings, intercourse, and exchange with his children. He is their free Father, not in a lofty isolation in which he

---

[52] *ChrL*, p. 85.
[53] Ibid.
[54] Ibid., p. 102.
[55] Ibid.
[56] Ibid.

would be the prisoner of his own majesty, but in his history with them as his free children whom he himself has freed. He does not just speak to them. He wills that he also be spoken to, that they also speak to him. He does not just work on and for them. As the Founder and the perfect Lord of this concursus . . . he wills their work as well. He for his part will not work without them. He will work only in connection with their work.[57]

It is crucial to Barth's point here that such an affirmation of the community of action between God and humanity does not entail the *limitation* of divine freedom, but rather its *specification*. A God 'condemned to work alone' is a prisoner of his own sovereignty. For Barth, however, God is not 'so omnipotent, or rather, so impotent, that as they call upon him, liberated and commanded to do so by him, he will not and cannot hear them, letting a new action be occasioned by them, causing his own work and rule and control to correspond to their invocation'.[58] And so, 'it is very proper for him . . . to let his action be co-determined by his children who have been freed for obedience to him'.[59]

The boldest feature of Barth's account here is the further refinement of the language of 'correspondence'. Earlier, he has talked of the activity of God as that which evokes human correspondences; now he reverses the direction, suggesting that to the human act of invocation there corresponds the divine act of hearing:

When God's children invoke him as Father, this is in no sense a venture, a mere gesture, a shot in the dark, an experiment, or a gamble. They do this as those who have a part in the history in which God is their partner and they are his partners, in which they are liberated for this action and summoned to it, in which there is also given to them the promise of his corresponding action and therefore of his hearing.[60]

[W]hen they pray on this ground . . . this cannot be done in uncertainty, hesitation, or doubt . . . but only with the confidence

---

[57] Ibid., p. 103.
[58] Ibid.
[59] Ibid., p. 104.
[60] Ibid.

that the Father, who *is* the Father, and they *are* his children, will hear and answer, corresponding to their action with his.[61]

He hears them . . . in such a way that he is to them the Greater, the Lord. It is as such that he corresponds to their invocation. Yet he does correspond to it; he hears and answers it.[62]

What is most striking here, and in other examples that could be adduced, is that prayer is a real movement from humanity to God. Clearly, it is a movement whose ultimate origins lie beyond the human agent in the gracious provision of God: we do not pray in our own name. Yet the expectation of hearing presupposes that we are not only recipients, but those who call, and whose calling is not in vain because it evokes the action of the divine Father.

A parallel may help to make the point. The basic theological intentions of the argument here are in many respects similar to those of H. H. Farmer's discussion of prayer in *The World and God*. Farmer suggests that revelation (as the action of God upon human selves) and prayer (as the responsive action of human selves to such action) are fundamental to any account of God and humanity as indissolubly personal:

To be livingly aware of God's approach to the soul as personal is not possible without there being some response which is already of the order of prayer; and to pray a prayer which is in the least degree lifted above the mere mechanical repetition of formulae is not possible without there being some sense of one's own life having significance for an ultimate reality of an actively personal kind. We confront here that duality or tension which is necessary to constitute a relationship specifically personal.[63]

Farmer was particularly cautious about the elimination of petition from prayer (from whatever motives) because of the ease with which that may lead us to jettison a dialogical account of God and humanity as persons in relation, in

---

[61] Ibid., p. 105.
[62] Ibid., p. 106.
[63] H. H. Farmer, *The World and God* (London, 1936), p. 129.

favour of some sort of 'impersonalistic monism'.[64] Petition
secures a place for humanity as actively participating in its
relation to God, since 'prayer ... must have act and will
at the centre of it'.[65] And so, ultimately, to talk about prayer
as an activity of human selves is to register the *status* of
humanity before God: 'so far from being a primitive immaturity', petitionary prayer 'is bound up with man's status
as a personal being called to find his true maturity in the
harmonizing of his will with God's'.[66]

Barth's idiom is obviously different – Christology and
covenant rather than 'personality' – but his underlying concern matches that of Farmer, namely a sense that prayer
as petition entails an affirmation of the creature as a voluntary self in relation to God. As the God who responds to
prayer,

[i]n his free grace God purges himself from the base suspicion
that he is an unchangeable, untouchable, and immutable deity
whose divine nature condemns him to be the only one at work.
By God's free grace these people are not marionettes who move
only at his will. They are given the status of subjects who are
able and willing to act, able and willing to do what is appropriate
to them in dealing with him, able and willing to call upon him
as the Father of Jesus Christ and therefore as their Father and
also as the Father of all men. In his free grace he orders them
to do what he has freed them to do, namely, to call upon him
as Father. By God's free grace, what they do when they obey his
command, their 'Abba, Father', becomes the basic act of the
Christian ethos.[67]

In sum, what has Barth said about 'life in this vocative'?
Such a life is 'miraculous', a fruit of the gratuity of the
Father's self-bestowal, and in no sense an extension or
modulation of our natural history, and therefore a matter
of *astonishment*. 'Only with great surprise, profound amaze-
ment, and even consternation and fright can one speak of
the fact that there may and should be this calling upon

[64] Ibid., p. 131.
[65] Ibid., p. 135.
[66] Ibid., p. 137.
[67] *ChrL*, p. 102.

God by Christians as his children', for 'we stand before the mystery of the covenant – in its own way no less a mystery than that of the incarnation and resurrection of the Lord'.[68] That there should be this form of life which wholly transcends our expectations of the possibilities of worldly occurrence is rooted in the activity of the Holy Spirit, that is, in the self-manifestation and self-giving of the risen Jesus Christ. 'In the Holy Spirit God has dealings with these people in such a way that he cannot continue to act one-sidedly.'[69] But if the Christian life is thus ec-centric, it is no less an ongoing 'life-history', and no mere series of unrelated eruptions of divine grace.[70] Once again: a consistent interpretation of the statement 'God is' will of necessity include a statement about the active life of Christian obedience, since:

It is his free grace alone – the grace they always need – that he wills to conduct those dealings, that intercourse and exchange with them, in such a way that he makes them his partners and himself their partner, that he forges so close a link between their invocation and his answering, their action and his. He willed this and did it when he brought them to know himself as Father and called them his children. In doing so he blocked the way back to the fiction that they were dealing with a self-enclosed deity that worked alone.[71]

'HALLOWED BE THY NAME!'

Father, do what thou alone canst do. See to it finally, perfectly, and definitively that thou and thy name are known – only known, and no longer in any place or to any person unknown. See to it that thy name is no longer desecrated but always and by everybody regarded as holy in the way that it is in fact holy as thy name that thou thyself hast sanctified. Dispel the fatal ambivalence of our situation.[72]

---

[68] Ibid., p. 89.
[69] Ibid., p. 90.
[70] Ibid., p. 94.
[71] Ibid., p. 105.
[72] Ibid., pp. 115f.

Thus Barth's paraphrase of the first petition of the Lord's Prayer which provides the text for paragraph 77 of *The Christian Life*, under the rubric 'Zeal for the Honour of God'. He expounds that petition as a cry to God to put to an end the regime of ambiguity, hesitancy, and vacillation in respect of God which characterises the public history of the world, the life of the Christian community, and above all the personal life of the Christian believer. Early in the exposition, it becomes evident that Barth does not envisage the putting aside of this 'ambiguous, divided, and ambivalent situation' as simply the work of God, as a divine self-sanctification;[73] it is also a call to God's covenant partners to assume responsibilities, involving a purposive redirection of the human will. Paragraph 77 falls, therefore, into the familiar structure which reflects the overarching concerns of the ethics of reconciliation: after a brief introduction on 'the great passion' of Christians for the honour of God (paragraph 77.1), 77.2 describes the situation of ambivalence; 77.3 describes God's act of hallowing his own name; 77.4 indicates the corresponding human ethos which flows from God's achievement.

Christians pray for the hallowing of God's name in a situation of ambivalence. That is to say, the context for their prayer is not the complete desecration of the name of God: Barth does not allow that ignorance of God is an absolute state of affairs parallel to God's self-sanctification. Rather, the situation in which 'God's intrinsically holy name is widely desecrated'[74] is, as it were, enclosed within a larger, more all-encompassing reality – the fact that God has *already* achieved the hallowing of his own name, and thereby eradicated the possibility, if not the absurd 'reality', of ignorance of God:

He is the God who in his concealment is not absent but present, not veiled but manifest. God is not anonymous. He has a name. He has made himself a name. He has made it known as his holy

[73] Ibid., p. 115.
[74] Ibid.

name. He has already hallowed it. He has already invested it
with honour, validity, radiance, and glory.[75]

As Barth traces through this ambiguity in the three spheres
of the world, the church and the individual Christian, it is
very important to recognise his idiosyncratic use of the term
'knowledge'. He distinguishes between 'objective knowledge'
and the 'subjective knowledge' which corresponds to it.
'Objective knowledge' is best thought of as the revelation
of the truth and reality of God in relation to the creaturely
world, which as such is independent of the subjective apprehension or appropriation of that revelation by human know-
ers (that is, independent of what we might more usually call
'knowledge'). This highly objectivist account of knowledge is
clearly an entailment of a prior conviction that God's act
of self-manifestation is noetically fundamental and has priority over the functioning or malfunctioning of human cognition or consciousness. Thus Barth argues that, in all three
spheres, the objective knowledge of God has cognitive precedence over the absence of its realisation in subjective acts
of knowing. As a result, the prayer for the hallowing of
God's name receives its orientation from God's accomplished
hallowing of his own name: it is not a prayer that God
will, as it were for the first time, hallow his own name, but
a prayer that God will finally establish in the subjective
realm that this hallowing has already and definitively
occurred in Jesus Christ.

Of the three forms of vacillation, we look at the world's
desecration of the name of God as an example of Barth's
pattern of argument. God is both known and unknown in
world history. God is 'very well known',[76] not simply through
Christian witness, but primarily through the objective orientation of humanity to God as Creator, for 'God has already
made himself known in his free grace, and already hallowed
his name . . . when it pleased him to determine for himself
and orient to himself the nature of man, his human essence,

---

[75] Ibid.
[76] Ibid., p. 119.

in its irreversibly good creation.'[77] In this 'hallowing', we have to do with 'the objective knowledge of God' to which 'there does not correspond with any reliability or continuity a subjective recognition and knowledge on the world's part'.[78] Crucially, however, Barth refuses to accord to this lack of subjective knowledge any kind of status: 'in all the secularity of his world as it is marked by man's subjective refusal, victoriously contradicting its contradiction, he is already as its Creator the God who is objectively well known to it'.[79] His ultimate reason for this is Christological: 'As we search for a knowledge of God in the world that is unequivocally achieved both objectively on God's side and subjectively on man's, as we look for a point where his name might be clearly and distinctly hallowed on *both* sides in and for the world, we can think only of the one Jesus Christ.'[80] Moreover, Jesus Christ's subjective realisation of the objective knowledge of God is inclusive; it includes all within its scope, thereby relativising ignorance of God – whether theoretical, practical or religious – by making it into an absurd contradiction of what is truly the case about us:

[H]e lived and lives for all men in the place of all. All people, therefore, are elected, justified, sanctified, and called in him. In his knowledge of God a decision is made concerning theirs. Their knowledge of God is enclosed in his. In him they too are men of God, and they are infallibly and irrevocably confronted with the God of man as their God too. Hence none among them has any reason or right to exist without the knowledge of God. In relationship to him, the world of humans must be defined as the world in which God has made himself known once and for all to all mankind and is thus once and for all well known to all men. Now that God has made himself known within the world in Jesus Christ, ignorance of God has been fundamentally outdated. It has become a brute fact devoid of all meaning or basis.[81]

---

[77] Ibid., p. 120.
[78] Ibid., p. 123.
[79] Ibid., p. 121.
[80] Ibid., p. 123.
[81] Ibid., p. 125.

In this situation, characterised by the continued presence of that ignorance of God which has already been set aside, what does it mean to pray for the hallowing of God's name? A number of things in Barth's answer to this question need to be noted.

First, the petition is a petition that God himself should sanctify his own name: even though paragraph 77.4 will talk at length of corresponding human acts of hallowing, there remains a proper sense in which the work of God is incommunicable:

[God] is himself asked to sanctify himself (since it is his name), to take into his own hands the matter of his outward differentiation, distinction, and honour, to bring about the triumph of the knowledge of himself over all the darkness of ignorance of himself. It is no mere question ... of a sanctifying of his name that will be done by those who know and confess him, which will be a work of the church and Christians ... what is at issue is the sanctifying of the name of God which is not our work but God's, so that we can only pray that it will take place.[82]

This point is reinforced when we remember that what is being prayed for here is no 'mere shift in the relationship between light and darkness, a mere expansion and increase in the knowledge of God and a corresponding decrease in the ignorance of God in the world',[83] but 'a total and definitive action'[84] which finally eradicates ignorance of God by manifesting that, in Jesus Christ, God was at work, 'dispersing the darkness, removing any relation of light to it, establishing the sole sovereignty of light, of the knowledge of God'.[85]

Immediately the question arises: if this complete hallowing of God's name has already taken place in Jesus Christ, in what sense is it a matter for whose fulfilment we are to pray? In line with Barth's familiar twofold affirmations in the area of eschatology, we need to say two things. First,

[82] Ibid., p. 158.
[83] Ibid., p. 159.
[84] Ibid., p. 160.
[85] Ibid., pp. 162f.

Jesus' life-history is 'the unique and definitive act whereby God himself hallows his name', and so 'the end of all God's ways, the eschaton'.[86] But, second, we need also to affirm that

there are . . . two times – a once and a then, a yesterday and a tomorrow – of this one perfect act of God. Our time, our present in division, is the time between these two times of the one act, of the one Word of God spoken in this act. What has still to come for us in terms of the then, the tomorrow that is still future, is the revelation of what took place in the history of Jesus, validly, efficaciously, redemptively, and correctively for the world, the church, and each individual.[87]

But again, we may ask, if the hallowing of God's name for which we pray is God's own affair, and if its basis is the already accomplished hallowing of God in Jesus Christ, what space remains for human action? Does Barth's construal of our present history as 'between these two times' of accomplishment and definitive manifestation render our acts superfluous? The way in which Barth addresses this question is highly instructive for how he thinks of human agency.

At one level, Barth is setting limits to the significance of our acts by distinguishing them from God's overwhelmingly efficacious act. The Christological–eschatological frame within which Barth sets human action means, very simply that '[o]ur part – what is required of us – what we have to contribute and do in the matter, can indeed only be ours . . . [I]t can only be done in our human place and our human manner, only within the limits of our human capabilities and possibilities'.[88] Nevertheless, it is very important that Barth develops his eschatology in an *ethical* context, for by doing so he underlines that, whilst God's eschatological action is properly incommunicable, it does evoke analogous human acts. Prayer for God's act is not passivity: since it springs from God's setting aside of the realm of vacillation

[86] Ibid., p. 163.
[87] Ibid., p. 167.
[88] Ibid., p. 170.

already accomplished in Christ, that prayer entails 'a final and profound disquiet'.[89] For:

What took place then is full of critical dynamic, preventing any easy pacification among those who perceive it, and constituting an irrefutable veto of the compromise of an ambivalence of light and darkness, not only at that time, but on into our present time too.[90]

Thus what is commanded of us is not only 'to look and wait' but also to act: to 'move toward the . . . act and word of God' from which we come and in whose perfection we rest. What kind of action is this?

Christians are to act with a zeal for God's honour which 'corresponds and is analogous to his divine act';[91] their hallowing is 'analogous . . . to the hallowing of God's name for which we pray';[92] 'as little human acts' our acts are 'not like the great acts of the great God, yet still, for all the unbridgeable gulf between them, not just unlike but similar'.[93] That is, to the prayer for the eschatological hallowing of God's name on 'the great and final day . . . the sabbath day of the light of God which abolishes all the division of the present',[94] there corresponds a modest and yet utterly real activity:

Those who really press and involve God with this petition in the expectation that he will answer it, as people who are seriously and fundamentally disquieted and startled, press and involve themselves too in their own place and manner as people and within the limits of their own human capabilities and possibilities. They declare, and within their limits take on responsibility, that in the matter about which they pray to God something will be done correspondingly by them.[95]

The language of 'correspondence' serves initially to limit the range and significance of our activity: we act 'only in

89 Ibid., p. 164.
90 Ibid., p. 165.
91 Ibid., p. 170.
92 Ibid., p. 172.
93 Ibid., p. 173.
94 Ibid., p. 168.
95 Ibid., p. 169.

our human place and our human manner', and so there can be no question of taking over the divine role. 'What God commands of us when he bids us pray for the hallowing of his name is certainly not that we should want to act or be like him.'[96] When we pray, we *pray* – look, that is, to another, and renounce any pretence to absolutism. Analogous action is anticipatory, referring beyond itself and in no sense a realisation or embodiment of that which God uniquely does. In this light, Klauspeter Blaser's interpretation of Barth's notion of analogous human action as 'mediation historique' is surely too strong:[97] Barth would reserve such a term for the agency of the Holy Spirit, and would restrict human ethical action to the more limited sphere of anticipatory testimony.

In addition to limitation, however, the language of correspondence also serves to *characterise* our acts. Since our acts are not wholly dissimilar to God's great act of revolt against the regime of vacillation, Christians exist in revolt; they 'cannot come to terms and be satisfied with the status quo':[98]

[U]ndertaken in obedience and ventured with humility and resoluteness, it [our work] will not just be unlike God's act but also like it, running parallel to it on our level, a modest but clear analogue to the extent that it is directed against the abomination that has already been defeated and removed in God's completed act in Jesus Christ and which will be visibly shown before the eyes of all to be a shattered power in the manifestation of Jesus Christ as the goal of our path. It is to this action of resistance against the desecration of God's name that we are summoned – this action which even in its humanity is similar, parallel, and analogous to the act of God himself.[99]

More specifically, the shape of this life in resistance is giving precedence to the Word of God. The description is

[96] Ibid., p. 171.
[97] K. Blaser, 'L'Ethique en tant qu' "Invocation de Dieu"', in *Karl Barth 1886–1968. Combats – Idées – Reprises* (Bern, 1987), pp. 179, 181. J.-L. Blondel misreads Barth in the same way: 'Prayer and struggle: Karl Barth's "The Christian Life"', *St. Luke's Journal of Theology* 23 (1980), p. 114.
[98] Ibid., p. 173.
[99] Ibid., p. 175.

deliberately restrained, over against more exalted descriptions such as 'the *lordship* of God's Word' which Barth considers, but then lays aside:

The phrase 'precedence of God's Word' is perhaps a little weak, yet it is appropriate ... when our task is that of trying to understand and characterize zeal for God's honour very plainly as an action which may be ascribed to us people, which is humanly possible ... Would we not be guilty of doing something that is unfortunately all too frequent in the language of the church, namely, filling our mouths with grandiose speech, saying too little in too big words, if we were to tell Christians that they had to establish that lordship and practice that subjection in their own lives. Would this ... be asking for something ethically attainable, something they could and would practice? To allow and give the Word of God the precedence over other constitutive factors in their lives – that is something that *can* take place.[100]

'Precedence', moreover, acknowledges that the Christian's choice and resolution to honour God's name is a choice which does not ignore other claims, but is set in the midst of them. There can be no question of the reduction of the moral life to a single principle, adherence to which constitutes the whole sum of obedience to God. 'We are', Barth writes in an important qualification, 'presupposing that the other, equivocal factors will always be present in the life of the Christian, will always be at work and speak too, will always claim him in their own ways'.[101] Barth's hostility to the regime of vacillation does not deny that the Christian is addressed by a plurality of claims, nor does it recommend a single-minded, but ultimately artificial, elimination of all but one claim, that of God's Word.[102] Furthermore, the Christian's resolution to honour God above all things does

---

[100] Ibid., p. 178. I have altered the translation of the third sentence: the ET reads: 'Would this *not* be asking for something ethically attainable ...?' (italics mine), which reverses the sense of the original: 'Sagte man ihnen damit etwas ethisch Belangvolles, d.h. etwas, was sie *praktizieren* können und werden?' (*Das christliche Leben*, p. 300). For a similar statement on the need for restraint in describing human sanctity, see IV/2, p. 524.

[101] *ChrL*, p. 178.

[102] In this connection, see D. Emmet, 'Singlemindedness', in *The Moral Prism* (London, 1979), pp. 104–14.

not obliterate or render uninteresting other roles and relations: as a Christian, 'I live and think also as a man who in soul is constructed and talented thus and thus: as Homo sapiens, Homo faber, Homo ludens, as father, businessman, teacher, as patriot with obligations here or there, as thinker oriented more or less idealistically or more or less positivistically, as a man with this or that political or aesthetic gift, and simply as a sexual being with all that that implies.'[103] Set in this situation, necessarily and inescapably so, the Christian can only grant to God's claim 'the position that is its due at the head of all the factors that claim us, when we resolve at all costs to hear its claim first and only then, as determined by this claim, the claims of the other factors'.[104]

Barth's treatment of the first petition of the Lord's Prayer, then, ranges over some of the ways in which the Christian's deeds are limited, fragmentary, lacking in that finality and absoluteness which can be predicated only of God's perfect act and its coming glorious revelation. Yet, for just this reason, the Christian may not be excused from action. His or her acts are certainly 'interim steps', with 'no more than provisional and relative significance and range'.[105] But: 'one thing . . . [the Christian] will never have cause to do, namely to refrain from action like the lazy servant'.[106] The treatment of sin earlier in the doctrine of reconciliation, we may recall, contains a lengthy meditation on human sloth, a passage which is remarkable above all for its sober observation of human habit and of the sheer mediocrity to which men and women condemn themselves.[107] Against this background, Barth's insistence upon 'rebellion and resistance against the regime of vacillation'[108] takes on sharper contours:

[103] *ChrL*, pp. 179f.
[104] Ibid., p. 179.
[105] Ibid., pp. 180f.
[106] Ibid., p. 181.
[107] IV/2, pp. 403–83. On this theme, see further my essay ' "The firmest grasp of the real": Barth on original sin', *Toronto Journal of Theology* 4:1 (1988), 19–29.
[108] Ibid., p. 174.

The Christian would be no true man, or would know himself poorly in his humanity if, apart from all that he sees outside himself, he did not see the whole stream of his own human thought and feeling, desire and will, flowing down strongly to the ocean wastes of compromise between light and darkness. But the Word of God, which has made him a witness to the light without shadow, wants from him the big but not impossible thing that precisely as a person, no matter what may be the result, he should not flow with the stream, but that following the lead of the Word and accepting its discipline, he should continually swim against it.[109]

The Christian's counter-ethos repudiates 'the status quo, the law of the eternal recurrence of all things'.[110] Barth's refusal of fate is not couched in the language of heroism, nor is it detached from realistic appraisal of circumstance. But it does affirm that the eschatological orientation of the Christian life – its occupation of the midway between reconciliation and redemption – means that Christians more than any others are to encourage what William Walsh once called 'resistance by the person to the encroachment of the context'.[111] The final, and perhaps the most remarkable, paragraph of *The Christian Life* explores further how the Christian 'presents himself to other men of the world as a nonconformist, as one who is zealous for God's honour, as a witness to what he, who is also a man of the world, has to advocate to others of his kind. He does this by offering to them the image of a strangely human person.'[112]

'THY KINGDOM COME'

Barth explores the theme of Christian rebellion in the section on 'the lordless powers' early on in the final paragraph of *The Christian Life*. He begins from an observation which has been made earlier in the *Dogmatics* in looking at 'The Sloth

---

[109] Ibid., p. 187.
[110] Ibid., p. 180.
[111] W. Walsh, *The Use of Imagination* (London, 1964), p. 29.
[112] Ibid., p. 204.

of Man': sin is not simply Promethean.[113] Sin is not only
bold disobedience, but also the impoverishment and belittle-
ment of the sinner, the sinner's reduction to inactivity,
and thus a counter-movement to the life-in-act which grace
empowers and commands. The sinner seeks an identity in
abstraction from, and opposition to, God's good order. Such
is the deceit of sin that the sinner believes opposing God
to be the path to self-mastery; but 'in no case does this result
in him becoming the lord and master of the possibilities of
his own life'.[114] On the contrary: the sinner finds himself in
the same trap as Goethe's sorcerer's apprentice: surrounded
by 'spirits with a life and activity of their own, lordless,
indwelling forces',[115] the sinner finds that '[p]arallel to the
history of his emancipation from God there runs that of the
emancipation of his own possibilities of life from himself:
the history of the overpowering of his desires, aspirations,
and will by the power, the superpower, of his ability'.[116]

To be sure, he thinks he can take them in hand, control them,
and direct them as he pleases, for they are undoubtedly the forces
of his own possibilities and capacities, of his own ability. In
reality, however, they escape from him, they have already escaped
from him . . . They act at their own pleasure, as absolutes, without
him, behind him, over him, and against him . . . In reality, he
does not control them but they him. They do not serve him but
he must serve them. He is the more their football and prisoner
the less he is aware of the reversal that has long since taken place
between him and them, and the more he still rocks himself in
the illusion of his lordship and mastery over them. If we are to
see the disorder and unrighteousness which corrupt human life
and fellowship, we must not only not deny, but consider very
seriously, not merely man's rebellion against God, but also the
rebellion unleashed by it, that of human abilities, exalting themselves as lordless forces, against man himself.[117]

---

[113] IV/2, pp. 403–83.
[114] *ChrL*, p. 214.
[115] Ibid.
[116] Ibid.
[117] Ibid., pp. 214f.

Humanity without God, that is, *suffers*, loses its proper agency in grasping after omnicompetence. For his examples, Barth turns to the public worlds of politics, finance, and ideology, and – not without a trace of comedy – to the worlds of fashion, sport, and transport. The machinery of state may cease to serve and instead may control human interests, for example, ceasing to function as an instrument of common human purpose and instead become 'a lordless force'.[118] Money may cease to be a mere useful medium of economic exchange, and become 'an absolutist demon, and man himself can only be its football and slave. Mammon . . . is no reality, and yet it is one – and what a reality!'[119] And so what sinners have fashioned somehow comes to slip from their grasp, assuming a wilful and necessary life of its own:

[I]t is he [the human person] who is at the helm, who pulls the levers, who presses the knobs. Nevertheless, they automatically and autonomously rumble and work and roll and roar and clatter outside him, without him, past him, and over him. He finds that he himself is subject to their law, which he has foreseen, and to their power, which he has released. Turning aside from God, he is himself displaced, that is, jerked out of his proper position in relation to these forces into one that is unworthy of him.[120]

If such is the human situation, what is the implication for Christian ethics? Simply this: the Christian is freed by God to be a rebel against the lordless powers which oppress humanity and rob humanity of its dignity and freedom. The person of faith rejects the regime of necessity, not being satisfied with the passivity of the sinner under the sway of pseudo-forces; and so the person of faith acts in a way which witnesses to the disenchantment of the world by the mighty action of God. In face of the plight of humanity, Christians

118 Ibid., p. 221.
119 Ibid., p. 224.
120 Ibid., p. 228.

are commanded to … move against this plight, to enter into conflict with it … From the pressure of this plight, people, if they are not free, can and should become free again. It does not correspond at all to God's will for them but contradicts it. People who know God's will – and Christians should be such people – cannot in any circumstances accept this plight as an unalterable reality … In all circumstances the Christian is summoned and in a position to rise up against it, to enter into conflict with it.[121]

The language here is striking, especially when we bear in mind that what Barth has in view is state order as one of the 'lordless powers'. So that we do not over-read Barth here, two matters need to be noted.

First, what he says about Christian rebellion in *The Lordless Powers* needs to be read alongside his other writings on political order and rebellion. If what he has to say here seems initially somewhat surprising, it may be because Barth's theology of the state generally emphasises law, order, and political stability. A characteristic definition of the civil community runs: 'Political systems are the attempts undertaken and carried out by men in order to secure the common political life of man by certain coordinations of individual freedom and the claims of the community, by the establishing of laws with power to apply and preserve them. Political organisation means a system of law based on power, a system of power in honour of law.'[122] The need for such order is rooted in human perversity and disorderliness: 'What is at issue is the preservation of the common life from chaos.'[123] And the Christian community is 'particularly conscious' of the fact that 'all men … need to have "kings"',[124] since the Christian community 'knows of man's presumption and the plainly destructive consequences of man's presumption … it knows him as a sinner, that is as a being who is always on the point of opening the sluices through which, if he were not checked in time, chaos and

121 Ibid., p. 211.
122 'The Christian community in the midst of political change', in *Against the Stream. Shorter Post-War Writings 1946–52* (London, 1954), p. 80.
123 Ibid.
124 'The Christian community and the civil community', in *Against the Stream*, p. 19.

nothingness would break in and bring human time to an end'.[125] Furthermore, Barth gives a strong *theological* basis to this notion of state order, for the state is 'created in Christ, through Him and for Him',[126] and is one of the constants of divine providence. Indeed, Barth argues that it is possible 'to regard the existence of the State as an allegory, as a correspondence and an analogue to the Kingdom of God which the Church preaches and believes in'.[127] All of this may give the casual reader the impression that Barth's account of the state is exhausted in the notions of power and order and is, therefore, inherently *conservative*. The impression soon disappears, however, on closer analysis. State power and order are always and only 'external, relative and provisional',[128] and there can never be a direct identity between revelation and any existing set of political arrangements: 'The various political forms and systems are human inventions which, as such, do not bear the distinctive mark of revelation, and are not witnessed to as such – and can, therefore, not lay any claim to belief.'[129] Whilst state order is analogous to the kingdom of God, the analogy relativises as much as it legitimises state order, for the eschatological disjunction between the heavenly city and its earthly analogue is such that the heavenly city is 'not . . . an ideal but . . . a real State – yes . . . the only real State; not . . . an imaginary one but . . . the only one that truly exists'.[130] This lack of any unbroken connection between state and divine kingdom is underscored by a reality to which Barth gives considerable attention in a 1938 lecture on *The Church and the Political Problem of Our Day*, namely the possibility that the state can go beyond what Barmen V called its divine *ordinatio* and put forward 'a claim to be in itself an unmediated, a divine power – *the* divine power'.[131] One immediate

---

[125] Ibid., p. 20.
[126] *Church and State* (London, 1939), p. 30.
[127] 'The Christian community and the civil community', p. 32.
[128] 'The Christian community and the civil community', pp. 19, 22.
[129] Ibid., p. 25.
[130] *Church and State*, p. 38.
[131] *The Church and the Political Problem of Our Day* (London, 1939), p. 40.

implication here is that the 'subjection' to the state required in Romans 13.1 needs very careful specification. Subjection 'does not mean directly and absolutely "to be subject to someone", but to respect him as his office demands',[132] and 'cannot possibly consist of an attitude of abstract and absolute elasticity towards the intentions and undertakings of the state'.[133] Christian loyalty to the state is 'the obedience of a free heart'[134] – that is, *critical* loyalty which has its absolute object of commitment elsewhere, in the coming kingdom of God, and which can never regard the state as having a final claim.[135] But a further implication is that we may not exclude political rebellion as a proper Christian attitude to the state when it exceeds its divine *ordinatio* and ceases to act in accordance with the limits of its office. Such rebellion is positive and not anarchic, seeking to restore a just state order. Thus, whereas Barth allows for 'armed rising against a regime that is no longer worthy of or equal to its task', such revolt is 'undertaken not to undermine but to restore the lawful authority of the State'.[136] The rule, as Barth puts it neatly in a post-war essay, is: 'One must begin with Romans 13 and not with Revelation 13.'[137] And yet 'Christians would be neglecting the distinctive service which they can and must render to the State, were they to adopt an attitude of unquestioning assent to the will and action of the State which is directly or indirectly aimed at the suppression of the freedom of the Word of God ... Christians would, in point of fact, become enemies of any State if, when the State threatens their freedom, they did *not* resist, or if they concealed their resistance.'[138]

---

[132] *Church and State*, p. 64.

[133] Ibid., p. 66.

[134] 'The Christian community and the civil community', p. 24.

[135] This lies behind what Barth says about participatory democracy and 'adult' styles of political life in 'The Christian community and the civil community', pp. 37f, and *Church and State*, pp. 78–81.

[136] 'The Christian community and the civil community', p. 41; cf *The Church and the Political Problem of our Day*, pp. 68, 78.

[137] 'The Christian community in the midst of political change: documents of a Hungarian journey', in *Against the Stream*, p. 98.

[138] *Church and State*, p. 69.

Though it would not be impossible to read what is said in *The Christian Life* as a move away from the theology of the state in Barth's earlier writings, it is doubtful if such a reading would do justice either to the details of his thinking in the 1930s and 1940s, or to the nuances of what is said in these late texts, in which the themes of rebellion and resistance are given a very specific interpretation. Because Barth has a very particular kind of revolt in mind, he has a particular answer to the question: how can the *Christian* be a person in revolt? A rebel, says Camus, is 'a man who says no, but whose refusal does not imply a renunciation. He is also a man who says yes as soon as he begins to think for himself.'[139] Rebellion, that is, is concerned with the retrieval of the self and its worth; it 'cannot exist without the feeling that somewhere, in some way, you are justified . . . In every act of rebellion, the man concerned experiences not only a feeling of revulsion at the infringement of his rights but also a complete and spontaneous loyalty to certain aspects of himself.'[140] This is why, in Camus' account, grace and rebellion cannot co-exist:

The rebel is a man who is on the point of accepting or rejecting the sacrosanct and determined on creating a human situation in which all the answers are human, or, rather, formulated in terms of reason. From this moment every question, every word, is an act of rebellion, while in the sacrosanct world every word is an act of grace. It would be possible to demonstrate in this manner that only two possible worlds can exist for the human mind, the sacrosanct (or, to speak in Christian terms, the world of Grace) or the rebel world.[141]

The world of grace, the heteronomous, 'sacrosanct' world, is always a place of diminishment and bondage; revolt of necessity creates 'a situation in which all the answers are human'.

Like that of Camus, Barth's account – which is one of the few significant treatments of revolt in recent theological

[139] A. Camus, *The Rebel* (Harmondsworth, 1956), p. 19.
[140] Ibid.
[141] Ibid., pp. 26f.

literature[142] – is notable above all for the significance which it accords to human action. For Camus (following Scheler) revolt is quite different from resentment in just this respect. Resentment is passive, self-involved 'auto-intoxication' – 'the evil secretion, in a sealed vessel, of prolonged impotence'.[143] The mainspring of revolt, on the other hand, is 'the principle of superabundant activity and energy'.[144] So also for Barth: Christian revolt is not a mere defensive gesture; it does not 'curve in upon itself';[145] it is not simply negative or a mere rejection of one possibility. It is active 'entry into the struggle for the actualization of a very different possibility'.[146] For both Barth and Camus, then, revolt entails the repudiation of historical necessity, and a positive assertion of human work as necessarily involved in the bringing about of a very different reality.

A deep divide between Barth and Camus, however, can be seen over the question of the *limits* to human activity. For Camus, human autonomy is axiomatic: 'rebellion plays the same role as does the *cogito* in the category of thought: it is the first clue'.[147] For Barth, it is quite otherwise: the Christian's revolutionary protest against human diminishment and his or her human attempt to realise a different actuality is inseparable from the prayer: 'Thy Kingdom come!' In this act of invocation 'may be seen the limit which is set for the kingdom of human disorder – set by that other kingdom which in the form of the prayer for its coming is not only distant but also near and already present'.[148] If the Christian maintains that 'the unrighteousness

---

[142] For a further example, see a variety of essays by Donald MacKinnon: 'Prayer, worship and life', in Mackinnon, ed., *Christian Faith and Communist Faith* (London, 1953), pp. 242–56; 'Lenin and theology' and 'Law, change and revolution', in *Explorations in Theology*, vol. 5 (London, 1979), pp. 11–29, 30–54; and 'Power politics and religious faith', in *Themes in Theology* (Edinburgh, 1987), pp. 87–109.

[143] Camus, *The Rebel*, p. 23.

[144] Ibid.

[145] *ChrL*, p. 206.

[146] Ibid., p. 207.

[147] Camus, *The Rebel*, p. 28.

[148] *ChrL*, p. 234.

and powers that he has unleashed and which oppress and afflict him [cannot] establish a definitive situation or represent an ineluctable fate', it is only because the Christian has been given freedom to call upon God.[149] And 'the freedom to call upon God is authentic freedom, not one of the inauthentic freedoms that man usually arrogates to himself'.[150] Revolt, therefore, takes its rise, not in the actualisation or preservation of the self, but in God's decisive act, in what Donald MacKinnon once called 'God's own revolt against the world He made'.[151]

Because human revolt is rooted in prayer for the coming of the Kingdom of God, Barth provides a lengthy statement of the priority of divine action. 'Thy Kingdom *come*' – the verb is of great importance, furnishing a focal term in Barth's exposition of how God's decisive act in establishing the Kingdom relates to human acts. Prayer for the *coming* of the Kingdom presupposes that the Kingdom is not within the horizon of possibilities realised through human action. It is rather 'the great new thing on the margin – yet outside and not inside the margin of the great horizon of all the perceptions and conceptions of us people who are people of disorder'.[152] The Kingdom is in one sense without analogies; it 'defies expression'.[153] In ethical terms, this means that prayer for the coming of God's Kingdom encloses human work within the prior work of God. For the Kingdom is 'independent of human will and act and different from all human works and achievements into whose sphere it enters. It is God's own independent action which limits all human history from outside, which is sovereign in relation to it.'[154]

More concretely, prayer for the coming of God's Kingdom is a possible venture only on the basis of the presence of the Kingdom in the person and work of Jesus Christ. ' "The

[149] Ibid.
[150] Ibid.
[151] D. M. MacKinnon, 'Prayer, worship and life', p. 248.
[152] *ChrL*, p. 237.
[153] Ibid.
[154] Ibid., p. 240.

Kingdom of God is at hand" means "the Word was made flesh and dwelt among us".'[155] In a set of paragraphs of considerable rhetorical force, Barth insists on the Christological *Er* and *Damals* – the absolute, irreducible singularity of Jesus Christ's person and acts as not simply the signs but the embodiment of the Kingdom:

He is the mystery that cannot be imprisoned in any system of human conceptuality ... *He* is God acting concretely within human history. *He* is the one who calls those who know him to obedient willing and doing ... *He* is the total and definitive limitation of human unrighteousness and disorder ... *He* at that time was in his history, on the path that he trod to the end in his time, the imminent kingdom of God.[156]

We must emphasise the 'he' ... Simply and solely *he himself*: accomplishing and completing God's work for the salvation of the world, that is, its reconciliation to God; speaking without reservation or subtraction God's Word to all people without exception; *he*, this man in the history of his life and word and work and passion and death. Whoever knew and loved and proclaimed him knew and loved and proclaimed the imminent kingdom of God. Speaking about God's kingdom could only mean telling his story.[157]

The New Testament writings ... and with the New Testament writings the New Testament community, all look back to the past of the history of the coming of Jesus and to the past of the drawing near of the kingdom of God as to an incomparably and uniquely great *then* ... The *then* which in its inexhaustibility they keep before them either directly or indirectly as they look back to it is the presupposition of the prayer 'Thy kingdom come.' They could at any rate pray this prayer to the extent that they could know what they were saying in it because the kingdom and its coming were not empty words to them but were a known factor as they looked back to this *then*.[158]

In view of all this, is not Camus' critique irrefutable? Is it possible, in the face of Barth's insistence upon the perfec-

[155] Ibid., p. 249.
[156] Ibid., p. 252.
[157] Ibid., pp. 252f.
[158] Ibid., p. 253.

tion and incommunicability of divine action, to think of the
worlds of grace and human action as other than antithetical?
Does not the primacy of invocation call into question the
very ethos which it is supposed to ground?

Barth's response, implicit within the last pages of *The
Christian Life* in the section 'Fiat iustitia!', is a little less taut
than the preceding discussion. But it contains the elements
of two main lines of argument.

First, there is reiteration of a point made throughout his
various discussions of prayer: since it is itself a form of
responsible human action, prayer cannot be divorced from
ethos. When Christians pray 'Thy Kingdom come', 'then
necessarily with their hearts and lips, caught up by what
they pray, their whole life and thought and word and deed
are set in motion, oriented to the point to which they look
in their petition.'[159] Prayer is not mere consent, not only a
calling upon the strengths of another, but that which actual-
ises the will and energies of the Christian and sets them
upon a specific path. But second, and more importantly,
Barth tries to sketch a way in which the world of grace
and the rebel world can exist alongside and in relation to
each other, each with its own sphere of operation. For
Camus, the recovery of the human agent necessarily entails
the deposition of God; for Barth, the question is rather one
of distinguishing properly between God and humanity, in
that way restoring to humanity its proper, 'de-absolutised'
role as agent.[160] Barth seeks to construct an account of the
relation of God and humanity which refuses the antithetical
alternatives of autonomy and heteronomy, preferring to think
of a set of analogical relations between the action of God
and human acts. Thus, for example, he suggests that, alongside prayer to God to establish his Kingdom, there is also
a properly human struggle for a properly 'human, not divine
righteousness':

---

[159] Ibid., p. 262.
[160] On this theme in Barth, see E. Jüngel, ' "... keine Menschenlosigkeit
Gottes. . ." Zur Theologie Karl Barths zwischen Theismus und Atheismus', in
Barth-Studien (Gütersloh, 1982), pp. 332–47, especially pp. 344–7.

That the latter [the Kingdom of God] should come, intervene, assert itself, reign, and triumph can never be the affair of any human action. Those who know the reality of the Kingdom, Christians, can never have anything to do with the arrogant and foolhardy enterprise of trying to bring in and build up by human hands a religious, cultic, moral, or political kingdom of God on earth. God's righteousness is the affair of God's own act.[161]

But, as with the refusal of sacramental status to baptism with water, so here: the apparent restriction of the mediatory scope of human action is intended to the praise of that action as truly human, and not as quasi-divine:

[P]recisely because perfect righteousness stands before them as God's work, precisely because they are duly forbidden to attempt the impossible, precisely because all experiments in this direction are prevented and prohibited, they are with great strictness required and with great kindness freed and empowered to do what they can do in the sphere of the relative possibilities assigned to them, to do it very imperfectly yet heartily, quietly, and cheerfully. They are absolved from wasting time and energy over the impassable limits of their sphere of action and thus missing the opportunities that present themselves in this sphere. They may and can and should rise up and accept responsibility to the utmost of their power for the doing of the little righteousness.[162]

Or again, the action of those who invoke the Kingdom is 'kingdom-like';[163] in relation to and correspondence with God's own act, 'the action of Christians may in its own way and within the limits of its own sphere be called and be a righteous action ... in its own place and manner.'[164]

On this basis, Barth hints at a conception of revolt which disentangles it from association with pure autonomy, in just the same way that his conception of divine grace has been disentangled from association with divine sole causality. Barth is deeply and unremittingly suspicious of the idea of human autonomy, which he reads as an evasion of the problem of sinful self-loss, not as a solution. 'Man himself

[161] *ChrL*, p. 264.
[162] Ibid., p. 265.
[163] Ibid., p. 266.
[164] Ibid.

suffers, and he fights tooth and nail against admitting this even to himself, let alone to others. He acts – this is the point of his disguises – as if he does not suffer.'[165] Christian revolt against the 'lordship of demons'[166] is simply the grace-given courage to identify and act within those spheres of life where we need not suffer, and, cheerfully and in good conscience, to leave the rest to God. If this is so, and if grace is properly to be construed as taking away from humanity not its proper agency, but its false self-divinisation, then God's acts can be seen as blessing rather than threat.

[165] Ibid., p. 269.
[166] Ibid., p. 270.

CHAPTER SEVEN

'The room of the gospel':
Barth's moral ontology

As we have looked in detail at Barth's late ethical writings, two major considerations have emerged. First, Barth's dogmatics has been shown to be what he claimed it to be: an *ethical* dogmatics, a dogmatics which consciously and consistently turns its attention to the realm of human action as a primary theme in theological reflection upon the covenant of grace, since 'the room of the gospel' is one in which there is 'room for us'.[1] Second, Barth's moral theology cannot be grasped apart from its *ontological* force. His answer to the question: what shall the Christian do? is rooted in an answer to a prior question: what is moral reality? This second observation highlights one of the points at which Barth diverges sharply from the theological and philosophical culture of modernity. One way of further articulating that divergence would be to say that, for Barth, ethics is rooted in *nature*. By 'nature' is meant, not a reality prior to or existing as a condition of possibility for 'grace', nor some general *humanum* which grace perfects or completes: of 'nature' in these senses, Barth's theology knows nothing. What is meant, rather, is simply nature as *that which is*. Barth believes that good human action is generated, shaped, and judged by 'that which is', and that 'that which is' is a Christological, not a pre-Christological, category. Correlatively, Barth believes that it is possible – indeed, urgently necessary – for human beings to come to apprehend a transcendent order of value if they are to conduct themselves

[1] K. Barth, 'Gospel and law', p. 11.

properly in the world. Such apprehension is not a matter of self-reflection or of any 'proposing' activities on the part of human agents, but is the fruit of scrupulous and ever-newly focussed attention to Jesus Christ in the perfection of his achievement and in his presence and activity in the power of the Holy Spirit. Transcendent value is, in other words, 'spiritually' apprehended, apprehended by faith. 'Nature' so apprehended is not – as it has become in the axiomatic contrast drawn by the modern Western moral tradition – the *antithesis* of freedom, but its ultimate root.

The same point can be phrased somewhat differently by speaking (in a phrase borrowed from Charles Taylor) of Barth's 'moral ontology'.[2] Within the terms of much modern moral theory, texts like Barth's, which operate in the classical mode of Christian ethics, are singularly difficult of access. Their implicit or explicit notions of the objectivity of morals are largely unavailable to us, or available only in positivist form. The apparent 'givenness' of certain moral realities which they propose is more likely to strike us as a projection of contingent historical and cultural arrangements, and not as a transcript of some universal moral order. We are, accordingly, more familiar with critical moral consciousness than with the idea of moral obligation impressed upon us *ab extra*. Above all, we most commonly identify the realm of the ethical with the realms of deliberative consciousness or spontaneous action. We are, in other words, no longer instinctively possessed of a moral ontology. Whilst we ordinarily undertake 'strong evaluation' in thinking about our behaviour[3] – that is, whilst we make desire-independent discriminations of right and wrong – we find it acutely

---

[2] C. Taylor, *Sources of the Self. The Making of Modern Identity* (Cambridge, Mass., 1989), p. 8. For Taylor's application of this analysis to a modern philosophical writer, see his essay 'Engaged agency and background in Heidegger,' in C. Guignon, ed., *The Cambridge Companion to Heidegger* (Cambridge, 1993), pp. 317–36. For a parallel reading of modernity, see E. Tugendhat, *Self-Consciousness and Self-Determination* (Cambridge, Mass., 1986).

[3] Ibid., p. 4. For a fuller treatment of this notion, see Taylor's earlier essays 'What is human agency?' and 'The concept of a person', in his *Philosophy and the Human Sciences. Philosophical Papers 1* (Cambridge, 1985), pp. 15–44, 97–114.

difficult to formulate the 'background picture'[4] on the basis
of which it makes sense to make such evaluations. 'Moral
space' (which is closely analogous to what we have earlier
called 'the moral field') is another term used by Taylor to
make much the same point. There is, he writes, an

essential link between identity and a kind of orientation. To know
who you are is to be oriented in moral space, a space in which
questions arise about what is good or bad, what is worth doing
and what is not, what has meaning and importance for you and
what is trivial and secondary . . . [W]e are only selves in so far
as we move in a certain space of questions, as we seek and find
an orientation to the good.[5]

What Barth offers in the ethics of the *Church Dogmatics* is
a moral ontology, an account of moral space. It is an
account of what the good *is*, rather than is *chosen* or *desired*
to be, for morality is a matter neither of consciousness nor
culture, but a matter of the way in which human agents
are oriented to a creative agency which is the genesis of
their own agency, and by which they find themselves both
challenged and fulfilled. Furthermore, agents are 'inside'
moral space: nothing in Barth's moral theory allows us to
believe that value is other than something which transcends
and surrounds us. To be 'inside' moral space in this way
is to be circumscribed by a morally textured reality which
is inexhaustibly independent of our private and public dispositions, which simply *is*.

These ontological considerations are important because of
the way in which they shed a good deal of light on two
issues which are central to making sense of Barth's ethics
and assimilating their radically anti-modern character. A
first issue concerns the nature of Christian theological ethics
as part of Christian dogmatics. Barth's dogged insistence
that Christian ethics is properly to be located within dogmatics – which distinguishes him from both 'liberal' and
'post-liberal' accounts of the task – is largely incomprehen-

---

[4] *Sources of the Self*, p. 3.
[5] Ibid., p. 28.

sible without reference to a set of theological and ontological convictions about the being and activity of God as the defining context for ethical theory. A second issue concerns Barth's moral anthropology, most crucially the question of moral freedom: does Barth's Christological theory of moral 'nature' simply eliminate the category of freedom, as many of his critics allege? Consideration of these issues, which have already surfaced at a number of points in the preceding exposition, will form the structure of the final chapter.

ETHICS, DOGMATICS, AND ONTOLOGY

Barth's procedure in the ethics of reconciliation, as we have seen, presupposes that the co-inherence of Christian ethics and Christian dogmatics is fundamental to securing the *Christian* character of moral theology. Accordingly, the theological description of good human action which Christian ethics undertakes occurs within the framework of that description of reality which is offered by Christian dogmatics in its reflection upon the Christian *Credo*. Moreover, the intellectual enterprise of 'doing Christian ethics' is itself wholly determined by that same reality as it is construed in the church's confession. Though Christian ethics is 'the attempt to answer *theoretically* the question of what may be called *good* human action',[6] it does not occur in some space outside the Christian confession and its apprehension of reality. Nor does its theoretical discourse seek to arrive at judgments concerning the possibility of Christian ethical reality claims. Theological ethics is neither agnostic nor sceptical about the existence of the good, nor reluctant to undertake a positive description of its character. Indeed, the primary task of theological ethics is just that: a steady description of what is taken to be the case by Christian faith. Such description is generally undertaken in close proximity, and by extensive appeal, to the language of Christian confession: Barth's use of the Lord's Prayer as a framework

---

[6] *ChrL*, p. 3.

for expounding the Christian Life is no mere incidental
device, but consistent with his understanding of the theological task as a whole. For theological ethics is not transcendental or critical inquiry into morals. It is explication of
that which is given to faith as faith hears and obeys the
command of the gracious God. Theological ethics, like all
theology, is dominated by the question: 'To what extent is
reality as the Christian believes it to be?'[7]

This procedure, most sharply described in Barth's *Anselm*
book and put to work throughout the *Church Dogmatics*, goes
a long way to accounting for Barth's unshakeable confidence,
which so exasperates some readers and puzzles others who
feel that it is out of all proportion to the scant labour
which Barth expends on establishing the grounds of such
confidence. The ethics of reconciliation betrays no anxiety
about the answerability of its opening question: 'What may
be called good human action?'[8] There is in Barth's ethics,
both as a whole and in each part, that 'characteristic absence
of crisis' which Barth noted in Anselm's theology, and which
surely marks his own.[9] Of course, the confidence of Barth's
rhetoric certainly says much about his personal and intellectual temper: both his life and his writings are rarely self-
effacing or articulations of doubt, even though they are
sometimes self-subverting. But the confidence, and the corollary freedom from the need to secure a generally warranted
basis of operations in Christian ethics, derives ultimately
from Barth's sense that such is the ontological force of the
Credo that the theologian 'always has the solution of his
problems already behind him'.[10] The ethics of reconciliation
contains no prolegomena, therefore, since Barth's doctrinal
affirmations about Jesus Christ as Word, as the self-
manifestation of God who is the ontic and noetic basis for

---

[7] K. Barth, *Anselm: Fides Quaerens Intellectum*, p. 27. Matheny, *Dogmatics and Ethics*,
pp. 46–59, 208f, lays considerable emphasis on the specifically *theological* ration-
ality at work in Barth's ethical method.
[8] *ChrL*, p. 3.
[9] *Anselm*, p. 26.
[10] Ibid., pp. 25f.

Christian theology, render prolegomena superfluous. Theological ethics is always already under way, its conditions of possibility already established from outside, the problem into which it inquires already resolved.

The essential character of this procedure will elude us, however, unless we read Barth's ethics 'realistically'. That is to say, we need to read Barth with an eye to his conviction that there are objects, events, states of affairs outside the Christian confession to which that confession refers. Already in looking at Barth's doctrine of revelation and Holy Scripture in chapter 1, we have seen how crucial this realism is to understanding his conception of theology. And what we have seen of Barth's characterisation of the moral field in chapter 3 shows the same to be true of his ethics: Christian moral theology is essentially an assertion that good human action is action which is most in accord with the way the world is constituted in Jesus Christ. Barth's ethics is not best interpreted as reflection upon an immanent world of moral *meaning*, but as a reflection upon a transcendent order of *being* and *value* organised around the grace of God in the gospel of Jesus Christ.

It is this which differentiates his work from recent writers on Christian theology and ethics who share his affirmations about the coinherence of the Christian ethos and the positivities of the Christian community's believing and behaving, but remain reticent at the point where Barth is unreserved: the utter priority – ontological and epistemological – of transcendent good. Hans Frei once described Barth as about the task of 'Christian-communal critical self-description of the community's language'.[11] As a way of articulating Barth's distance from the procedures of theological revisionism, this is acute. But it can succeed as a reading of Barth's moral theology (and, in fact, of his theology as a whole) only if we are clear that for Barth the Christian

---

[11] H. Frei, 'Barth and Schleiermacher: divergence and convergence', p. 196. In *Types of Christian Theology* (New Haven, 1992), p. 92, Frei speaks similarly of 'communal Christian self-description', which is 'a matter of being able to use words like faith, hope and love in the context of the Christian community'.

community is most appropriately understood not as a natural state of affairs, a contingent social, cultural and linguistic entity, but as a *spiritual* reality, wholly referred to Jesus Christ. And even if we are firm at this point, to describe Christian theology as the 'self-description of the community's language' may suggest too strong an interest in the proximate realities of the church's acts of confessing, and too weak a sense of the preponderant massiveness of that which is confessed. For theology and theological ethics are, on Barth's account of the matter, responsible only derivatively and secondarily to a religious province of meaning and the activities of its inhabitants. Their primary responsibility lies elsewhere: to the personal presence and activity of God.

Barth's ethics are, therefore, not 'hermeneutical', in that they do not limit their description to what Paul Ricoeur calls 'a culturally contingent symbolic network',[12] nor do they renounce the search for an 'ultimate foundation'.[13] Of course, Barth has no foundationalist ambitions; he does not believe that theology is about the business of elaborating better warrants for Christian moral convictions than those with which that conviction operates in its ethical performance. But his renunciation of such ambition is not made on the grounds of the contingency of all worlds of moral meaning in their irreducible plurality. On the contrary: ethical foundationalism is rejected because it is an attempt to substitute mere constructs for the given foundations of the Christian ethos: God, Christ, revelation, Spirit, church. This is why Barth's ethics has in some respects a curiously premodern tone. Frei, again, correctly notes that:

Barth sounds like a traditional metaphysician who wants to make *theological* information do service for what in the eighteenth century used to be the duty of school metaphysics – to tell us about the realities of God, world and soul corresponding to our ideas of them.[14]

---

[12] P. Ricoeur, *Oneself as Another* (Chicago, 1992), p. 25.
[13] Ibid.
[14] H. Frei, *Types of Christian Theology*, p. 45.

But Frei is surely mistaken when he goes on to suggest that 'the impression is misleading'.[15] On the contrary: what we have seen of his ethical writing suffices to convince that Barth's work is not really comprehensible unless we think of him as in important respects working like a traditional metaphysician, and not simply as busy exhibiting 'the rules or fragments of rules implicit in the ruled use of language which is the sign system of the sociolinguistic community called the Church'.[16]

All of this amounts to a cumulative suggestion that ontological considerations are crucial in understanding both the method and the content of Barth's ethics, whose leading motif is the self-existence of God. 'Dogmatics', wrote Barth – and here he includes ethics –

in each and all of its divisions and subdivisions, with every one of its questions and answers, with all its biblical and historical assertions, with the whole range of its formal and material considerations, examinations and condensations, can first and last, as a whole and in part, say nothing else but that God is.[17]

What can be learnt from this for the task of constructing Christian ethics?

'When theologians turn their attention to ethics', writes Trutz Rendtorff, 'they do not enter an uninhabited house in which they can settle down without regard to the others who dwell there. They share this house with many other disciplines.'[18] Barth, by contrast, presses us to consider Christian ethics, not as an example of a generic theory of morality, but as a 'positive' intellectual discipline. The positivity of ethics is rooted in the fact that moral action, and reflective moral activities such as deliberation, approbation, and disapprobation, are not independent of a particular understanding of what is the case in the world. In so far as the Christian confession offers a distinctive account of

---

[15] Ibid.
[16] Ibid. Frei admits something of this point about Barth in 'Conflicts in interpretation', *Theology and Narrative. Selected Essays* (Oxford, 1993), pp. 163f.
[17] II/1, p. 258. See further Matheny, *Dogmatics and Ethics*, pp. 133–55.
[18] T. Rendtorff, *Ethics*, vol. 1 (Philadelphia, 1986), p. 23.

what is the case in the world, it engenders a distinctive ethos. Once again, this is not simply to repeat the assertion – by now fairly well established in moral philosophy and theology – that 'morality' is inseparable from the historical determinateness of 'tradition'. It is true that, without further specification or qualification, general terms such as 'ethics' or 'morals' can steal our attention away from the important distinctive features which are basic to grasping how moral traditions function. Moreover, from one point of view, we are unwise to continue talking of '*the* moral point of view and *the* language of morals, rather than asking of any particular moral concept or belief, "Whose concept or belief is this?" and "What is the particular historical and social setting in which it arose and flourished?"'[19] Again, it is certainly the case that any sharp separation of judgments of value from judgments of fact ignores the way in which moral judgments are bound up with beliefs about what the world is like, so that (to put the matter formally) expressions of intention 'offer descriptions of characterizations of one's action which entail beliefs about the way the world is'.[20] But the positivity which Barth presses us to attribute to Christian moral theology is of a different order. The positive character of Christian moral theology is not a function of the historical character of moral traditions; nor does it emerge out of analysis of the proximate phenomena of belief in their relation to morals. Christian moral theology is positive in that it takes its rise in the *positum*, the given reality of God's action to which the gospel testifies. If Barth's procedure is instructive, therefore, it is not so much at the formal level of renewing our appreciation of the embeddedness of Christian ethics in that network of language, practices, and beliefs which we call moral tradition, but at the *dogmatic* or *ontological* level. Put very simply: he invites

---

[19] A. MacIntyre, 'Moral philosophy: what next?', in A. MacIntyre and S. Hauerwas, eds., *Revisions* (Notre Dame, 1983) p. 6.

[20] S. Sutherland, 'Religion, ethics and action', in S. Sutherland and B. Hebblethwaite, eds., *The Philosophical Frontiers of Christian Theology* (Cambridge, 1982), p. 164.

his readers to begin talk of human agency with talk of the reality-constituting acts of God.

A Christian account of the moral field is wholly determined by the – ontological – conviction that 'God is'. That conviction, which is to be construed as 'God acts', articulates the unique, incommunicable character of God's action as the action of a free and sheerly necessary being. But language about God and the acts of God also has an ordering function: it operates as a 'fundamental orientation for all action'.[21] Confession of the reality of God in his acts contains a description of created reality as structured in such a way that certain patterns of intentional activity on the part of human agents are in accord with how the world is. 'God's action is thereby spoken of in such a way that God's action is designated as the ground of possibility of human action.'[22] Language about God is therefore a means of moral orientation, a fundamental reference point in mapping and traversing the moral field – though only in so far as such language points us to a personal divine agent of absolute and inexhaustible priority. If Barth has continuing significance for Christian ethical theory, it is in large measure because of the utter seriousness and single-mindedness with which he pursues this single train of thought.

ORDER AND FREEDOM IN MORAL ANTHROPOLOGY

If talk of God functions in this way, offering a 'fundamental orientation' for Christian ethical theory, how does it shape the way in which we are to think of human agents? What kind of ontology of the acting person is Barth recommending?

First, Barth's moral anthropology is essentialist. This is not because he considers that there is some detachable 'essential' human nature which is prior to a person's life-act and into which that life-act can be resolved. Barth's point

[21] C. Schwöbel, 'Die Rede vom Handeln Gottes im christlichen Glauben', *Marburger Jahrbuch der Theologie* I (1987), 62.

[22] Ibid., p. 63.

is more that to be a human person is not simply to produce oneself in a process of self-shaping, but rather to discover oneself within an ordered reality which is governed by God's dealings with creation in Jesus Christ. And so, as we have seen, in his initial sketch of the character of the moral field near the beginning of *The Christian Life*, Barth asserts without equivocation that the question of the nature of the human agent 'is answered in Jesus Christ'.[23] It is, in other words, entirely possible to say what a human agent *is*. The full import of Barth's point can be seen by a contrasting passage from Sartre's *Being and Nothingness*:

To say that the for-itself has to be what it is, to say that it is what it is not while not being what it is, to say that in it existence precedes and conditions essence or inversely according to Hegel, that for it 'Wesen ist was gewesen ist' – all this is to say one and the same thing: to be aware that man is free. Indeed, by the sole fact that I am conscious of the causes which inspire my action, these causes are already transcendent objects for my consciousness; they are outside. In vain shall I seek to catch hold of them; I escape them by my very existence. I am condemned to exist forever beyond my essence, beyond the causes and motives of my act. I am condemned to be free.[24]

The ethical consequence of Sartre's location of human freedom in the opposition of existence and essence is a denial of any teleology to human agency in which agents have given ends, in pursuit of which they become what they are. Sartre goes on:

[P]eople will posit ends as transcendences, which is not an error. But instead of seeing that the transcendences there posited are maintained in their being by my transcendence, people will assume that I encounter them upon my surging up in the world; they come from God, from nature, from 'my' nature, from society. These ends ready made and pre-human will therefore define the meaning of my act even before I conceive it, just as causes as pure psychic givens will produce it without my even being aware of them.[25]

---

[23] *ChrL*, p. 21.
[24] J.-P. Sartre, *Being and Nothingness* (New York, 1966), p. 567.
[25] Ibid., p. 568.

Thus, in a crucial sentence, Sartre proposes: 'Freedom is precisely the nothingness which is *made-to-be* at the heart of man and which forces human reality *to make itself* instead of *to be.*'[26] Over against this, Barth envisages the human agent as occupying an allotted space, as filling out a given role, discovering selfhood in giving active consent to the creative and redemptive works of God.

This leads to a second feature of Barth's moral anthropology, namely its ecstatic character. True humanness is not a quality of which we can in any straightforward way claim to be proprietors. To be human is to stand in relation to Jesus Christ and to be a participant in his history. '[E]ach man as such – not just the man who knows him but also the man who scarcely knows him or knows him not at all – has a part in his history and without it would have no history of his own.'[27] Or again, Barth can claim of each person, confessing Christian or not, 'The decision concerning his true human being was taken from all eternity and also in time on Golgotha, long before he is ready (or not ready) to recognize it and to honour it with his own decision.'[28] Like Luther, Barth in his moral anthropology is hesitant to affirm that the moral self is unambiguously a centre of attribution.[29] Luther's hesitancy is cast in the idiom of the doctrine of justification, most especially the anthropological consequences of forensic or alien righteousness; Barth's is articulated in terms of a conviction of the ontological preponderance and inclusiveness of the history of Jesus Christ. The common core of both, however, is a notion that moral selfhood is derived from, and intimately bound to, a source external to the self, and that the severing of that bond leads to incalculable moral losses. Moreover, that bond between the moral self and God, brought to dogmatic expression by language about the Holy Spirit, constitutes the only context

---

[26] Ibid.
[27] *ChrL*, p. 20.
[28] Ibid., p. 21.
[29] See here especially W. Joest, *Ontologie der Person bei Luther* (Göttingen, 1967), pp. 233–74.

in which it is proper to attribute goodness to human action. Only when this is grasped can we begin to make sense of Barth's material on topics such as allegiance in the baptismal fragment, or rebellion in *The Christian Life*.

One very serious counter-question to Barth cannot be evaded: does not his essentialist anthropology, with its vision of moral identity derived *ab extra*, make his account of human action one of the 'abortive attempts to stifle freedom under the weight of being'?[30] Do we not find in Barth's moral ontology 'an empire of the real order that is sovereignty of servitude'?[31] However firmly Barth may affirm the reality of contingent activity, his affirmations seem to many readers to be thoroughly outweighed by the sheer massiveness of God's reality in Jesus Christ. In his recent study of Barth's ethics, for example, Nigel Biggar perceives an incoherence in Barth's doctrine of grace. Barth, it is argued, is unable consistently to hold to his account of human freedom, since 'human beings are ultimately determined by God's grace, and . . . their liberation is in the end an inexorable necessity'.[32] In consequence, Barth has 'a notion of human freedom that is more apparent than real',[33] because '[i]n making persistent error ultimately impossible, it [that is, Barth's determinism] removes the deep and mysterious seriousness of human moral responsibility, and accordingly diminishes human dignity'.[34]

There are, nevertheless, a number of reasons why Barth's moral anthropology does not collapse under such a critique. One is the sheer extent and richness of his description of human moral action: if the exposition in the preceding chapters has shown anything, it is that, for Barth, dogmatics is disoriented from the beginning if it fails to give attention to the human moral world. But, more importantly, the critique persists in characterising moral freedom in a way

---

[30] J.-P. Sartre, *Being and Nothingness*, p. 568.
[31] G. Bataille, *Theory of Religion* (New York, 1992), p. 77.
[32] N. Biggar, *The Hastening that Waits*, p. 5.
[33] Ibid.
[34] Ibid., p. 162.

which is hostile to Barth's extensive reordering of the notion. Lurking within the critique is a notion of freedom as a kind of spiritual neutrality, as some arena in human life or consciousness in which we are able to exist and operate in relative isolation from the formative activity of God.[35] Barth's doctrine of baptism and his account of the shape of Christian agency in *The Christian Life* are predicated on a quite different understanding of freedom. For him, moral freedom is consent to the necessary character of the moral order of God: it is 'situated freedom'.[36] Freedom is not primarily to be identified with will or choice considered as ends in themselves, or as quintessential marks of human dignity whose removal spells the end of serious consideration of the substance of humanity. Nor is freedom best envisaged as discontinuity or independence from the order of things.[37] Contingent, willed occurrence and the liberty of human agents, though unquestionably significant to Barth and described by him with vividness as proper objects of theological interest, are important not because they alone must bear the burden of providing evidence of human moral stature, but because they find themselves within the sweep of God's saving dealings with humanity:

[The human agent] lives by what God is, by what he is in the word of his grace for this people and therefore also for him. He thus lives by God's eternal mercy, whose power is that God, faithful in his affirmation, love, and election, has in the freedom of his lovingkindness made him also free. To have freed him is to have reconciled him to himself; to have reconciled him is to have justified him so that he can stand before him; to have

---

[35] Very curiously, Biggar (*The Hastening that Waits*, p. 4) criticises J. Macken, *The Autonomy Theme*, for failing to distinguish spiritual freedom from the liberal notion of formal freedom of choice, even though Biggar's own critical reflections on Barth tend to trade upon the same lack of distinction.

[36] For this notion and its application in the analysis of modern understandings of selfhood and moral agency, see C. Taylor, *Hegel and Modern Society* (Cambridge, 1979), pp. 135–69, and his *Hegel* (Cambridge, 1975), pp. 537–71.

[37] On this theme, see G. Grant, *Philosophy in the Mass Age* (Toronto, 1960), and the excellent commentary by J. O'Donovan, *George Grant and the Twilight of Justice* (Toronto, 1984), especially pp. 28–46.

sanctified him, so that he can live with and for him; and to have called him, so that he can serve him as a witness.[38]

Barth there describes particular moments of the classical Protestant 'order of salvation' in terms of its moral-anthropological dimensions: standing before, living with and for, serving as witness. And it is in such activities (rather than in occupancy of some anterior 'unaligned' space) that human freedom is disclosed. Barth continues:

He has the freedom to be this man who is justified before God, sanctified for him, and called by him. He only has this freedom – everything else called freedom is unfreedom – but he really has it. He has it in the fulfilment of his destiny by creation whereby he is from God and to God. He has it in the order of his being by creation whereby he is fellow man of fellow man. He has it as the content of his structure by creation as soul of his body. He has it as the meaning of his existence by creation in his restricted time. Whoever he may be, he has it in all circumstances, in every conceivable condition and situation in which he may find himself. As man he is always and everywhere to be addressed in terms of it. He may and can be this man, and as he makes use of this freedom, he is this man. He does not have this freedom of himself, however; he has it only as God's gift.[39]

Finally, to label the theology of grace which lies behind Barth's ethics 'deterministic' is to pass over the thorough reconstruction of the idea of divine sovereignty which Barth undertakes in many long passages in the doctrines of revelation, God, creation, and reconciliation, as well as in the structure of his the-anthropology considered as a whole. It is here – in the trinitarian-incarnational affirmation of 'God with us' and in its anthropological consequences – rather than in any abstract notion of divine determination that we find the driving force of Barth's ethical writings. From this vantage point, Gerhard Ebeling's critique of Barth's theology as 'the ethicising of Christianity' becomes readily understandable, even though it is in other respects highly unsatis-

[38] *ChrL*, p. 22.
[39] Ibid.

factory.[40] Ebeling quite correctly perceives that Barth – unlike Luther – insists that 'the human person – in correspondence to God – is an agent whose being is in activity'.[41] But Ebeling is surely mistaken to draw the conclusion that Barth's 'taking up of ethics into dogmatics' leads to 'the conversion of dogmatics into ethics'.[42] If Ebeling's account does not satisfy, it is not simply because he underestimates the seriousness with which Barth wants to speak of the *passivity* of the believer.[43] It is also because Ebeling, in his correct but rather rudimentary observation of Barth's anthropology, assumes that the only possible outcome of Barth's argument is compromise of the sovereignty of grace. In effect, Ebeling's argument is a mirror-image of Biggar's: though the terms are reversed, it still trades upon the alternative *either* God's action *or* ours. The whole thrust of Barth's ethics, in its covenantal structure, is to deny that we are forced to choose.

Barth's moral vision, his picture of the world of human agents and acts, is organised – apparently rather precariously – around two seemingly contradictory themes which we might call 'order' and 'rebellion'. That is, ethics counsels at one and the same time an obedient acceptance of assigned roles within a necessary order which is not of the agent's creation and an energetic refusal of fate. We can only understand how this can be so when we are attentive to the way in which the ethics of the *Dogmatics* as a whole, and of the doctrine of reconciliation in particular, redefine both themes.

---

[40] G. Ebeling, 'Karl Barths Ringen mit Luther', in *Lutherstudien III: Begriffsunter-suchungen – Textinterpretationen – Wirkungsgeschichtliches* (Tübingen, 1985), pp. 428–573.

[41] Ibid., p. 555.

[42] Ibid., p. 557.

[43] On Ebeling's account, in Barth 'faith itself . . . is understood as a human act' (ibid., p. 554), whereas Luther 'understands faith as God's work in the human person, who is accordingly in every sense a receiver' (p. 556). The contrast is excessively bald, in view of Barth's tying of faith to the vicarious character of the humanity of Jesus and to the activity of the Holy Spirit. For more nuanced accounts of the contrast between Barth's and Luther's accounts of passivity and moral spontaneity, see E. Jüngel, 'Gospel and law' and K. Stock, *Anthropologie der Verheissung. Karl Barths Lehre vom Menschen als dogmatisches Problem* (Munich, 1980), pp. 95–115.

'Order', the given reality of value which is the command of God, is not leaden fate or some external causality which simply sweeps us along, but God's personal address which, as command, is invitation and empowerment, entitlement and resource. 'Rebellion' is not wilful moral *creatio ex nihilo*, but rather that assertive human testimony to what *is* (in Christ) over against what falsely claims to be. Furthermore, this coinherence of order and rebellion in Barth's work is rooted, as we have seen, in the variety of uses of Christology in his work. Jesus Christ relates to the human agent not only as substitute, rescuer, giver of status, but also as assigner of roles and model of performance. Being a moral agent thus involves both quietly and cheerfully working within a given order, and struggling against the waste caused by humanity's perverse refusal to acknowledge the good command of God. This vision – Augustinian-Calvinist in temper, though modified in favour of a greater sense of the range of human responsibility and more dense in its portrayal of the human world – is one of the most powerfully anti-modern statements by a Christian theologian since the Enlightenment. Hans Blumenberg remarks that modernity is predicated on 'the elimination of the premise that the world has a particular quality for man that in effect prescribes his basic mode of behaviour'.[44] Refusing this elimination constitutes the continuing resourcefulness of Barth's ethical thought.

---

[44] H. Blumenberg, *The Legitimacy of the Modern Age* (Cambridge, Mass., 1983), p. 143.

Select secondary bibliography

Balthasar, H. U. von, *The Theology of Karl Barth* (San Francisco, 1992).

Biggar, N.,'Hearing God's command and thinking about what's right: with and beyond Barth', in N. Biggar, ed., *Reckoning with Barth* (Oxford, 1988), pp. 101–18.

The Hastening that Waits. Karl Barth's Ethics (Oxford, 1993).

Blaser, K., 'L'Ethique en tant qu' "invocation de Dieu"', in *Karl Barth 1886–1968. Combats – Idées – Reprises* (Bern, 1987), pp. 171–81.

Blondel, J.-L., 'Prayer and struggle: Karl Barth's "The Christian Life"', *St. Luke's Journal of Theology* 23 (1980), 105–15.

Busch, E., *Karl Barth. His Life from Letters and Autobiographical Fragments* (London, 1976).

'Introduction', in H.-M. Rumscheidt, ed., *Karl Barth in Re-View. Posthumous Works Reviewed and Assessed* (Pittsburgh, 1981), pp. x–xxviii.

Cochrane, A. C., 'Markus Barth – an unBarthian Barthian. The place of the doctrine of baptism in the *CD*', in D. Y. Hadidian, ed., *Intergerini Parietis Septum* (Pittsburgh, 1981), pp. 39–50.

Collins, A., 'Barth's relationship to Schleiermacher: a reassessment', *Studies in Religion/Sciences Religieuses* 17 (1988), 213–24.

Dalferth, I. U., 'Karl Barth's eschatological realism', in S. W. Sykes, ed., *Karl Barth. Centenary Essays* (Cambridge, 1989), pp. 14–45.

'Theologischer Realismus und realistische Theologie bei Karl Barth', *Evangelische Theologie* 46 (1986), 402–22.

Daveney, S. G., *Divine Power. A Study of Karl Barth and Charles Hartshorne* (Philadelphia, 1986).

Demura, A., 'Zwingli in the writings of Karl Barth – with special emphasis on the doctrine of the sacraments', in E. A. McKee, and B. G. Armstrong, eds., *Probing the Reformed Tradition* (Louisville, 1989), pp. 197–219.

Dickinson, C. C., 'Church Dogmatics IV/4', in H.-M. Rumscheidt, ed., *Karl Barth in Re-View. Posthumous Works Reviewed and Assessed* (Pittsburgh, 1981), pp. 43–54.

Dinkler, E., 'Die Taufaussagen des Neuen Testaments. Neu untersucht im Hinblick auf Karl Barths Tauflehre', in F. Viering, ed., *Zu Karl Barths Lehre von der Taufe* (Gütersloh, 1971), pp. 60–153.

Ebeling, G., 'Karl Barths Ringen mit Luther', in *Lutherstudien III: Begriffsuntersuchungen – Textinterpretationen – Wirkungsgeschichtliches* (Tübingen, 1985), pp. 428–573.

Ford, D. F., *Barth and God's Story* (Frankfurt/M, 1981).

Frei, H., 'Barth and Schleiermacher: divergence and convergence', in *Theology and Narrative. Selected Essays* (Oxford, 1993), pp. 177–99.

Types of Christian Theology (New Haven, 1992).

Graf, F. W., 'Die Freiheit der Entsprechung Gottes. Bemerkungen zum theozentrischen Ansatz der Anthropologie Karl Barths', in T. Rendtorff, ed., *Die Realisierung der Freiheit. Beiträge zur Kritik der Theologie Karl Barths* (Gütersloh, 1975), pp. 76–118.

Greive, W., *Die Kirche als Ort der Wahrheit. Das Verständnis der Kirche in der Theologie Karl Barths* (Göttingen, 1991).

Gunton, C., 'No other foundation. One Englishman's reading of *Church Dogmatics*, Chapter V', in N. Biggar, ed., *Reckoning with Barth* (Oxford, 1988), pp. 61–79.

'The triune God and the freedom of the creature', in S. W. Sykes, ed., *Karl Barth. Centenary Essays* (Cambridge, 1989), pp. 46–68.

Hauerwas, S., *Character and the Christian Life* (San Antonio, 1975).

'On honour: by way of a comparison of Barth and Trollope', in N. Biggar, ed., *Reckoning with Barth* (Oxford, 1988), pp. 145–69.

Herlyn, O., *Religion oder Gebet?* (Neukirchen, 1979).

Hübert, H., *Der Streit um die Kindertaufe* (Frankfurt/M, 1972).

Hunsinger, G., *How to Read Karl Barth. The Shape of his Theology* (Oxford, 1991).

'Beyond literalism and expressivism: Karl Barth's hermeneutical realism', *Modern Theology* 3 (1987), 209–23.

'Truth as self-involving. Barth and Lindbeck on the cognitive and performative aspects of truth in theological discourse', *Journal of the American Academy of Religion* 61 (1993), 41–56.

'A response to William Werpehowski', *Theology Today* 43 (1986), 354–60.

Jeanrond, W., 'Karl Barth's hermeneutics', in N. Biggar, ed., *Reckoning with Barth* (Oxford, 1988), pp. 80–97.

Jenson, R., 'Karl Barth', in D. F. Ford, ed., *The Modern Theologians*, vol. 1 (Oxford, 1989), pp. 23–49.

Jüngel, E., *The Doctrine of the Trinity. God's Being is in Becoming* (Edinburgh, 1975).

'Gospel and law: the relationship of ethics to dogmatics', in *Karl Barth. A Theological Legacy* (Philadelphia, 1986), pp. 105–26.

'Karl Barth's Lehre von der Taufe. Ein Hinweis auf ihre Probleme', in *Barth-Studien* (Gütersloh, 1982), pp. 246–90.

'Thesen zu Karl Barths Lehre von der Taufe', in *Barth-Studien* (Gütersloh, 1982), pp. 291–4.

'Zur Kritik des sakramentalen Verständnisses der Taufe', in *Barth-Studien* (Gütersloh, 1982), pp. 295–314.

' "...keine Menschenlosigkeit Gottes..." Zur Theologie Karl Barths zwischen Theismus und Atheismus', in *Barth-Studien* (Gütersloh, 1982), pp. 332–47.

'Theologische Existenz – Erinnerung an Karl Barth', *Evangelische Kommentare* 19 (1986), 258–60.

'Invocation of God as the ethical ground of Christian action', in *Theological Essays* (Edinburgh, 1989), pp. 154–72.

Kelsay, J., 'Prayer and ethics: reflections on Calvin and Barth', *Harvard Theological Review* 82 (1989), 169–84.

Klappert, B., *Promissio und Bund* (Göttingen, 1976).

Kreck, W., 'Karl Barths Tauflehre', in F. Viering, ed., *Zu Karl Barths Lehre von der Taufe* (Gütersloh, 1971), pp. 11–26.

Krötke, W., 'Gott und Mensch als "Partner". Zur Bedeutung einer zentralen Kategorie in Karl Barths Kirchlicher Dogmatik', in E. Jüngel, ed., *Zur Theologie Karl Barths*, *Zeitschrift für Theologie und Kirche*, Beiheft 6 (1986), 158–75.

Kühn, U., *Sakramente* (Gütersloh, 1985).

Lindbeck, G., 'Barth and textuality', *Theology Today* 43 (1986), 361–76.

Macken, J. *The Autonomy Theme in the 'Church Dogmatics': Karl Barth and His Critics* (Cambridge, 1990).

Marshall, B., *Christology in Conflict. The Identity of a Saviour in Rahner and Barth* (Oxford, 1987).

Matheny, P. D., *Dogmatics and Ethics. The Theological Realism and Ethics of Karl Barth's 'Church Dogmatics'* (Frankfurt/M, 1990).

McGrath, A. E., 'Karl Barth als Aufklärer? Der Zusammenhang seiner Lehre vom Werke Christi mit der Erwählungslehre', *Kerygma und Dogma* 30 (1984), 273–83.

McGrath, A. E., 'Karl Barth and the articulus iustificationis. The significance of his critique of Ernst Wolf within the context of his theological method', *Theologische Zeitschrift* 39 (1983), 349–61.

Moltmann, J., *The Trinity and the Kingdom of God* (London, 1981).

Mottu, H., 'Les sacrements selon Karl Barth et Eberhard Jüngel', *Foi et Vie* 88 (1989), 33–55.

Quadt, A., 'Die Taufe als Antwort des Glaubens', *Theologische Revue* 6 (1968), 468–74.

Rae, S. H., 'Law, gospel and freedom in the theological ethics of Karl Barth', *Scottish Journal of Theology* 25 (1972), 412–22.

Rendtorff, T., 'Der ethische Sinn der Dogmatik. Zur Reformulierung des Verhältnisses von Dogmatik und Ethik bei Karl Barth', in T. Rendtorff, ed., *Die Realisierung der Freiheit. Beiträge zur Kritik der Theologie Karl Barths* (Gütersloh, 1975), pp. 119–34.

Roberts, R. H., 'Barth's doctrine of time: its nature and implications', in *A Theology on Its Way? Essays on Karl Barth* (Edinburgh, 1991), pp. 1–58.

Rosato, P. J., *The Spirit as Lord. The Pneumatology of Karl Barth* (Edinburgh, 1981).

Rumscheidt, H.-M., 'The first commandment as axiom for theology', in J. Thompson, ed., *Theology Beyond Christendom. Essays on the Centenary of the Birth of Karl Barth* (Allison Park, 1986), pp. 143–64.

Schellong, D., 'Der Ort der Tauflehre in der Theologie Karl Barths', in D. Schellong, ed., *Warum Christen ihre Kinder nicht mehr taufen lassen* (Frankfurt/M, 1969), pp. 108–42.

Schlüter, R. *Karl Barths Tauflehre* (Paderborn, 1973).

Smail, T. A., 'The doctrine of the Holy Spirit', in J. Thompson, ed., *Theology Beyond Christendom. Essays on the Centenary of the Birth of Karl Barth* (Allison Park, 1986), pp. 87–110.

Stirnimann, H., 'Karl Barths Tauffragment', *Freiburger Zeitschrift für Philosophie und Theologie* 15 (1968), 3–28.

Stock, K., *Anthropologie der Verheissung. Karl Barths Lehre vom Menschen als dogmatisches Problem* (Munich, 1980).

Thiemann, R., 'Response to George Lindbeck', *Theology Today* 43 (1986), 377–82.

Torrance, T. F., 'The one baptism common to Christ and his church', in *Theology in Reconciliation* (London, 1975), pp. 82–105.

Viering, F., ed., *Zu Karl Barths Lehre von der Taufe* (Gütersloh, 1971).

Villette, L., *Foi et Sacrement 2: De Saint Thomas à Karl Barth* (Paris, 1964).

Vogel, T., ' "Unterweisung in der Kunst des richtigen Fragens nach Gottes Willen und des offenen Hörens auf sein Gebot": Ansatz der Ethik und des ethischen Argumentation bei Karl Barth', in H. Köckert, and W. Krötke, eds., *Theologie als Christologie* (Berlin, 1988), pp. 121–35.

Webster, J., ' "Assured and patient and cheerful expectation": Barth on Christian hope as the church's task', *Toronto Journal of Theology* 10 (1994), 35–52.

'The Christian in revolt: some reflections on *The Christian Life*', in N. Biggar, ed., *Reckoning with Barth* (Oxford, 1988), pp. 119–44.

' "The firmest grasp of the real": Barth on original sin', *Toronto Journal of Theology* 4 (1988), 19–29.

W. Werpehowski, 'Command and history in the ethics of Karl Barth', *Journal of Religious Ethics* 9 (1981), 298–320.

'Narrative and ethics in Barth', *Theology Today* 43 (1986), 334–53.

West, C. C., 'Baptism in the reformed tradition', in R. T. Bender, and A. P. F. Sell, eds., *Baptism, Peace and the State in the Reformed and Mennonite Traditions* (Waterloo, 1991), pp. 13–35.

West, P., 'Karl Barth's theology of work: a resource for the late 1980s', *Modern Churchman* 30 (1988), 13–19.

Weth, R., 'Taufe in den Tod Jesu Christi als Anfang eines neuen Lebens' in H. Deuser et al., eds., *Gottes Zukunft – Zukunft der Welt. Festschrift für Jürgen Moltmann zum 60. Geburtstag* (Munich, 1986), pp. 147–58.

Williams, R., 'Barth on the triune God', in S. W. Sykes, ed., *Karl Barth. Studies of his Theological Method* (Oxford, 1979), pp. 147–93.

Willis, R. E., *The Ethics of Karl Barth* (Leiden, 1971).

'Some difficulties in Barth's development of special ethics', *Religious Studies* 6 (1970), 147–55.

Wingren, G., *Creation and Law* (Edinburgh, 1961).

Theology in Conflict. Nygren, Barth, Bultmann (Edinburgh, 1958).

Index